Language Teacher Emotion Regulation

PSYCHOLOGY OF LANGUAGE LEARNING AND TEACHING: 30

Language Teacher Emotion Regulation

An Exploration in Japan

Sam Morris

MULTILINGUAL MATTERS
Bristol • Jackson

DOI https://doi.org/10.21832/MORRIS9131
Library of Congress Cataloging in Publication Data
A catalog record for this book is available from the Library of Congress.
Names: Morris, Sam, author
Title: Language Teacher Emotion Regulation: An Exploration in Japan/ Sam Morris.
Description: Bristol; Jackson: Multilingual Matters, 2025. | Series: Psychology of Language Learning and Teaching: 30 | Includes bibliographical references and index. | Summary: "This book is the first comprehensive work on language teacher emotion regulation, filling a salient gap in the literature on teacher emotions and wellbeing. It explores the strategies language teachers use to regulate their emotions, their motives for doing so and the contextual factors influencing their decisions"— Provided by publisher.
Identifiers: LCCN 2025000238 (print) | LCCN 2025000239 (ebook) | ISBN 9781800419124 paperback | ISBN 9781800419131 hardback | ISBN 9781800419155 epub | ISBN 9781800419148 pdf
Subjects: LCSH: Language and languages—Study and teaching—Psychological aspects | Language teachers—Psychology | Emotions | Well-being | English language—Study and teaching—Japan—Case studies
Classification: LCC P53.7 .M67 2025 (print) | LCC P53.7 (ebook) | DDC 418.0071—dc23/eng/20250305
LC record available at https://lccn.loc.gov/2025000238
LC ebook record available at https://lccn.loc.gov/2025000239

British Library Cataloguing in Publication Data
A catalogue entry for this book is available from the British Library.

ISBN-13: 978-1-80041-913-1 (hbk)
ISBN-13: 978-1-80041-912-4 (pbk)

Multilingual Matters
UK: St Nicholas House, 31–34 High Street, Bristol, BS1 2AW, UK.
USA: Ingram, Jackson, TN, USA.
Authorised Representative: Easy Access System Europe – Mustamäe tee 50, 10621 Tallinn, Estonia, gpsr.requests@easproject.com.

Website: https://www.multilingual-matters.com
X: Multi_Ling_Mat
Bluesky: @multi-ling-mat.bsky.social
Facebook: https://www.facebook.com/multilingualmatters
Blog: https://www.channelviewpublications.wordpress.com

Copyright © 2025 Sam Morris.

All rights reserved. No part of this work may be reproduced in any form or by any means without permission in writing from the publisher.

The policy of Multilingual Matters/Channel View Publications is to use papers that are natural, renewable and recyclable products, made from wood grown in sustainable forests. In the manufacturing process of our books, and to further support our policy, preference is given to printers that have FSC and PEFC Chain of Custody certification. The FSC and/or PEFC logos will appear on those books where full certification has been granted to the printer concerned.

Typeset by Techset Composition India(P) Ltd, Bangalore and Chennai, India.

Contents

Acknowledgements		ix
Copyright Notice		xi
Acknowledgement of Financial Support		xiii
Foreword		xv

1. Introduction to Language Teacher Emotion Regulation — 1
   - 1.1 Why a Book on Emotion Regulation? — 3
   - 1.2 My Entry into Emotion Regulation — 4
   - 1.3 An Overview of the Book — 6

2. Theoretical Perspectives on Emotion Regulation — 8
   - 2.1 Introduction — 8
   - 2.2 Defining Emotions — 9
   - 2.3 Defining Emotion Regulation — 14
   - 2.4 Frameworks for Emotion Regulation Motives and Strategies — 19
   - 2.5 Lessons Learned: A Preliminary Language Teacher Emotion Regulation Model — 22

3. Emotion Regulation in Applied Linguistics — 25
   - 3.1 Introduction — 25
   - 3.2 Socioemotional Competencies and Emotion Regulation — 28
   - 3.3 Emotional Labour and Emotion Regulation — 30
   - 3.4 Well-Being and Emotion Regulation — 34
   - 3.5 Emotion Regulation in Applied Linguistics — 37
   - 3.6 Lessons Learned: The State of the Field — 43

4. The Non-Japanese Teacher in Japan — 45
   - 4.1 Introduction — 45
   - 4.2 English in Japan — 46
   - 4.3 The Japanese University — 48
   - 4.4 The Non-Japanese University Teacher — 51
   - 4.5 Lessons learned: Who is the Non-Japanese University EFL Teacher in Japan? — 55

5	A Study of Emotion Regulation	56
	5.1 Introduction	56
	5.2 People and Places	57
	5.3 Designing a Study of Emotion Regulation	61
	5.4 Rolling Up My Sleeves: Collecting and Analysing the Data	66
	5.5 Lessons Learned: Studying Emotion Regulation	74
6	Environment	76
	6.1 Introduction: Teachers Moulding Their Environment	76
	6.2 Characteristic Situational Strategies and Motives	77
	6.3 Contextual Factors Affording and Shaping Situational Strategies	84
	6.4 Complex Considerations	90
	6.5 Lessons Learned: Power Over Our Environment	94
7	Attention	96
	7.1 Introduction: Teachers' Points of Focus	96
	7.2 Characteristic Attentional Strategies and Motives	97
	7.3 Contextual Factors Affording and Shaping Attention Deployment	99
	7.4 Complex Considerations	102
	7.5 Lessons Learned: Attention and Emotion	107
8	Cognition	108
	8.1 Introduction: Teachers Regulating Their Thoughts	108
	8.2 Characteristic Cognitive Strategies and Motives	109
	8.3 Contextual Factors Affording and Shaping Cognitive Change	115
	8.4 Complex Considerations	122
	8.5 Lessons Learned: Empathy at the Heart of Cognitive Change	128
9	Response	129
	9.1 Introduction: Teachers Regulating Their Responses	129
	9.2 Characteristic Response Modulation Strategies and Motives	130
	9.3 Contextual Factors Affording and Shaping Response Modulation	134
	9.4 Complex Considerations	140
	9.5 Lessons Learned: Holistic and Responsive Emotional Displays	147
10	Conclusion: Language Teacher Emotion Regulation	149
	10.1 Goal 1: The Voices of Practicing Professionals	150
	10.2 Goal 2: The Language Teacher Emotion Regulation Model (LTERM)	153

10.3 Goal 3: Lessons for the Field	156
10.4 Concluding Remarks	162
Appendices	163
References	170
Index	185

Acknowledgements

The writing of this book could hardly have been more filled with emotion, surviving house moves, illnesses, the birth of my daughter and the COVID-19 pandemic. It has been as much a journey of learning to regulate my own emotions as learning from the participants! Throughout the project I have received immeasurable support and I extend special thanks to the following people.

Firstly, to Jim King, who has been a wonderful guide over the past eight years. Jim always seems to know the next point to consider, the next person to speak to and the next paper to read. I am extremely grateful for his unwavering belief in this project.

I would like to express my thanks to the editors, Sarah Mercer and Stephen Ryan, for their belief in this book. I am also grateful to Laura Jordan, Rosie McEwan, Constance Collier-Qureshy and Flo McClelland at Multilingual Matters for all of their support in bringing the manuscript to print.

I wish to thank all of my friends and colleagues. I am especially grateful to Martin Mielick, Daniel Hooper, Satchie Haga and Richard Sampson for their useful comments on various drafts. I am also very grateful to the anonymous reviewers, whose suggestions improved the manuscript immensely.

There were a large number of management and support staff at the participating university who enabled this research to take place. Without them, the book would not exist, and I am thankful for their help in negotiating access, ethics and a whole host of administrative red tape.

The participants who took part in the study were all extremely gracious in lending me their time and their stories. I am very grateful to them for their enthusiasm.

Finally, I would like to extend my gratitude to my family. To my parents, Linda and Ray, who have always supported me in my academic and life choices. The past six years have been especially difficult, and I am forever grateful to you for believing in me. I would like to also thank my parents-in-law, Toshie and Nobuyoshi for their limitless encouragement.

To my wife and my daughter, who all of this is for. Your unwavering support for this project is the only reason it was finished. Thank you for lifting me whenever I was down.

Copyright Notice

The dataset of the study published in this book has also been explored in two other publications:

Elements of chapters 6, 7 and 9 have previously been discussed in Morris, S. (2022) Performing motivating and caring identities: The emotions of non-Japanese university teachers of English. In M. Mielick, R. Kubota and L. Lawrence (eds) *Discourses of Identity: Language Learning, Teaching and Reclamation Perspectives in Japan* (pp. 341–358). Palgrave Macmillan.

Elements of chapters 6, 8 and 9 have previously been discussed in Morris, S. and King, J. (2023) University language teachers' contextually dependent uses of instrumental emotion regulation. *System 116*, 103080

Acknowledgement of Financial Support

I was fortunate to be awarded a grant from the Japan Society for the Promotion of Science to fund this project, and I extend my gratitude to them – JSPS KAKENHI Grant Number JP19K00856. Any opinions, findings and conclusions or recommendations expressed in this material are those of the author and do not necessarily reflect the views of JSPS nor MEXT.

Foreword

Jim King
University of Leicester

Despite experience teaching in language schools across Europe and Australia, plus spells at other Japanese universities, in the early 2000s I found myself facing one of the most difficult classes of my career. From the moment I walked in to Class 2B, there was a palpable sense of resistance from this group of second-year Japanese learners of English. Closed body language, averted eyes, whispered sniggers and minimal-to-no participation. It all felt rather awkward and personal. No matter how much energy and enthusiasm I put into my lessons, they remained cold and unresponsive with a barely contained hostility seeming to simmer under the surface. I remember feeling completely nonplussed by this, as I'd always considered myself to be quite a charismatic educator with strong engagement and classroom management skills. I soon learned that Class 2B deeply missed their first-year teacher and resented my presence as an unwelcome replacement. The clue to what was happening presented itself one day early in the term when I came to class to find that half the students were wearing T-shirts with their former teacher's beaming mugshot emblazoned across the front. This was a clue hard to miss! Class 2B's indifference tested my confidence and patience in ways I hadn't expected at that stage of my career. It became a real dilemma that played on my mind: should I let my feelings show, being real and honest in my emotional displays, or should I suppress them, knowing that certain emotions, such as open frustration or anger, tend not to be considered appropriate for teachers to publicly display in Japanese classroom settings, particularly when done so by a foreigner? In the end, I relied on emotion regulation to navigate both my own feelings and the classroom dynamic. I re-framed my thinking, reminding myself that the rejection was more about the group's difficulties dealing with change and grief about the loss of their former tutor than about me as a person or teacher. Rather than letting disappointment dictate my response, I focused on maintaining a calm and positive presence. I made a conscious effort to stay cheerful and engaging, even when their reactions, or lack of them, stung. I adjusted my expectations, understanding that winning over Class 2B would take time. I made space for their emotions, showing them that I was not there to replace their beloved former teacher but to provide them with a different and equally valuable experience. Slowly, I started to see some changes, such as a hesitant answer here or a small laugh there. It would be inaccurate to say that there was a happy-ever-after ending in which Class 2B and I suddenly became the best of friends, but by the end of the course, we were able to focus on the important business of making progress in language learning (and the journey to the classroom no longer felt like a walk to the gallows for me!). This experience reinforced for me that emotion regulation isn't just about suppressing affective responses entirely; it's about managing them in ways that support both teacher well-being and student learning. Had I let my frustration show too much, I might have deepened Class 2B's resistance. But by carefully balancing authenticity with emotional restraint, I was eventually able to create an environment where trust could grow and learning could happen.

Research into language teacher psychology is experiencing something of a boom at the moment, with the publication of a number of influential anthologies in recent years (e.g., Gregersen & Mercer, 2022; Gkonou et al., 2020; Martinez Agudo, 2018; Mercer & Kostoulas, 2018). Sam Morris's book does an excellent job of building upon and extending this previous work via his innovative study of how and why language teachers regulate their emotions. He provides a new and exciting framework which carefully considers the dynamic interplay between intra- and interpersonal factors helping to shape teachers' emotional experiences, showing how personal histories, social relationships, institutional demands and so on, all interact within the 'social crucible' (King & Morris, 2022: 313) of the language classroom. To do this Sam draws from an impressive set of data sources: many hours of observations within Japanese university English classrooms, multiple interviews with experienced language teachers and a data corpus of over 300,000 words. Using psychologist James Gross's (1998) seminal ideas about how we use various strategies to regulate our emotions as its theoretical base, the study provides a fascinating insight into the emotional dimension of teaching English within a culturally and institutionally distinct setting. Sam uses participant testimony to good effect, giving these teachers a voice about how they manage their emotions in the face of interacting learners and negotiating relationships with them. I've previously called for the emotional aspect of teaching to be better addressed on training programmes, highlighting the need for improved working conditions and teacher well-being support mechanisms (see King, 2016; King et al., 2024). The contents of this book make that call all the more compelling. I only wish *Language Teacher Emotion Regulation: An Exploration in Japan* had been available to help guide me all those years ago as I struggled to deal with my affective response to the behaviour of students in Class 2B...

References

Gkonou, C., Dewaele, J.-M. and King, J. (eds) (2020) *The Emotional Rollercoaster of Language Teaching*. Multilingual Matters.

Gregersen, T. and Mercer, S. (eds) (2022) *The Routledge Handbook of the Psychology of Language Learning and Teaching*. Routledge.

Gross, J.J. (1998) The emerging field of emotion regulation: An integrative review. *Review of General Psychology* 2 (3), 271–299.

King, J. (2016) "It's time, put on the smile, it's time!": The emotional labour of second language teaching within a Japanese university. In C. Gkonou, D. Tatzl and S. Mercer (eds) *New Directions in Language Learning Psychology* (pp. 97–112). Springer.

King, J. and Morris, S. (2022) Social interaction. In T. Gregersen and S. Mercer (eds) *The Routledge Handbook of the Psychology of Language Learning and Teaching* (pp. 313–324). Routledge.

King, J., Almukhaild, H., Mercer, S., Mairitsch, A., Babic, S. and Sulis, G. (2024) Teacher emotions and the emotional labour of Modern Language (ML) teachers working in UK secondary schools. *International Review of Applied Linguistics in Language Teaching* 62 (3), 1213–1235.

Martínez Agudo, J.D. (ed.) (2018) *Emotions in Second Language Teaching: Theory, Research and Teacher Education*. Springer.

Mercer, S. and Kostoulas, A. (eds) (2018) *Language Teacher Psychology*. Multilingual Matters.

PSYCHOLOGY OF LANGUAGE LEARNING AND TEACHING

Series Editors: **Sarah Mercer**, *Universität Graz, Austria* and **Stephen Ryan**, *Waseda University, Japan*

This international, interdisciplinary book series explores the exciting, emerging field of Psychology of Language Learning and Teaching. It is a series that aims to bring together works which address a diverse range of psychological constructs from a multitude of empirical and theoretical perspectives, but always with a clear focus on their applications within the domain of language learning and teaching. The field is one that integrates various areas of research that have been traditionally discussed as distinct entities, such as motivation, identity, beliefs, strategies and self-regulation, and it also explores other less familiar concepts for a language education audience, such as emotions, the self and positive psychology approaches. In theoretical terms, the new field represents a dynamic interface between psychology and foreign language education and books in the series draw on work from diverse branches of psychology, while remaining determinedly focused on their pedagogic value. In methodological terms, sociocultural and complexity perspectives have drawn attention to the relationships between individuals and their social worlds, leading to a field now marked by methodological pluralism. In view of this, books encompassing quantitative, qualitative and mixed methods studies are all welcomed.

All books in this series are externally peer-reviewed.

Full details of all the books in this series and of all our other publications can be found on http://www.multilingual-matters.com, or by writing to Multilingual Matters, St Nicholas House, 31–34 High Street, Bristol, BS1 2AW, UK.

1 Introduction to Language Teacher Emotion Regulation

Christie is a mid-career teacher working at a private language school in Southern Spain. She has taught secondary-age learners for at least 10 years, and though she enjoys the challenge of engaging her students, she sometimes struggles when they are truly unmotivated. Christie's main difficulty is that her students do not study English by choice. Most are forced to take classes by their parents or feel external pressures to study a foreign language for reasons they do not fully understand. This year, a pair of tight-knit teenagers have caused her particular trouble. The students chat incessantly, ignore instructions and respond negatively to requests to remain on task. Christie faces an emotional dilemma. Should she show anger in her classes to communicate her displeasure? Or would it be better to exhibit warmth and understanding, to let the students know that their struggles are recognised, but that their attention is needed on the task in hand?

Carlos is a highly experienced teacher employed at a university in the USA, where he teaches a content-focused course that combines English instruction alongside political theory. Carlos spends hours sourcing videos and planning interesting activities for his classes, and he is grateful that he is able to combine his passion for politics with his passion for language learning. Given the content focus of his course, there are inevitably times when he has to deal with very serious topics in the classroom, and today's lesson on political upheaval is likely to be both resonant and sobering for many of his students. Carlos too faces an emotional dilemma. How should he manage his emotions in front of students, who may themselves experience stress, frustration and anxiety towards the topics? Would intense emotions be needed, or indeed welcome, in conveying the seriousness of the topics under discussion? Would a lighter touch be preferable, a little humour and perhaps some smiles to lighten the mood?

Alina is a recently qualified teacher of English who will soon begin a first job working with highly motivated learners at a private language school in Korea. Since she is new to the country and also to the profession, Alina feels conflicted, not only about which grammatical points to teach, which vocabulary items to include and which classroom activities to use, but also about which kind of emotional persona to bring to the classroom. Alina wants to present herself as a lively, caring and personable teacher, but after noticing that her Korean colleagues adopt a strict tone she begins to reconsider. Alina also faces an emotional dilemma. Should she perform to Korean or American ideals of a 'good teacher'? Would young people in Korea respond to a teacher who presents themselves and their subject as something fun, lively and carefree? Alina's concerns simmer and she begins to question her whole assumptions on teaching young learners. Is it even desirable for teachers to engage with students warmly? Or is it perhaps better to use stern emotions, performing the role of the 'teacher as authority' to prevent potential issues from ever arising?

Christie, Carlos and Alina are not real teachers, but the situations they find themselves in are extremely common. Every working moment, language teachers make complex emotional decisions to negotiate their circumstances. Such decisions depend on the teacher's reading of the room and the goals they are trying to achieve. They are informed by social, cultural and institutional pressures, and filtered through the teacher's life experiences. If we consider the situations of Christie, Carlos and Alina (and indeed any number of incidents from our own classrooms), it becomes very clear that the emotions a language teacher feels and displays has important consequences, both for themselves and for the students in the room. In the face of such challenges, it would be terrible indeed if teachers lacked power and agency to make choices regarding their emotions. Fortunately, however, language teachers have a great degree of influence over emotions through *emotion regulation*.

Emotion regulation is a relatively recent concept arising from the traditions of psychoanalysis and coping in the 1980s (Gross, 1999). The field has significantly grown since then, but the core psychological principles have remained stable. Emotion regulation is achieved through attentional, behavioural and cognitive actions known as *emotion regulation strategies* (Gross, 2014, 2015; Koole, 2009) which are employed for a diverse range of intrapersonal and interpersonal reasons known as *emotion regulation motives* (Gross, 1998, 2015; Tamir, 2016; Tamir et al., 2020). Emotions can be regulated in innumerable ways. Individuals can strengthen them, weaken them, extend them or shorten their lifespan. They can prevent emotions from taking form or generate desired emotions into being. They can also manipulate the symptomatic outcomes of emotions: the facial expressions, physiological changes and motivations that appear to flood through the body once an emotion takes hold (Gross, 2014). Emotion regulation is ubiquitous, and almost every emotional experience is regulated in one way or another (Koole, 2009; Parrott, 2007). For language teachers, therefore, emotion regulation is 'something of a full-time job' (Goleman, 1995: 57).

1.1 Why a Book on Emotion Regulation?

In recent years, there has been an explosion of interest in L2 student and teacher emotions in the field of applied linguistics, and since I began thinking about this project in 2016 at least three edited volumes and two special issue journals have been released (see De Costa *et al.*, 2018; Gkonou *et al.*, 2020a; Martínez Agudo, 2018a; Prior & Haneda, 2023; Simons & Smits, 2021). Among these papers, emotion regulation has been continually posited as an important language teaching skill that needs further attention in reflective practice and training programmes. Nevertheless, there remains no full, detailed exploration of how and why experienced language teachers might regulate their emotions, of how cultural and contextual features influence their decision-making, or of the lessons that can be learned from experienced teachers' emotion regulation experiences.

Although it is true that individuals have control over their emotions, that is not to say that all language teachers share this power equally. Indeed, an individual's ability to regulate their emotions is dependent on a myriad of factors. Teachers all have unique childhoods, learning experiences and teaching histories that guide their emotional behaviour. They are also all subject to a variety of external pressures, their emotions being squeezed by sociocultural moods, by institutional demands, by expectations from managers and parents, and of course by the needs and attitudes of the students themselves. How do these factors intertwine with teachers' emotion regulation decision-making? A greater understanding is surely beneficial to all language teachers.

In this book I offer a theoretical framework of language teacher emotion regulation and explore the impact that contextual features such as personality, history, institutional guidelines and societal pressures have on experienced teachers. The focal point of the book is a study of 15 experienced non-Japanese English as a foreign language (EFL) teachers who all taught at the same Japanese university. I met with each teacher numerous times, interviewing them about their general beliefs on classroom emotions, observing their lessons to see their emotions in action, and using stimulated recall sessions to access their in-class thoughts and regulation decision-making. After 45 hours of observation and 45 interviews, I amassed a corpus of more than 300,000 words from which to draw conclusions. It is from this corpus that I believe this book achieves its three most important goals – to give practicing professionals a voice on their emotional experiences, to formulate a model of language teacher emotion regulation and to present lessons for stakeholders in the field so that teachers, trainers, researchers and institutions can more ably understand this important skill.

1.2 My Entry into Emotion Regulation

Similar, perhaps, to the imagined difficulties experienced by Christie, Carlos and Alena, my own interest in emotion regulation stems from a critical incident early on in my university teaching career. Although I was already a reasonably experienced teacher when I entered the tertiary sector in Japan, having worked for 10 years at various private language schools in Asia and Europe, the first years of my university experience were emotionally demanding. One day, during my very first semester, I was working in my office and struggling to grade a student's paper. The student in question was clearly (at least to me) very motivated. They were engaged in lessons and completed tasks diligently. They shared ideas freely and encouraged their classmates to speak in English as much as possible. They often approached me with questions and self-selected to spend time after class in the autonomous learning centre at the university, where they met with other students and teachers to practice speaking. The student was, in every sense, the embodiment of an 'active learner', the kind of self-motivated and autonomous risk-taker that is sought by the Japanese government (Ito, 2017). Yet despite all of this, the student's written homework was quite poor, and I, as their teacher, needed to give them a failing grade.

I felt a range of emotions at this prospect which manifested in different ways at different times. While grading in my office I felt a low-level of unease driven by thoughts that a failing grade might cause the student to feel demotivated. Yet, when handing back the grade I felt extreme stress. I remember being unable to make eye contact with the student during the class and recall making a conscious decision that day to wait until the end of class before returning grades, meaning that there would be little time for questions or queries. I tried to process my emotions by discussing my concerns with my more experienced colleague. Through these conversations I came to understand something important – my colleague did not share my negative feelings, maintaining an emotional distance from students, and grading with seemingly little difficulty. At the time I was struck deeply by the fact that my emotional response was not universal.

I now know that the actions I took throughout this incident were emotion regulation strategies. My decisions to avoid eye contact and delay giving feedback were attempts to attenuate the stressful emotions I was feeling, while my conversations with my colleague were attempts to reinterpret my experiences and find a new way forward. I was clearly experiencing a high degree of emotional dissonance. My desire to motivate my student was wrestling with my notions of professional responsibility and my need to protect my own emotional health. These tensions were themselves influenced by multiple contextual factors. There was for example, the fact that the semester in question was the first time that I was singularly responsible for the direction, learning and assessment of a class.

There was my previous work experience, which primarily took place in financially driven contexts, where my role required me to protect students from negative emotions. Of course, there was also my own language learning history at play – memories of a high school French teacher reporting disappointment in my language ability at a parents' evening. These factors certainly informed my emotions and my attempts to regulate them.

What relevance then, does this narrative have to this book and my beliefs that underlie it? In the first case, it highlights that investigations of emotion regulation should be descriptive rather than prescriptive. Given that any teacher's emotional experiences are driven by their own histories, beliefs, experiences and interpretations, any attempt to define what teachers *should* be doing emotionally in the classroom has the potential to antagonise. This is a perspective shared by other researchers (e.g. Cowie, 2011; Day & Leitch, 2001; Gkonou *et al.*, 2020b; Gkonou & Mercer, 2017). Certainly, I do not think that my approach to grading was either better or worse than my colleague's, but by discussing the issue I obtained greater understanding of our dual perspectives. It is my belief, therefore, that investigations of emotion regulation should be driven by a desire to unearth, explore and explain the experiences of others. To afford an empathetic understanding such that any reader may be able to reflect themselves on the relevance of testimony to their own situations.

Secondly, the narrative highlights that language teaching is, essentially, a social practice (e.g. Batstone, 2010; Breen, 1985; Hall, 1995; King & Morris, 2022). Classroom language learning is almost wholly driven by interaction, either by students interacting with the teacher, or by students interacting with peers in the presence of the teacher. Given that emotions themselves are essentially socially emerging phenomena (Boiger & Mesquita, 2012), it is logical to accept that almost everything a language teacher does in the classroom will be, to varying degrees, influenced by emotions, either their own or their students' (a conclusion I echo from Zembylas, 2002). In my example above, it was clear that my emotions were shaped by past interactions and equally shaped future interactions. Emotion regulation is not simply a way for teachers to manage the unwanted emotions they experience but also a tool with which they may support their students to learn languages in a most effective way.

This point is relevant to a third belief: that teaching is a job requiring the skilful *use* of emotions. The choice of the word 'use' here is deliberate. Just as an accountant uses a computer to calculate a tax bill and a carpenter uses a lathe to shape wood, a teacher uses their emotions to engage their students, present content effectively and meet the responsibilities of the profession. Teachers' emotion regulation actions enact change within themselves and their students, and I agree with other researchers who have suggested that emotion regulation should be considered a teacher competence (e.g. Brackett *et al.*, 2010; Corcoran & Tormey, 2012; Gkonou & Mercer, 2017; Hagenauer & Volet, 2014; Hosotani &

Imai-Matsumura, 2011; King et al., 2020; Yin & Lee, 2012; Yin et al., 2013). Language teachers have important and unique emotional responsibilities: language teaching is dominated by interactive methodologies, takes place in multicultural classroom landscapes and requires a high degree of empathetic understanding on the part of the teacher (Gkonou & Mercer, 2017). The fostering of second language literacy can bring about profound changes in the way that students perceive the world and their place within it, but to do this successfully, teachers must manage their own fears, anxieties, joys, guilts, stresses, angers, excitements and frustrations in ways which support rather than impede learning.

1.3 An Overview of the Book

Like all good books, I believe that different readers will find different things to enjoy in the nine chapters that follow. Of course it can be read from cover to cover, and perhaps this is the best way to approach the text for those new to the topic of teacher emotions. Yet, each chapter has been designed to meet a particular goal, and can be read singularly or out of turn for those targeting a particular facet or feature of emotion regulation. Broadly speaking, the book is split into two halves. Chapters 2, 3 and 4 explore theoretical concerns, whereas Chapters 5–10 describe and discuss the study.

Those looking for a theoretical understanding of emotions and emotion regulation need look no further than Chapter 2. There it will be seen that teacher emotions and emotion regulation need to be recognised as being both intrapersonal and interpersonal phenomena. In simple terms, an intrapersonal perspective sees emotions and regulation as being experienced within an individual, with teachers exerting control over a variety of psychological, physiological and behavioural emotional symptoms. These experiences, however, cannot be divorced from surrounding interpersonal social contexts, which exert control over both the emotions that are experienced and how they are subsequently managed. This chapter will introduce a key framework of emotion regulation from general psychology, called *the process model of emotion regulation* (Gross, 1998, 2014, 2015). According to this model, the actions which individuals take to regulate their emotions are termed emotion regulation strategies. There are an enormous number of such strategies which Gross groups into four groups: *situational strategies*, which are actions targeting the real-world catalysts of emotions; *attention deployment strategies*, which are actions targeting the attentional systems; *cognitive change strategies*, which are actions targeting cognition; and *response modulation strategies*, which are actions targeting the experiential, behavioural and physiological responses after an emotion has emerged. Each of these strategy types will be explained along with relevant examples from general psychology and teaching.

Those interested in an overview of the current literature on emotion regulation will enjoy Chapter 3. In this chapter I review the existing work in education and applied linguistics. Emotion regulation does not exist in a bubble, and it is attended to in a range of parallel fields including socio-emotional literacy, emotional labour and language teacher well-being. Papers from each of these areas will be critically discussed along with studies that have placed emotion regulation strategies and motives at the heart of their investigation, leading readers to a thorough grounding in current knowledge.

Many may be unfamiliar with the Japanese context, and the purpose of Chapter 4 is to bring readers up to speed with university education in Japan. In addition to describing the purpose and goals of tertiary education, I discuss the roles occupied by non-Japanese teachers and their emotional responsibilities. This chapter sets the scene for the second half of the book.

At this point the book then moves onto the central study. Those looking to understand how emotion regulation might be investigated in the language classroom will find use from Chapter 5, which explains the methodological decision-making. The qualitative study that I conducted had three main aims: to explore the emotion regulation strategies employed by the teachers, the motives they regulated their emotions in aid of and the contextual factors that influenced their decision-making. This chapter will help the reader to understand the exploration of the data in the remaining chapters.

The discussion of the data that was obtained takes place in Chapters 6–9. Each chapter deals with a different target of emotion regulation actions. In Chapter 6, I present the data related to how the participants regulated their environment. This chapter has much to say about the ways that institutional freedom and control influence language teachers' emotion regulation abilities, and consequently their well-being. In Chapter 7, I discuss how the participants regulated their attention, and in Chapter 8, I explore how the participants regulated their thoughts. In Chapter 9, I analyse how the participants regulated their emotional expressions, and this chapter is particularly relevant to those interested in the topic of emotional labour.

In the final chapter of the book, I turn my attention back to the most important goals of the book, summarising the voices of the participants, presenting a model of language teacher emotion regulation and providing lessons for the field. When reflecting upon the theoretical knowledge presented in the first half of the book, and the data-based conclusions in the second, numerous questions emerge. Thus, I end by considering the most important of these: How can language teachers understand their own emotion regulation practices more deeply, and make more adaptive choices for themselves and their students? Must institutions do more to support the emotional demands of teaching? How should researchers best explore emotional decision-making? And finally, where should we go next?

2 Theoretical Perspectives on Emotion Regulation

2.1 Introduction

I am lucky enough to teach a content-based course on emotions to undergraduate learners in Japan. Students study a wide range of topics including the role of emotions in intercultural communication, the impact of stress on health, and (of course) the importance of emotion regulation. Over the six-year history of the course, I have been asked one question far more than any other, usually in the first few weeks: 'Are we studying psychology, biology or sociology?' I love this question. It illustrates the breadth of the field of emotions and underscores the value of emotion study to both natural and social sciences. I always respond by telling my students that emotions are attended to in a range of academic domains, and that it is useful to understand emotions from different perspectives. I believe that this is true for studying language teacher emotion regulation too.

In this chapter I explore definitional and theoretical perspectives of emotion and emotion regulation. Broadly speaking, research has tackled a wide range of foci, including the evolutionary purposes of emotions, the processes of emotion arousal, the psychological features of emotions and the functions of emotions in human lives. I explore many of these in the sections to come. Like other researchers working in the field of applied linguistics (e.g. King & Ng, 2018), I view emotions to contain both intrapersonal (i.e. that emotions exist within a person) and interpersonal (i.e. that emotions are externally influenced by a person's surroundings) components, and I extend these ideas by asserting that emotion regulation also be viewed from intrapersonal and interpersonal perspectives. In the first half of the chapter, I return to first principles and present definitions of both emotions and emotion regulation from these two positions. These are necessarily technical discussions, but I aid the reader by providing real world examples from the language classroom. In the second half of the chapter, I introduce the core psychological features of emotion regulation and present a discussion of how emotion regulation strategies and motives can be taxonomized. These two halves lead to the presentation of a tentative model of language teacher emotion regulation which can support the reader of this book to follow the remaining chapters. The model is presented in a preliminary form in this chapter, and completed later in Chapter 10.

2.2 Defining Emotions

Before considering how emotions are regulated, it is important first of all to understand what exactly an emotion is, and that is the purpose of this section. In defining emotions, we must of course also define what emotions are not. Emotions are not feelings. Emotions are physical changes that occur in our body, sometimes unconsciously, whereas feelings are subjective mental representations of emotions (Scherer, 2005). Emotions are therefore a more technically accurate word to describe the chemical and behavioural changes that occur when we experience a feeling like anger. Emotions are also not moods. Emotions are of higher intensity than moods, which tend to last for longer periods (Rosenberg, 1998) and lack a clear instigating event (Gross, 2014). Finally, emotions are not stress. Stress is, of course, discussed in this book, but as an umbrella term representing a group of negative emotions that have an impact on our mental health (Kyriacou, 2001).

I begin by exploring the definition of emotions from an *intrapersonal* perspective. Here I am concerned with the ways in which emotions are experienced and managed within an individual.

2.2.1 Emotions from an intrapersonal perspective: Appraisal theories

From an intrapersonal perspective, appraisal theories of emotion offer the best descriptive model, since appraisals are widely considered to reflect the internal psychological processes of emotions (Russell, 2014). According to these theories, emotions are aroused and managed through *cognitive appraisals* – evaluations of whether an event that an individual encounters is considered to be personally relevant (Arnold, 1959; Lazarus, 1991; Moors, 2014; Moors *et al.*, 2013; Ochsner & Gross, 2014; Scherer, 2001; Suri & Gross, 2016). Appraisals are considered to be natural responses to environmental stimuli that help individuals to manage their well-being (Moors *et al.*, 2013).

Appraisals are typically modelled as four-stage processes. When an individual meets an internal or external stimulus event, and their attention is guided towards it, the event will be appraised. Should the event be considered relevant, an emotion will be triggered. This process is called the *situation–attention–appraisal–response* cycle (Gross, 2015; Ochsner & Gross, 2014; Suri & Gross, 2016). A simple classroom example of this process might be when two students begin to chat idly off topic (situation), the teacher notices (attention), evaluates the situation as impacting their teaching (appraisal) and then experiences frustration (response).

In my description above, the notion of 'attending to' and 'appraising' something could be interpreted to suggest conscious effort; however, I think it is important to understand that appraisals operate on and across different levels of processing (see, for example, Ochsner & Gross, 2014; Scherer, 2001, 2009; Suri & Gross, 2016). Ochsner and Gross (2014) describe three levels in depth. At the lowest and most primitive neural level, *core evaluations* occur. Here, appraisals are processed implicitly with close similarities seen to the notion of survival instincts. On this level, simple connections between events, consequences and behaviour are made (lion = dangerous = avoid). On a higher schematic level, *contextual valuations* take place. Here an appraisal is guided by contexts and memories, including the social, historical and motivational circumstances surrounding the individual and the event. These contexts determine whether an emotional stimulus will impact an individual positively or negatively at a given time, and consequently, whether the stimulus should be attended to or avoided. Contextual valuations use more cognitive processing than lower-level appraisals owing to the higher degree of effort required to analyse the environment. Finally, at the highest level of appraisal, *conceptual evaluations* are made. Here, emotions are driven by their relationship to abstract and verbalisable constructs. Two students chatting idly, for example, may be connected to the concept of 'rudeness' which will subsequently influence a (potentially negative) emotional path for a teacher. In sum, appraisals may be conscious and deliberate, or unconscious and spontaneous, depending on the levels of processing involved. Language teachers may, therefore, experience very automatic appraisals when teaching or they may make more conscious appraisals driven by their interpretations of behaviours and events. An important overarching principle that must also be highlighted is that appraisals are mostly individualistic. With the exception of the very primal core evaluations, appraisals are driven by any person's own unique experiences. For language teachers this means that classroom-based appraisals are highly influenced by any teacher's past learning and teaching experiences, as well as by their more general life path.

2.2.2 Emotions have five components

What actually happens to a person while they are experiencing an emotion? Ekman and Cordaro (2011: 366) describe the impact of emotions as a 'cascade of changes' through the body and mind. Formally speaking, these changes are called *emotion components* (Russell, 2014; Shuman & Scherer, 2014; Thoits, 1989, 2007). Five of these components are described most commonly. Following the appraisal of an event (component 1), a person will experience physiological changes in their body (e.g. sweating, blood pressure changes – component 2); uncontrollable expressional changes to the face (e.g. smiling, frowning – component 3); action tendencies, which are motivational reactions to the stimulating event (e.g. a desire to flee, a desire to be alone – component 4); and a subjective feeling that they describe using language (e.g. when experiencing an emotion we attribute a label like 'fear' or 'anger' within our mind – component 5) (Scherer, 2001, 2005, 2009). These five components interact bidirectionally with each other continually across an emotional episode.

Emotions impact us for a reason, and each of the five components contribute to the evolutionary functional purposes of emotions in different ways (Shuman & Scherer, 2014). The function of the appraisal is to support an individual to understand and make meaning from an event being experienced, and it allows teachers to understand the causes and effects of emotion-inducing events. The function of the physiological change is to regulate and support the body for action. It may do this, for example, by increasing the blood flow to a teacher's face and upper body so that they may be more able to respond to a difficult circumstance. The function of the facial expression component is to communicate feelings and intentions to others. A frown by the teacher may communicate to students that their behaviour is inappropriate. The function of the motivational component is to make an individual take action in a fast and unconscious manner. It can be recognised in a teacher's urge to raise their voice to deal with classroom misbehaviour. Finally, the subjective feeling component functions as a monitor of an individual's internal state and the way they perceive and interact with the environment. It allows teachers to continually assess the path of their emotions as they play out. Through these five componential functions, emotions support teachers to negotiate their classrooms and places of work.

From an internal, intrapersonal perspective, emotions are driven by appraisals and cause componential changes, but this emerging model paints only half a picture. Appraisal models do not take account of the external features that influence emotional paths. To better understand the role of context we must also look to interpersonal models of emotions.

2.2.3 Emotions from an interpersonal perspective: Social constructivist perspectives

'Emotional experiences and their meaning to the individuals involved do not occur in a vacuum' (Schutz & DeCuir, 2002: 130), so we should consider the role that social and cultural factors play in supporting and inhibiting language teachers' emotions. The interpersonal dimension of emotions is most ably served by constructivist paradigms. Constructivist positions stress that emotions arise from the brain's attempts to make sense of contextual information by comparing external stimuli to an individual's past experiences and predicting the most adaptive path forward (Barrett, 2017). Emotions therefore are not hardwired, nor shared universally amongst people of different cultures, but are constructed in the moment to help individuals respond to emerging stimuli (Barrett, 2017; Mesquita, 2022). Constructivist positions again support the idea that language teachers' emotions are uniquely wed to their own personal histories: to the wealth of experiences, education and critical incidents that have impacted them in their past.

Equally, constructivist positions emphasise the dynamic and social nature of emotion. Boiger and Mesquita (2012), for example, highlight that the majority of emotions experienced in the modern world occur during human interactions. Emotions serve pragmatic functions within these interactions to help individuals and interlocuters take meaning from the experiences. The authors describe that emotions are constructed through an 'iterative and an ongoing process that unfolds within interactions and relationships, which derive their shape and meaning from the prevailing ideas and practices of the larger sociocultural context' (2012: 222). In other words, emotions emerge as they are co-constructed during exchanges by actors who are subject to a range of external contextual pressures: by display rules and expectations on ideal behaviours that are informed by notions of culture (Barrett, 2014; Mesquita *et al.*, 2016), and by power dynamics that guide the required emotional output within a relationship (Hochschild, 1983; Kemper, 1981; Shuman & Scherer, 2014).

Boiger and Mesquita (2012) outline three nested contexts within which emotions emerge: moment-to-moment interactions, developing and ongoing relationships and sociocultural contexts. At the lowest interactional level, emotions are continually constructed and managed by the participants involved in a social exchange. As an interaction progresses, the emotions being experienced are sculpted by the linguistic and gestural tools used in the communication. Thus, when a teacher and a colleague speak, their emotions are afforded or constrained by the semiotic signals they receive from each other. If one advances a facial expression indicating annoyance, this will be appraised by the other in a particular way, causing them to adapt their own communication. This adapted communication will then be reinterpreted by the original speaker. We can see that emotions are continually shaped by both parties, who construct their own meanings from their interpretations of the exchanges.

On the middle relationship level, any emotions being experienced are afforded and constrained by both the history of the relationship, and also the potential futures that the relationship may have. Different emotions will be afforded among actors with a positive and long-term relationship to those with a short-term or combative relationship. Within these relationships patterned or unusual behaviours may have a significant impact on emotional episodes, with actors able to differentiate between what is 'normal' and what is not. Equally important, is that the hierarchical structure of the participants will dictate to a considerable degree the types of emotions they will experience (Lively & Weed, 2016); thus, a teacher, typically in a stronger hierarchical position than a student, may feel bound by the relationship to construct and project particular emotions, and equally the student, in the weaker position, may feel a similar pressure.

On the highest sociocultural contextual level, emotions are intimately wed to the prescribed social norms of the group culture. This may be on a community scale, such as in the emotions deemed appropriate for organisational cooperation in business contexts, or on a larger national scale, such as in the degree to which a culture allows expressive components of emotions to flourish. The impact of culture and structure on emotions is often exemplified through the concept of Arlie Hochschild's 'feeling rules' (1983), unwritten sociocultural guidelines that sculpt emotional exchanges in interactions. Such rules dictate various facets of emotions including the degree of intensity of emotions that are allowed to be displayed, the valence (direction – positive or negative) of acceptable emotions, and the duration of emotions. They may be considered similar in manner to other socially constructed rules such as etiquette. Feeling rules are 'learnt' through various forms of socialisation throughout infancy, adolescence and adulthood, with significant adults (caregivers, teachers etc.) taking on a crucial role in affirming the emotions of the very young (Barrett, 2017; Lively & Weed, 2016). On a national scale, emotions are managed according to the requirements of the value system of that culture. For example, research shows that cultures that place value on group-level harmony and on hierarchical power levels (such as Japan) tend to suppress their emotions more often than those from individualistic cultures (such as 'the West') (Matsumoto et al., 2008; Tsai et al., 2006).

Let me end this section by summarising what we may learn about teachers' emotions from the various theories that I have introduced thus far. Firstly, from an intrapersonal perspective we can learn that teachers' emotions are episodic processes powered by appraisals of events as advantageous or disadvantageous. Such appraisals may be implicit or explicit and may occur across multiple levels of processing. Secondly, we can learn that emotions serve functional purposes for teachers through five componential changes. Emotions help them communicate their desires through facial expressions, make behavioural changes and enable meaningful understanding of classroom events. Thirdly, from an interpersonal perspective, we can learn that teachers' emotions are shaped within cultures. Their emotions emerge in interactions, and are influenced by their past experiences, by their relationships and by larger sociocultural pressures. I hope it is clear from the discussion thus far that any model of emotions should take both the intrapersonal (internal) and interpersonal (external) perspectives into account.

2.3 Defining Emotion Regulation

Although I have explored definitions of emotions, the topic of this book is emotion regulation. I now wish to define emotion regulation and consider how it builds upon the ideas discussed thus far.

Within literature, the impression is often given that emotions and emotion regulation involve distinct mechanisms, with one system built upon another. But in truth, emotions and emotion regulation are hardly separable (Koole, 2009; Parrott, 2007). This means that emotion regulation also contains intrapersonal and interpersonal dimensions. I explore these dimensions first before giving an explanation of the four core features of emotion regulation.

2.3.1 Emotion regulation from an intrapersonal perspective

In the same way that appraisals drive emotions, appraisals also drive emotion regulation. Earlier I explained that when individuals place attention on events, they appraise them. In fact, appraisals are continually reoccurring. This means that as emotions take form, individuals constantly appraise them to understand whether they are moving in an adaptive or maladaptive direction (Gross, 2015; Ochsner & Gross, 2014; Suri & Gross, 2016). If an individual appraises an emerging emotion as being unwelcome, they may take action to modify the course of that emotion. This action is what we can understand to be emotion regulation.

I will illustrate this with a simple example. When we imagine a teacher dealing with a non-responsive student, it is easy to imagine that the teacher may feel any or all of a range of negative emotions: frustration, anxiety, stress or perhaps even fear. During such circumstances, a teacher continually appraises their emerging emotional states and evaluates whether their response is appropriate. As the teacher experiences and monitors the emotion, they may take action to move it into more adaptive forms. Across time, any emotion may be regulated into a new emotion, which can itself be regulated into a shorter/longer/hidden emotion. Imagine the language teacher of the inattentive student that makes an angry outburst, who then becomes embarrassed at their anger, who then tries to hide their embarrassment from the class by putting on a brave face, who then wishes to move on from the whole sorry episode and decides to just get on with the class.

So how about the emotional components? What roles do they play in emotion regulation? Simply put, the components function as targets of emotion regulation processes, and individuals are able to modify any or all of them (Gross, 2015). For example, a teacher who is feeling angry, may target the expressional component only, masking their frown and hiding their annoyance from the class. Alternatively, the same teacher may target their cognition and try to change how they are appraising the environmental stimulus causing the emotion. Emotional components are important because the componential targets of emotion regulation behaviour contribute to the way that emotion regulation actions are understood and taxonomized, and this is something that I will discuss in more detail later in this chapter.

2.3.2 Emotion regulation from an interpersonal perspective

When we turn to interpersonal perspectives, I deduce that social constructivist theories play an important conceptual role in EFL teachers emotion regulation in two ways. Firstly, these perspectives show that the emotion regulation actions taken by teachers are guided by past experiences, frequently performed within interactions, and to a great degree informed by their relationships with students and peers. Any interactions are themselves situated within relational histories, and subject to pressures arising from the cultures of the classroom, institution, political system and society at large. Since language teachers may be working outside cultures they were raised in, it must be deduced that their regulation during interactions is continually informed by their understanding and interpretations of both their first and host cultures, which develop ontogenetically across their working lifetime.

Secondly, social constructivist theories suggest that emotion regulation actions themselves can be tied to the sociocultural context (Mesquita et al., 2014). It may be, for example, that a particular form of emotion regulation is encouraged or discouraged by the context of work. Teachers may work in a culture where colleagues frequently vent their stresses to each other, and while any individual teacher might not wish to take part in this form of emotional release, they may nevertheless find themselves drawn towards this practice through group socialisation.

What becomes clear from the interpersonal perspective is that unfolding emotions and emotion regulation actions cannot be extricated from the context in which they arise, and that consequently, models of language teacher emotion regulation must include a contextual component.

2.3.3 The core features of emotion regulation

In the discussion thus far, I have very much focused on the theoretical definitional discourse of emotions and emotion regulation. Emotion regulation, however, is a very practical affair. Individuals make conscious efforts to regulate their emotions using a variety of cognitive, attentional, psychological and behavioural actions, and it is both useful and important to understand the key psychological features of emotion regulation.

The literature on emotion regulation in general psychology indicates that there are four core features of emotion regulation which emerge consecutively: motives, goals, strategies and outcomes (Gross, 2014; Tamir, 2016). These are what I discuss in this section.

2.3.3.1 Emotion regulation motives

Any act of emotion regulation begins with a *motive* for the regulation: a tangible reason or desired end result of the emotion regulation process. Emotion regulation is motivated since individuals employ it for functional purposes: they use it to manage their well-being, to enact identities and to influence the behaviour of others, among other things (Tamir, 2016; Tamir *et al.*, 2020). A prototypical motive for language teacher emotion regulation might be 'to increase my general sense of well-being' or 'to change the behaviours of my students'.

Emotion regulation motives are a very important feature of emotion regulation. Understanding why a teacher might choose to regulate their emotions can help when assessing the success and impact of their regulation.

2.3.3.2 Emotion regulation goals

Once a motive has been established, a *goal* for emotion regulation must be activated. Where motives refer to the functional outcome of emotion regulation, goals refer to the emotional outcome. They typically correspond with desired changes to the valence, length or strength of emotions. A prototypical language teacher emotion regulation goal might be 'to increase the strength of my happiness' or 'to hide the expression of my anger'.

The valence of emotions can be influenced in four ways. Both positive and negative emotions can be either up-regulated (enhanced) or down-regulated (attenuated) (Gross, 2014), and it is important to note that individuals often hold different beliefs in relation to their management of positive and negative emotions (Bryant, 2003). In other words, a teacher's ability (or perceived ability) to be able to reduce their negative emotions as a way to cope with stress does not predict that same person's ability to enhance the positive moments of their life.

2.3.3.3 Emotion regulation strategies

Once emotion regulation motives and goals have been activated, teachers need to actually modify the emotions they are experiencing. The actions they do so with are known as emotion regulation *strategies*.

Emotion regulation strategies can be of varying complexity, and can focus on the external environment, the attentional systems, cognition, or the componential outcomes of emotional episodes. For example, one common strategy is known as *reappraisal* (e.g. Gross, 1998, 2014), and it involves the manipulation of the appraisal component of an emotion. When employing this strategy, an individual changes how they feel about an emotional stimulus. For example, a language teacher might reappraise a badly behaving student as 'usually well-behaved', to attenuate emerging negative emotions. Another common strategy is called *expressive suppression* (e.g. Gross, 1998, 2014) and it involves the concealing of the expressional component of an emotion. For example, a teacher may wish to hide their displays of anger from the class by adopting a neutral expression. There are a huge number of possible emotion regulation strategies and these are usually taxonomized into various groups, more of which is discussed later in this chapter.

Emotion regulation strategies are often applied in advance of or during an emotional event (Gross, 1998, 2014), but they have also been shown to be applied following an event (Bryant, 2003; Quoidbach *et al.*, 2015). The timing of the strategy may be critical for both short- and long-term outcomes for well-being in teachers. For example, teachers may sacrifice short term hedonic benefits to meet long-term pragmatic aims, or vice versa, may choose a regulation strategy which deals with issues in the short term at the cost of negative consequences later on (Tamir, 2016).

Individuals can employ multiple strategies at a time when regulating their emotions. In fact, Heiy and Cheavens (2014) found that individuals tend to employ, on average, seven strategies to regulate instances of emotion. The authors theorised that some strategies, while not powerful when used alone, may increase in value when paired with others. Heiy and Cheavens's work also concluded that contextual decisions played a critical role in the choice and number of emotion regulation strategies that may be employed. For example, the authors found that individuals use more strategies to up-regulate excitement and love, than they do for amusement and excitement. Heiy and Cheavens's work suggests that when teachers and researchers explore emotion regulation, they need to account for the use of multiple emotion regulation strategies, each of which may play more or less dominant roles in the regulation and may be contingent upon contextual circumstances.

2.3.3.4 Emotion regulation outcomes

The final core feature of emotion regulation is known as the *outcome*, and it refers to the actual changes that are made to any emotion. Emotion regulation outcomes can be observed in two locations. *Intrinsic emotion regulation* outcomes are observed in the experiencer (the teacher has regulated their own emotions), and *extrinsic emotion regulation* outcomes are observed in others (the teacher has regulated the emotions of the students) (English & Eldesouky, 2020; Gross, 2014; McRae & Gross, 2020).

2.3.3.5 Implicit and explicit emotion regulation

Having explored the four key features of emotion regulation, I would like to introduce one more important characteristic of emotion regulation – its implicit and explicit nature. Briefly speaking, exploring emotion regulation (either our own or others') can be challenging because conscious knowledge of an emotion regulation motive, goal, strategy or outcome, may sometimes be hard for an individual to access.

In research literature, emotion regulation is usually described prototypically as an explicit act, something that is both conscious and deliberate, but emotion regulation can also take place implicitly without awareness. Explicitness and implicitness are not binary states but may be reflected along a continuum mediated by the degree of conscious effort required to initialise the regulation process, and the degree of conscious awareness and monitoring that take place throughout (Braunstein et al., 2017; Gyurak et al., 2011). Explicit emotion regulation requires conscious effort to initialise it, and throughout there remains some level of awareness and monitoring by the individual. Conversely, implicit regulation is initiated automatically, and lacks any form of monitoring or awareness on the part of the individual.

The degree of implicitness of emotion regulation behaviour is an important concept, because researchers in general psychology have suggested that frequent use of particular emotion regulation actions can result in increased automaticity over time (Gyurak & Etkin, 2014; Gyurak et al., 2011). This automatisation implies that effective emotion regulation behaviour, if it can be isolated, is a skill that language teachers can learn through training and instruction.

2.3.3.6 Considerations for researching emotion regulation

I would like to finish this section by highlighting some important considerations for any readers who may themselves wish to investigate emotion regulation in their own teaching contexts.

Firstly, I think it is important to give attention to all four of the core features of emotion regulation. In fact, many past studies of emotion regulation have tended to limit their discussion to goals, strategies and outcomes. This is perhaps a consequence of the fact that motives are a relatively new addition to models of emotion regulation, but emerging evidence suggests that the success of strategies cannot be isolated from motives (e.g. Tamir, 2016; Tamir et al., 2020).

Secondly, many studies of adults, particularly those focusing on teachers, limit their discussion of emotion regulation to intrinsic directions (e.g. Ghanizadeh & Royaei, 2015; Haeussler, 2013). Although this choice means that research is pragmatically easier, researchers must remember that a significant amount of emotion regulation behaviour by language teachers has inevitable extrinsic outcomes on students, and moreover, that language teachers may regulate their emotions with the express motive of influencing students.

Thirdly, notions of implicitness and explicitness suggest important consequences for emotion regulation research. By definition, they suggest that explicit forms of emotion regulation are accessible to research subjects. Consequently, researchers will be able to uncover and describe explicit uses of emotion regulation alongside their varying motives, goals, strategies and outcomes. Furthermore, these notions suggest that there will be acts of implicit emotion regulation which originated as an explicit act. This means there is the potential for researchers to be able to access the participants' knowledge of some habitual emotion regulation behaviours which were once employed in a conscious manner. Finally, these notions suggest that some highly implicit forms of emotion regulation may be out of reach of participants. Therefore, researchers are unlikely to be able to access the most unconscious forms of emotion regulation. These three consequences have important implications for methodological decisions. To investigate emotion regulation most successfully, researchers should consider methods which not only access participants' beliefs, but also their thought processes during instances of regulation. Introspective methods are likely to achieve this second aim.

2.4 Frameworks for Emotion Regulation Motives and Strategies

In the final section of this chapter, I will discuss how emotion regulation strategies and motives might be taxonomized. Given that there are potentially limitless motives and strategies that teachers may employ to regulate their emotions, categorisation systems help to identify, isolate and analyse behaviours, producing data which can then be used to inform training programmes. I will discuss two forms of categorisation in turn. Firstly, the categorisation of emotion regulation motives, and secondly the categorisation of emotion regulation strategies.

2.4.1 How do we categorise emotion regulation motives?

Emotion regulation motive is actually rather a new concept and there exists only limited empirical data on the higher-order motives that influence individuals' emotion regulation. In particular, work by Tamir and colleagues (Mauss & Tamir, 2014; Tamir, 2016; Tamir et al., 2020) goes some way to demonstrating the potential reasons why people might regulate their emotions. Tamir (2016) proposed a taxonomy for emotion regulation motives based on an analysis of published empirical data. Under this taxonomy, motives for emotion regulation fit into two broad categories: *hedonic considerations* and *instrumental considerations*.

Hedonic considerations serve two basic physiological purposes: *prohedonic motives*, which refer to the desire to increase pleasure and decrease negative emotions for the benefit of well-being, and *contrahedonic motives*, which refer to the desire to decrease positivity and increase negative emotions to enhance discomfort and pain. Prohedonic motives are considerably more common than contrahedonic motives, which are most commonly employed for masochistic gratification, or when facing a choice between short but acute pain and long but muted pain (Tamir, 2016). Given the considerable stress that affects the education sector, pro-hedonic motives are likely to be an important regulation motive for language teachers. Teachers regulating their emotion within this category will do so during those times they want to experience more joy and happiness in their work and relationships.

By contrast, instrumental considerations concern attempts to achieve outcomes which are unrelated to emotional states. Within this umbrella concept, *performance motives* refer to when people regulate their emotions to complete a task in a more effective manner, such as when a teacher wishes to 'pump themselves up' before entering a difficult class. *Social motives* refer to emotion regulation that helps form or manage relationships, such as when a teacher wishes to support a struggling student by displaying warmth. *Epistemic motives* refer to when emotion regulation verifies an individual's self-image, such as when a teacher wants to project themselves as being professional by hiding feelings of anger. Finally, *eudaimonic motives* refer to the use of emotions to contribute to an individuals' need to feel autonomy and mastery. Tamir (2016) observes that eudaimonic motives are least well served by evidence in general psychology, with only indirect evidence of their existence.

At present, Tamir's taxonomy offers the best starting point for considering why language teachers might regulate their emotions, but since it is modelled on everyday lives, it is not ideally suited for the situated work that language teachers do. Indeed, one hope for this book is to generate a more relevant taxonomy for language teacher emotion regulation motive, a goal which I return to in the concluding chapter.

2.4.2 How do we categorise emotion regulation strategies?

The work on emotion regulation strategy categorisation is very developed, and Gross's (1998, 2014, 2015) process model is undoubtedly the most influential categorisation system within the general psychological literature (and also in applied linguistics).

This framework closely follows the situation-attention-appraisal-response cycle of emotion that I described earlier. Remember, this cycle suggests that when an individual encounters an emotion-inducing situation, their attention will be drawn to the source, and they will appraise it. Should they deem the source to be personally relevant, an emotional response may be triggered. Gross's process model posits that individuals can apply emotion regulation strategies to target each stage of the situation, attention, appraisal and response timeline, and defines five categories of emotion regulation strategy that may be employed to do so. *Situation selection* and *situation modification* strategies target the situational stage of the process, *attention deployment* strategies target the attention stage, *cognitive change* strategies target the appraisal stage and *response modulation* strategies target the response stage. Below, I offer a brief illustration of each category of strategy.

2.4.2.1 Situation selection

Situation selections strategies are employed before an emotional event takes place and refer to an individual's attempts to agentively attend to or avoid a source of emotion. A teaching-related example of this kind of strategy would be when an EFL teacher deliberately avoids teaching an uninteresting textbook to prevent feeling boredom, or when a teacher chooses to employ an activity that they find entertaining so that they can experience more joy.

2.4.2.2 Situation modification

Similarly to situation selection, situation modification strategies target the external world; however, they are more immediate, being employed to modify an emotional stimulus in real time in order to change an emerging emotion. A teaching-related example of a situation modification strategy would be when a teacher stops a boring activity short to reduce negative emotions, or when a teacher extends a fun activity to lengthen positive emotions.

2.4.2.3 Attentional deployment

Emotion regulation strategies focusing on attention involve movement of the attentional systems either towards or away from a source of emotion. Teaching-related examples include when a teacher decides to divert their attention away from an off-task student to relieve frustration, or divert their attention towards a diligent student to increase satisfaction.

2.4.2.4 Cognitive change

Cognitive change strategies target appraisals and involve adjustments to how an individual appraises an emotional stressor. A teaching-related example may be when a teacher reduces frustration towards an off-task student by deliberately thinking about negative events that the student is experiencing in their personal life. They could, for example, remind themselves that the student is particularly busy, or under stress. They could also remind themselves that negative emotional responses are unproductive.

2.4.2.5 Response modulation

Response modulation strategies are the final category, and they are employed at a late stage in the emotion generation process. These strategies target the neurophysiological, motivational, subjective feeling and motor expression components of an emotion. In other words, these strategies are used to control the symptoms and expression of emotions. A teaching-related example of this strategy might be when a teacher tries to hide joy from a student by stifling their smile, or when a teacher reduces the symptoms of anger by breathing deeply.

2.4.2.6 On the use of Gross's process model

Although it is not the only taxonomy of emotion regulation strategies, Gross's model is very useful for considering emotion regulation in language teaching. In addition to giving consideration to the situation–attention–appraisal-response cycle and the components of emotions, the model acknowledges the role that external contexts play on emotions, containing categories which show how the environment can be manipulated in order to regulate emotional experiences. Consequently, I believe the model gives consideration to both the intrapersonal and interpersonal dimensions of emotion regulation.

Some have criticised Gross's model for being too simplistic, particularly in its assertion that emotions always adhere to the situation, attention, appraisal and response timeline (Koole, 2009, perhaps, takes this stance most strongly). Personally, I view Gross's model to be a heuristic, and certainly agree it lacks dynamic complexity. It fails to appreciate how a teacher, in their busy working life, applies emotion regulation strategies over longer time-periods, before, during and after emotional experiences. One example of this may be the use of cognitive change strategies. Gross's model suggests that these strategies occur at the point of appraisal, but it is easy to imagine that cognitive change could take place much later, say, when a teacher has returned to their office and reflected on the situation. One way that we can resolve this issue is by acknowledging that emotion regulation strategies can be employed across more dynamic timelines. Precedent for this exists in a model based within positive psychology. Quoidbach *et al.* (2015) expanded on work by Bryant (2003) to apply three temporal elements to emotion regulation strategies. This model proposed that a positive emotional event could be *anticipated* from the past, *savoured* in the present and *reminisced* about from the future. Such temporal concepts are relevant for considering language teacher emotion regulation because they illustrate how language teachers might complexly regulate their emotions in advance of and proceeding emotional events.

2.5 Lessons Learned: A Preliminary Language Teacher Emotion Regulation Model

Throughout this very technical chapter I have endeavoured to pull out the key ideas from the theoretical literature that are relevant to studies of emotion regulation in language teaching. These threads are all theoretically sound, but to successfully investigate emotion regulation amongst language teachers it seems important to have a conceptual model that is tailored specifically to that target group. To that end, in Figure 2.1,

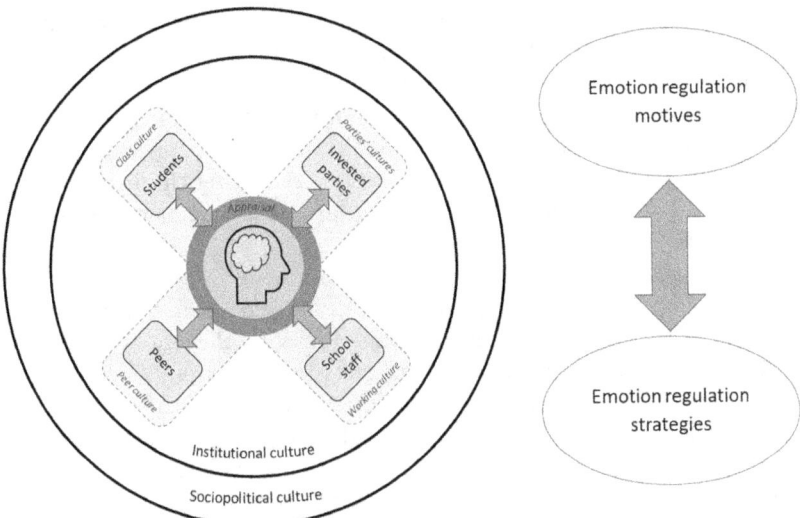

Figure 2.1 The preliminary language teacher emotion regulation model (LTERM-P)

I provide the Preliminary Language Teacher Emotion Regulation Model (LTERM-P).

The LTERM-P postulates that language teachers' emotions and acts of emotion regulation have intrapersonal (internal) and interpersonal (external) dimensions. The intrapersonal dimension of emotion and emotion regulation is, as appraisal theories describe, an internal process of appraisal and action that causes five componential changes to an individual. This dimension is represented by the teacher at the centre of the diagram, with the thought bubble representing the fact that appraisals and subsequent emotional responses are driven by a language teacher's subjective memories of their past experiences. In the circle surrounding the teacher, the word 'appraisal' represents the mediating mechanism between the teacher's real-world experiences and their internal experienced emotions.

The interpersonal dimension is, as social constructionist models postulate, an affordance and constraint of emotional experiences and regulation driven by competing external contexts. Remember that emotions emerge over interactional, relational and sociocultural levels. Interactions are represented by the bidirectional arrows, highlighting that emotions are regulated continually as interactions play out. The relationships are represented by the dashed boxes which connect the EFL teacher to each of their key contacts. EFL teachers are likely to have important emotional relationships with numerous stakeholders. They will have relationships with students, which will be afforded and constrained by the culture of each particular class; they will have relationships with other teachers, which are bound up in their peer cultures; they will have relationships with school staff (such as managers and administrators), which will be subject to varying forces of work culture; and they have relationships with various invested parties (such as parents or sponsors), which will each be bound by a unique culture. The sociocultural level is represented by the two circles on the outside of the diagram, reflecting the institutional, social and political cultures that bind languages teachers' emotional experiences.

Language teachers regulate their emotions using various strategies, for particular motives. Strategies and motives are represented in the circles included on the right side of the diagram. Presently the circles are incomplete: work in general psychology suggests that individuals regulate for hedonic and instrumental reasons using five categories of strategy, but what specific motives and strategies might language teachers use? How can we start filling in the gaps? In the concluding chapter of this book, I return to this model to fill in these missing details that emerged in my study, but in order to situate my work in the wider field, I next look for clues in the existing literature on emotion regulation in applied linguistics and language teaching.

3 Emotion Regulation in Applied Linguistics

3.1 Introduction

When my interest in emotion regulation first began, I found that there was very little literature that specifically spoke to and about language teachers. Hints and general conclusions could be gleamed from literature in general education contexts, and indeed my early writing focused mainly in this area. I always felt though, that the meaningful differences between language teaching and general education meant that the comparisons could only be surface deep. Fortunately, the past few years have seen a surge in interest in emotion regulation, and we now have some evidence of the strategy choices language teachers make and the impact of their emotion regulation. In this chapter I synthesise what is known about language teacher emotion regulation and evaluate previous approaches to its study. Throughout this chapter I make an important overall argument: there is now a sizeable body of work alluding to the fact that emotion regulation is a crucial facet of a language teacher's work, and yet, a paucity of studies that pay attention to emotion regulation in situated contexts, particularly in the Japanese tertiary sector. I begin by considering why the emotional requirements of second language teaching can be distinguished from teachers in other subjects, and then provide a short history of research focusing on language teacher emotions.

3.1.1 The emotion regulation requirements of second language teachers

It is undoubtedly true that language teachers share many features of their work with teachers of other subjects such as maths, history and art. Teachers in all subjects are expected to plan, execute and manage classes in ways which maximise the successes of students. It is also certainly true, however, that every subject has its own peculiarities that provide both opportunities and challenges for teachers. Therefore, an important question to consider is whether studies of emotion regulation in general education contexts can be applied to language education. Although it would be small minded indeed to suggest that studies in general education do not hold value, it is important to recognise that second language education has a particularly unique emotional facet, meaning that any emotion regulation competence for second language teachers may be distinct to those applied to general education contexts.

Firstly, although all education is social (Hargreaves, 1998; Nias, 1996), it can be said that second language education is uniquely so. Gkonou and Mercer (2017) astutely observe that this is visible in at least three features of the profession. Firstly, they note that second language education is dominated by communicative language teaching. Success in this highly interactional method is based largely on the dynamics of the class group, of which the teacher plays a guiding role in facilitation. Secondly, they point out that second language education frequently takes place in multilingual and multicultural classroom landscapes. Such classrooms require complex emotional decision-making skills to successfully navigate. Finally, they acknowledge that second language teaching has a common goal of fostering intercultural intelligence in students. This goal requires a high degree of empathetic understanding on the part of the teacher, as well as the ability to foster such understanding in learners.

In addition to the aforementioned social dimension of second language teaching, unique emotion regulation skills are required to address the secondary effects of the performative nature of communicative learning. Since individuals are frequently required to speak during classes in limited linguistic codes, the classroom is highly face-threatening (Arnold & Brown, 1999), and communication reticence can be a particularly damaging problem (King, 2013a, 2013b). It should therefore be recognised that the language classroom involves higher levels of anxiety than other subjects (Cutrone, 2009; MacIntyre & Gardner, 1989), and that second language teachers are able (and indeed, are required) to mitigate these issues through good teaching practice (see e.g. Dörnyei, 2001).

Finally, the subjects of study in foreign languages are themselves inherently emotional, and this provides unique challenges for EFL educators. This is because 'language teaching is never about skills training devoid of emotional content. Rather, teachers engage in ethically charged emotional work when they elect to focus on knowledge and skills that they believe are vital in shaping students' literate identities as socially and morally responsible citizens of the world' (Loh & Liew, 2016: 272). In other words, language teachers have a high moral and emotional responsibility for the selection of appropriate classroom topics and materials.

In sum, second language teaching likely has its own emotion regulation requirements because of its high degree of sociality, its performative learning styles and the emotional qualities of its content. Consequently, while work in general educational contexts is likely to be of value, there is a need to recognise that language teachers will regulate their emotions for very unique motives, and that they will be influenced by very unique contextual factors.

3.1.2 A short history

Until the most recent decade, teacher emotions rarely featured in literature within applied linguistics, a fact that has been commented upon by numerous other researchers (e.g. Dörnyei & Ryan, 2015; Gkonou *et al.*, 2020b; Martínez Agudo, 2018b). The earliest studies were, perhaps unsurprisingly, dominated by the study of learner emotions – particularly anxiety. Throughout the 80s and 90s, studies explored how this emotion correlated with a range of negative outcomes including test performance (Aida, 1994; Horwitz, 1986; MacIntyre & Gardner, 1989, 1994; Oya *et al.*, 2004), language proficiency (Matsuda & Gobel, 2004) and self-esteem (Horwitz *et al.*, 1986; Oxford, 1999). Research on learners inevitably filtered into work on language teacher anxiety and studies have repeatedly highlighted that feelings of inadequacy and linguistic insecurity are not limited to students (e.g. Bekleyen, 2009; Horwitz, 1996; Rajagopalan, 2005).

I see the isolation of discrete emotions such as anxiety as problematic, however, if there is not also work that attends to the full complexity of emotions. Teachers are not limited to one emotion. They experience a huge range of positive and negative emotions, often in the same class period and sometimes in the same moment! Despite pioneering work in general education and multiple calls to recognise the importance of teachers' emotional experiences (see e.g. Hargreaves, 1998, 2000, 2005; Nias, 1996; Zembylas, 2002, 2003, 2004), it is rather surprising that it wasn't until Cowie's (2011) qualitative exploration of nine language teachers in Japan that saw the emotional lives of teachers treated in a holistic manner. Cowie's work showed that teachers experience a plethora of positive and negative emotions in their work, that teachers' emotional experiences evolve across time, that power structures have a visible impact on language teacher emotions, and that emotions are enacted in the performance of socially defined identity roles. Personally, I think Cowie's work is very important. It highlighted what was possible in emotion research and paved the way for future contextually situated studies.

Since 2011, it is no understatement to say that interest in the emotional lives of language teachers has exploded. This has been driven in part by a movement towards greater consideration of language teacher psychology in general and also by increased interest in positive psychology in second language acquisition. White (2018: 19) has even gone so far to call the current period an 'emotional turn in applied linguistics', and it is hard to disagree given that research into language teacher emotions is now moving at great speed in diverse directions. Emotion regulation is not an isolated skill, but one that is connected to other emotional constructs including socioemotional intelligence, emotional labour and emotional health. These are worth exploring in depth, and I address each here before turning my attention to those studies that target emotion regulation directly.

3.2 Socioemotional Competencies and Emotion Regulation

One of the major growth areas in applied linguistics that is relevant to emotion regulation is socioemotional competencies. These kinds of competencies are important because when teachers have sufficient control and understanding of their own and their students' emotions, they are able to successfully achieve classroom goals (Dewaele et al., 2018), while simultaneously performing professionalism (Gkonou & Miller, 2021) and maintaining positive working relationships in the face of intense stress (Gkonou & Mercer, 2017; Nias, 1996; Zembylas, 2004).

Socioemotional competencies can be broken down into two separate skills: a social intelligence and an emotional intelligence. Social intelligence has a very long history stretching back to the 1920s (Lievens & Chan, 2017), and it refers to the ability for individuals to create and manage meaningful relationships with others. Within frameworks of social competence, emotion regulation features most prominently in notions of *self-presentation*. This is a concept that recognises that a successful member of society needs to display prosocial emotions with others (Goleman, 2006). Within social intelligence, emotion regulation therefore functions primarily as a tool for managing the expressional component of emotions within interactions.

Emotional intelligence is probably a more widely recognised construct. It has popularity in the business world as well as amongst the general population, particularly since the publication of Daniel Goleman's (1995) worldwide bestseller *Emotional Intelligence: Why it Can Matter More Than IQ*. Within emotional competence, emotion regulation is listed directly as one of four key emotional skills, and it operates at a high level of cognitive complexity (Mayer & Salovey, 1997).

There has been some controversy over whether social and emotional intelligence refer to identical constructs (Lievens & Chan, 2017), but Goleman (2006) argues, I think successfully, that considering them as one and the same diminishes the important role that social competence plays in interactions. In a similar vein, Gkonou and Mercer (2018) suggest that emotional intelligence is primarily intrapersonal in nature, whereas social intelligence is primarily interpersonal in nature, and while this is likely a simplification with regards to the way that emotion regulation functions within these relevant intelligences, it does highlight the chief concern of each construct.

3.2.1 Socioemotional competencies within applied linguistics

A range of studies in applied linguistics have provided three important considerations for language teacher emotion regulation. Firstly, quantitative explorations have generally shown that increased emotional intelligence positively correlates with other desirable teacher traits and outcomes. Dewaele *et al.* (2018) for example, explored the emotional intelligence of 513 language teachers and found that higher levels of emotional intelligence had a positive impact on self-reported creativity, classroom management and teaching ability; however, the authors acknowledge that their participants' self-reporting of classroom outcomes should be further verified through objective means. Similarly, Amirian and Behshad (2016) showed that language teachers' emotional intelligence was statistically linked to their self-efficacy, whereas Ghanizadeh and Moafian (2009) found that increased levels of emotional intelligence significantly correlated with student reports of successful teaching. In this latter study, those teachers who were able to build rapport and create mutually supportive atmospheres were able to have the most powerful influence over students. These studies paint the picture that emotional intelligence, and by association, emotion regulation, is an important feature of successful language teaching; however, the quantitative nature of the papers offers limited information regarding the real-world uses of emotion regulation.

A second and potentially more valuable research direction has been a series of qualitatively focused explorations of the impact of emotional and social intelligences on teachers' classroom behaviours. Here, Gkonou and Miller (2017) explored how teachers use their emotions to negotiate instances of learner anxiety. One way that this was done was through the participants deliberately expressing overtly maternalistic emotions towards students. These actions served to support students while also enabling teachers to perform a desired identity. One important complication revealed in the study was a tension experienced by the teachers as they attempted to balance relaxed but firm atmospheres within the classroom. A similar tension was also reported by Gkonou and Mercer (2017) in a large-scale investigation of socioemotional intelligence in secondary school language teachers. There, they defined the 'teacher paradox' (2017: 35), the potentially contradictory need for teachers to maintain warm, friendly relationships while also treating students with equality and professionalism. These kinds of studies have a high degree of relevancy to emotion regulation because they highlight that emotion regulation is performed by language teachers in aid of social motives, and equally that language teachers feel competing pressures to display different emotions to students at different times.

Finally, a third research direction has qualitatively investigated the emotional honesty of teachers' interactions and the effect this has on students. Emotional honesty is an important concept for emotion regulation since it concerns the performance and (perhaps) exaggeration of emotional displays through response modulation strategies. Within general educational contexts, teachers have viewed honesty as a positive outcome that enables students to view teachers as 'fully human beings' (Sutton, 2004: 387). Honesty is also achieved through instances where language teachers voluntarily share information about their personal lives with classes, and these instances are known as *acts of self-disclosure*. Although acts of self-disclosure are usually positioned as a relational act, I would also position them as an emotional act since they have been shown repeatedly to have a positive impact on learners' emotional states (Cayanus & Martin, 2008; Cayanus *et al.*, 2009; Elahi Shirvan & Taherian, 2021) and satisfaction (Song *et al.*, 2016). Not all teachers have reported a need for emotional honesty, suggesting that this is dependent on internal beliefs. In one study in Japan for example, a teacher reported consciously distancing themselves from their students, and even lying to them on occasion, such that they felt their students knew nothing truthful about them at all (see King, 2016b).

In sum, studies pertaining to socioemotional competencies in language teachers reveal that language teachers employ their emotions in aid of socially motivated emotion regulation goals, and they suggest some of the important internal- and classroom-level contextual factors that apply pressure to teachers with regards to their emotion regulation decision-making. As may be noted from their lack of presence in the above discussion, these studies do not attend strongly to emotion regulation strategy use, but simply allude to the regulation of facial expressions. This is neither unsurprising, nor a criticism of the studies, which do not present themselves as dealing with emotion regulation. However, work in socio-emotional intelligences and emotion regulation can complement each other well, and build on each other's strengths.

3.3 Emotional Labour and Emotion Regulation

Language teachers are responsible to multiple stakeholders: their students, parents, managers, institutions, governments and to society as a whole. This is true not only with regards to the content they teach and the teaching methods they employ, but also with the emotions that they display within the classroom. In Japan, where I teach, I am not alone in feeling an intrinsic pressure to present myself as cheerful, warm and kind. Although anger is not forbidden in any formal sense, there is an unwritten rule that discourages me from displaying anger towards the students. Teachers in every situation feel these kinds of emotion rules, which are known formally as *emotional labour*.

Emotional labour rose to prominence in industrial and organisational psychology following the publication of Arlie Hochschild's *The Managed Heart: Commercialisation of Human Feeling* (1983). Therein, Hochschild reflected on the lives of cabin attendants working in the United States, paying attention to the manner in which they were expected by their employers to control their emotions in the course of their work. Hochschild coined the term 'emotional labour' to refer specifically to the variety of feeling rules which prescribed the emotions that workers needed to display while working. The teaching profession has long been thought to contain a significant amount of emotional labour, which is explicitly and tacitly imposed by institutions, governments and society at large.

The prescriptive nature of emotional labour inevitably means that individuals can sometimes experience the 'wrong' emotions, or they can feel them too strongly or weakly, or at incorrect times. For example, I mentioned above that many teachers in Japan (especially non-Japanese teachers) often feel a tacit need to display warm emotions, but teachers experience a wide range of emotions in their daily life. There are, of course, times when language teachers do not feel truly positively enough to meet the expectations placed upon them. This disconnect between what is expected and what is actually felt is certainly a catalyst for emotion regulation.

In relation to these kinds of situations, Hochschild proposed two mechanisms for understanding how individuals meet the emotional labour rules of their employment: *deep acting* and *surface acting*. Deep acting refers to instances in which individuals induce and also attempt to internalise and fully realise their desired emotional state, whereas surface acting refers to when individuals fake the outward display of the required emotions. A third mechanism, *genuine expression*, has also been included in more recent work (e.g. Glomb & Tews, 2004; Taxer & Frenzel, 2015; Yin, 2016; Yin *et al.*, 2013), referring to when individuals display emotions freely with only minimal regulation.

Emotional labour was originally proposed to account for the unrecognised emotional requirements of customer service work, jobs which are typically performed by those of a lower social status. Unsurprisingly, Hochschild thus positioned emotional labour as a form of stress, detrimental to a worker's health as the mental effort required to manage emotional displays moved resources away from other psychological processes. Yet the work of teachers differs substantially from that of customer service professions and these days emotional labour is considered in more nuanced terms. In particular, various researchers have proposed that emotional labour in education may have a positive component (see e.g. Gkonou & Miller, 2017; Hargreaves, 1998; Humphrey *et al.*, 2015; King, 2016b; Miller & Gkonou, 2018). Emotional labour can be seen as a positive aspect of the job in a number of circumstances. Firstly, when teachers are able to achieve their own goals through their emotion work it is likely to have a positive effect on their well-being (Hargreaves, 1998). Secondly, when teachers achieve the emotional display expectations of the students, it is likely to result in smooth and comfortable interactions (Ashforth & Humphrey, 1993). Thirdly, since the language classroom is a source of immense anxiety for learners (e.g. Cutrone, 2009; Horwitz *et al.*, 1986; MacIntyre & Gardner, 1989; Oxford, 1999), it is likely that appropriate emotional displays can help to reduce negative feelings about language learning (Gkonou & Miller, 2017). Fourthly, when teachers invest in their students and care for their learning, emotional rewards can be experienced even in difficult circumstances (Gkonou & Miller, 2023; Miller & Gkonou, 2018). Finally, there is growing evidence that instances of genuine expression have a net positive effect on workers (Humphrey et al., 2015). Despite the potential for positive emotional labour, studies in applied linguistics most frequently take a tacitly negative stance (e.g. Acheson et al., 2016; Benesch, 2017; King, 2016b; Loh & Liew, 2016; Song, 2021). Nevertheless, when considering the emotion rules that ELT teachers are subject to, it is important to take into account that the meeting of such rules may have a positive effect on the teacher and students.

Finally, it is worth pointing out that some authors such as Ashforth and Humphrey (1993) and Grandey (2000) have proposed that the processes behind emotion regulation and emotional labour reflect two sides of the same coin. The reasoning behind this assertion is that surface acting and deep acting are very similar to response modulation and cognitive change respectively. Nevertheless, quantitative research does not yet fully support this notion (e.g. Lee et al., 2016). In truth, there are very meaningful differences between emotional labour and emotion regulation – emotional labour concerns itself with the rules of emotional display, but emotion regulation explores a broader set of motives and strategies and offers a more robust framework for understanding how emotions are managed. It therefore seems appropriate to continue to view them as distinct concepts.

3.3.1 Emotional labour within applied linguistics

Having defined emotional labour, I am now in a position to consider the findings from explorations of emotional labour in applied linguistics. Emotional labour is a very popular construct for investigating language teachers' emotional lives, with Benesch (e.g. 2017, 2018, 2020) taking a leading role in the field. Benesch's work on the emotional labour performed by teachers working in a publicly funded university in the US revealed that negative emotional labour can be driven to a large degree by conflict between teacher beliefs and institutional guidelines on course management. In Benesch's most major work (2017), emotional labour and emotional dissonance emerged as the participants negotiated testing, attendance and grading policies which they felt were unfair to their second language learners. Other studies, such as that of Gkonou and Miller (2017 – see also Miller & Gkonou, 2018), have emphasised the relational aspect of emotional labour; in particular, that the ethic of care that exists between teachers and their students has the potential to generate emotional stress.

Emotional labour research is clearly very contextual. Loh and Liew (2016), for example, highlighted the impact of Singaporean governmental policy and wider culture on language teachers' emotional labour. They particularly called out the country's high focus on assessment as creating emotional stress for language teachers as they negotiated exam success alongside other classroom goals. Yarwood (2020) too, drew attention to the industry-level contextual pressures that gave rise to emotional labour in private language schools in Japan, where the commercialised nature of English education forced teachers to sometimes prioritise customer satisfaction over language improvement.

King's (2016b) investigation of the emotional labour experienced by five EFL teachers working at a university in Japan is also extremely important, and I address it in detail here because of its relevance to the study that is described later in this book. King's study reveals the specific emotional display rules that EFL teachers in Japan are subject to and illustrates the relevance of the emotional labour tradition to emotion regulation research. Firstly, regarding Japan-specific rules, King found that his participants felt a strong need to take on a caring role in their work, with one even describing their position as a 'third parent' (2016b: 102) to the students. King noted also that the high degree of caring emotions performed by participants reflected traditional notions of teacher identity in Japanese culture, that teachers grew into their roles as caring instructors gradually over time and that some teachers might feel stress because of the effort required to consistently be caring. It becomes clear from the paper that it is neither natural nor a certainty that instructors will be able or willing to adopt the role expected of them by the Japanese context. This is an important point. It reflects the ontogenetic qualities of emotion regulation behaviour, and also suggests that there are potential benefits for discussing emotional identity roles in reflective practice and training sessions, which would help teachers to recognise and consider their emotional responsibilities and conflict.

Secondly, regarding the connection between emotional labour and emotion regulation, King (2016b) found that his university English as a foreign language EFL teachers felt a responsibility to frequently suppress their emotions (particularly negative) from students lest they affect the classroom atmosphere (much like my own experiences). The participants seemingly had an intrinsic awareness of the need to build strong social relationships in order to teach quality classes; however, they still reported experiences of frustration and anger at students' behaviour. In particular, teachers found themselves having to suppress strong negative emotions when dealing with students who were reticent to speak. This unproductive behaviour is a prevalent issue in the Japanese context (King, 2013a, 2013b), and one with which even experienced teachers continue to grapple with emotionally (Morris & King, 2018).

Finally, the notion of 'teacher as motivator' emerged as a strong prescribed role for the teachers in his study. The participants reported feeling they needed to instil a love of foreign language study through the up-regulation of their positive emotional displays. Teachers were requested to be 'bright, engaging and enthusiastic' (King, 2016b: 105) when interacting with students, and the participants internalised these sentiments in their identity as university teachers. While a positive classroom atmosphere is certainly a justifiable and even desirable goal, this emotional labour appeared to take a toll on King's participants who recognised that in meeting such feeling rules, their professional status within the university was left damaged: it was the responsibility of the foreign English teachers alone to be the 'entertainers' of the school, whereas Japanese colleagues were expected to take on more serious roles.

King's study makes it clear that emotional labour rules are highly pervasive and influential in the work of EFL teachers at universities in Japan. The participants in his study had seemingly internalised many of the feeling rules of their work, which in turn affected their teaching and identity as second language teachers. Work in the emotional labour tradition, then, is highly relevant to the work of researchers investigating emotion regulation behaviour, since it provides contextualised examples of the emotion regulation goals that teachers desire or are required to meet. In the case of the non-Japanese EFL teacher, such rules seemingly relate heavily to institutionalised ideals of the 'teacher' and the 'non-Japanese language teacher' within Japanese society.

In describing this study in detail, I hope to have highlighted the strengths of emotional labour research, as well as its weaknesses. Emotional labour studies provide intricate and detailed contextual data about the emotional feeling rules teachers aim to adhere to. However, since the focus in the emotional labour tradition is on deconstructing these rules, less time can be spent on identifying the specific emotion regulation behaviours that teachers employ. King's work, for example, reveals more about why teachers might feel the need to manage their emotions than about how they actually do so. How do teachers regulate their emotions to meet emotional responsibilities in ways that do not lead to them to become emotionally exhausted? How does the manner in which they do so change as teachers become more experienced in the Japanese context? Emotion regulation research compliments the emotional labour tradition by considering these questions in more depth.

3.4 Well-Being and Emotion Regulation

So far in this chapter I have tried to show that the topics of socioemotional competences and emotional labour have a very high degree of relevance to studies of emotion regulation. Given the well-documented levels of stress and attrition associated with the teaching profession, there is one other important contemporary research direction which I think is deserving of attention, and that relates to subjective well-being. This research direction has numerous important ties to emotion regulation which I will document below. In particular, quantitative studies have attempted to correlate trait emotion regulation behaviour with positive outcomes for psychological health, while qualitative studies have explored how emotion regulation functions as a supportive psychological resource.

3.4.1 Trait emotion regulation behaviour and well-being

One of the most widely researched areas in which emotion regulation has been proposed to support an individual's well-being is through consideration of their habitual emotion regulation. Most commonly, this has been conducted through predictive modelling of two emotion regulation strategies, the cognitive change strategy of reappraisal and the response-modulation strategy of emotive suppression. These two strategies are favoured because of early work by Gross and John (2003), who suggested that those with a tendency to reappraise in times of emotional difficulty (reappraisers) had an 'enviable affective profile' (2003: 356) over those who tend to suppress (suppressors). Over a series of five progressive studies with undergraduate students (with participant numbers ranging from 145 to more than 700), Gross and John showed that individuals who tended to use reappraisal lived psychologically healthier lives. These individuals experienced and expressed more positive emotions, and fewer negative emotions. They scored higher in tests of well-being and general life satisfaction, and had more optimism and self-esteem. Conversely, individuals who tended to suppress their emotions (both positive emotions and negative emotions) had more maladaptive outcomes. They experienced and expressed positive emotions less often and experienced more negative emotions. Suppressors further correlated more poorly with factors of well-being, and had lower levels of self-esteem, optimism and life satisfaction. Although reappraisal and suppression are often the two strategies selected for research, it has been suggested that situational, attentional and cognitive change strategies are all inherently healthier than response modulation strategies (Nyklíček et al., 2011).

Confirmational studies have taken place in both general education and second language teaching contexts, and it seems that these studies, although sometimes mixed, generally support the notion that reappraisal is more adaptive than suppression. For example, on the affirmative side, studies by Fan and Wang (2022), Lee et al. (2016), Kafetsios et al. (2012), Azari Noughabi et al. (2022) and Yin et al. (2016) found that positive outcomes such as job satisfaction, professional success and enjoyment correlated positively with the habitual use of reappraisal, whereas negative outcomes such as emotional exhaustion correlated with the habitual use of suppression. Moreover, Ghanizadeh and Royaei (2015) surprisingly found that both reappraisal and suppression correlated with decreases in burnout in a sample of 153 EFL teachers in Iran, and concluded that a general ability to regulate emotions can support positive outcomes for teachers.

By contrast, some evidence has been less certain. For example, while Chang (2013) found that teachers who regulated through suppression had higher levels of burnout and Kafetsios *et al*. (2012) correlated suppression with emotional exhaustion, neither could confirm that reappraisal had a reducing affect. Chang (2013) suggested that her inconclusive results may be explained by the fact that the common measurement system for reappraisal and suppression, the Emotion Regulation Questionnaire (Gross & John, 2003), was designed for everyday life, and does not capture the complex, motivated ways that teachers manage their emotions as part of their daily job. In other words, Chang suggested that there is a need to develop a quantitative tool that acknowledges that there may be times when teachers need to employ suppression to meet professional responsibilities. Chang's claim is supported by other authors who have recognised that the adaptability of suppression is likely to be contextual (Mauss & Tamir, 2014; Tamir, 2016), and may not be maladaptive when used by teachers in a controlled manner to meet instrumental goals (Hagenauer & Volet, 2014).

3.4.2 Emotion regulation and psychological resources for well-being

In addition to the quantitative studies, there is a second major research thread that suggests emotion regulation contributes to language teacher resilience. Much of this work is based within the positive psychology tradition, and is built upon theoretical notions that individuals have a set of resources that help balance their well-being. Hobfoll (1989, 2001), suggested that stress is a subjective reaction that results from (a) a loss of these resources, (b) the potential for loss of these resources or (c) the failure to gain new resources despite an investment of these resources. Similarly Fredrickson's (2000, 2001) highly influential broaden-and-build theory proposes that positive emotions broaden behavioural and cognitive action choices, simultaneously increasing an individual's range of physical, intellectual, social and physiological resources. Frederickson (2001) highlights interest, for example, as forging an appetite for exploration and supporting the intake of new information. Emotion regulation is important from this perspective of resources because if teachers are able to increase the quality and quantity of their positive emotional experiences, they may potentially be more able to deal with the stresses of the profession.

Within applied linguistics, resources and emotion regulation have been integrated by Kostoulas and Lämmerer (2018, 2020), who explored how language teachers might reconfigure their psychological resources to build resilience. In their work, they include emotion regulation as a specific example of what they call a *learned strategy* – a behaviour that can be employed at will and developed over time. According to their model, such learned strategies interact with relatively innate *inner strengths* and mediating *external support* in a dynamic system of growth. The authors illustrate this by describing the case of Peter, a teacher who drew upon friends and family, upon his cheerful disposition and upon his confidence to regulate emotions to adaptively construct resilience during a teaching practicum (Kostoulas & Lämmerer, 2020). Recent quantitative work in the Iranian context lends credence to Kostoulas and Lämmerer's model, with Namaziandost *et al.* (2022) showing that a teachers' generalised ability to regulate their emotions may correlate with their degree of immunity towards emotional stressors.

The fact that emotion regulation has been modelled as 'learned' in resilience studies highlights that emotion regulation ability may be developed through focused training programmes. To that end, important work has begun to be taken to support teachers in the growth of their emotion regulation capabilities in aid of improved well-being. Gregersen *et al.* (2020) described how they attempted to apply a week-long cognitive change intervention with an in-service teacher working in West Africa. The teacher participant received instruction on how she should reinterpret and reframe negative emotional stressors that she encountered in her work, and she wrote focused journal entries searching for positive outcomes from stressful events. Although the teacher participant was able to successfully reframe negative events in more than half of the occasions when she was prompted to do so by the research procedures, the intervention itself was considered a failure when the teacher had been unable to continue to employ the strategy after study was concluded. Although the intervention in this case was unsuccessful, the researchers identified some important factors for consideration in future training: namely, that a week-long intervention may not be enough to change teachers' long-standing habits on the way they approach emotional stressors, and equally, that the extent and nature of particular stressful situations may be more or less suited to such interventions. Consequently, this study has taken important first steps in understanding how emotion regulation skills might be taught and taken up by language teachers.

3.5 Emotion Regulation in Applied Linguistics

So far in this chapter I have explored three highly relevant areas: socio-emotional competencies, emotional labour and well-being. In each case, I have shown that these research directions hold important theoretical and empirical connections to emotion regulation. The main topic of this book is, however, emotion regulation, and it is time to explore this topic more directly. In this section of the chapter I am going to discuss those studies that have directly targeted emotion regulation skills and strategies. I begin with work in general education, and then move to language education.

3.5.1 Studies of emotion regulation in general education

Studies in general education have explored the use of emotion regulation in a range of settings including primary education in Japan (Hosotani

& Imai-Matsumura, 2011), secondary education in the US (Sutton, 2004) and China (Yin, 2016), and higher education in Australia (Hagenauer & Volet, 2014). Although these studies have only limited applicability to language education, they highlight four important considerations.

Firstly, the studies have undoubtedly shown that emotion regulation strategies are an important way that teachers protect their emotional health. In an especially potent study, Hauessler (2013) explored whether the emotion regulation actions employed by primary and secondary teachers in Germany could lead them to becoming resilient to emotional stressors. Haeussler's work was successful in identifying how participants pro-actively regulated their positive emotions to prepare for and mitigate future negative emotional experiences. They did this, for example, by reappraising difficult circumstances and by employing humour. Although the study did not actively attempt to address contextual affording factors, one of the most important findings of Haeussler's study was that institutional and governmental support can empower teachers to feel more motivated and less threatened by the potential for negative emotions in their work.

Secondly, studies in general education have shown that emotion regulation actions are employed for a range of purposes that extend beyond psychological health. The most major utility raised is to influence student behaviours. Teachers in Japanese elementary schools (Hosotani & Imai-Matsumura, 2011) and Chinese secondary schools (Yin, 2016), for example, have reported regularly up-regulating and faking their anger when disciplining students. Genuine displays of negative emotions have also been reported as effective in controlling classes because they force students to empathise with the teacher's position (Yin & Lee, 2012). Papers in general education literature have not yet adopted the work of Tamir and her colleagues (see Mauss & Tamir, 2014; Tamir, 2016; Tamir et al., 2020) in viewing emotion regulation as a motivated activity, and while participants have reported that emotion regulation may help them to build strong relationships with their learners and project a professional self-image (e.g. Hagenauer & Volet, 2014; Hosotani & Imai-Matsumura, 2011; Sutton, 2004; Yin, 2016; Yin & Lee, 2012), instrumental, social and epistemic motives are currently underserved.

Thirdly, studies in general education have revealed the highly contextualised nature of emotion regulation decision-making. Yin and Lee (2012), for example, have shown that 'passion' is a defining characteristic of the teaching profession in China. Teachers take their passion seriously, committing to professional improvement and putting student success ahead of their own well-being. Contextual factors exist at the classroom level too, with participants in Hosotani and Imai-Matsumura (2011) taking personalities and relationships into account when considering whether to display or suppress emotions so that they can best serve individual student needs.

Finally, the studies have revealed some of the potential tensions that may impact teachers in their emotion regulation decision-making. Of particular interest is the notion of balance – teachers have reported the need to balance their desire to motivate learners with their desire to protect their well-being (Acheson *et al.*, 2016), to balance their use of displays of praise with their displays of anger (Hosotani & Imai-Matsumura, 2011; Sutton, 2004), and to balance their use of emotional suppression with their use of emotional honesty (Hagenauer & Volet, 2014; Sutton, 2004; Yin & Lee, 2012).

3.5.2 Studies of emotion regulation in applied linguistics

Moving on from the literature in general education, I now explore the literature specifically within applied linguistics that has sought to understand language teacher emotion regulation. One important quantitative study has attempted to formulate an inventory of emotion regulation strategies for language teachers. Heydarnejad *et al.* (2021) conducted semi-structured interviews with 22 teachers working in Iran to inform an inventory of 27 common emotion regulation strategies, categorised by strategy type, that may be employed by language teachers. The inventory was then later tested with 534 high school and 476 university EFL teachers, revealing salient differences in emotion regulation strategy use in the two contexts. Among the findings was the fact that suppression was more common in the high school setting, while attention deployment, reappraisal and situation modification were more common in the university setting. The authors assigned this result to the varying learning goals and teaching styles used in the two groups.

Heydarnejad *et al.*'s study is very important because it has taken the first step in creating an inventory of emotion regulation strategies for language teaching, and their taxonomy is a useful list of emotion regulation strategies that language teachers employ. One observation that can be made about the inventory is that it attends only to the regulation of negative emotional states. In other words, the inventory does not attend to the fact that emotion regulation can be used by participants to generate, maintain and increase positive emotional states. Consequently, there is still a need to understand more deeply about the kinds of strategies that language teachers employ for the regulation of positive emotions.

Greater attention to emotion regulation in language teaching has actually been paid in qualitative studies. In a key paper, Talbot and Mercer (2018) adopted emotion regulation as a conceptual framework in their study of 12 language teachers from Japan, the US and Australia. In the interview-led research, the authors uncovered numerous relevant contextual factors that enhanced the well-being of teachers. Students, for example, were found to be a source of great joy, particularly when relationships and interactions were positive, and the teachers took meaning from their profession, recognising it as important for society. The participants also spoke about a number of negative stressors including administrative responsibilities, workloads and the precarious nature of their positions. Talbot and Mercer raised the important point that contextual factors can complexly cause both positive and negative emotional experiences simultaneously. Colleagues and collaboration, for example, were found to cause stress for the participants, but were also a source of support during difficult times.

The study also revealed some of the important emotion regulation strategies that were employed by the participants in hedonically motivated instances of emotion regulation. With regards to the regulation of negative emotional experiences, cognitive change strategies were found to be most widespread. The teachers reported to actively reframing classroom stressors and to making downward social comparisons with less fortunate colleagues, which allowed them to recognise the positive characteristics of their own circumstances. Talbot and Mercer (2018) also commented on the use of problem-directed action, an umbrella term for situational strategies that aim to make proactive changes to dealing with negative stressors. The participants, for example, took steps to avoid people they did not care for, and modified grading systems to reduce stress. The broad nature of problem-directed action suggests it may be a relevant and useful concept for situated studies of emotion regulation. With regards to the regulation of positive emotional experiences, Talbot and Mercer reported on the use of savouring, an attention deployment strategy through which participants took time to appreciate and enjoy aspects of their work. They also discussed the use of gratitude: more than half of the teachers in the study reported to thinking about, feeling and expressing gratefulness for their work and the opportunities it provided.

Overall, Talbot and Mercer's work reveals much about the ways that teachers might regulate their emotions for hedonic motivations. They have highlighted numerous important considerations related to how emotion regulation might intersect with well-being, such as making the recommendation that future attempts at intervention should focus not only on the elimination of negative emotions, but also on the amplification of positive emotional experiences.

A second relevant study is that of Gkonou and Miller (2023), who explored emotion regulation from a relational perspective. Their study used interview data from 50 teachers in four countries (US, UK, Germany, Norway) to investigate how emotion regulation was driven by and simultaneously influenced relationships with students and peers. The study revealed three important conclusions. Firstly, the authors showed that participants were able to experience positive regulatory benefits by choosing to be present and attending to classroom relationships. By working with students and supporting them, the participating teachers were able to generate a sense of satisfaction and emotional reward. Secondly, the study showed that language teacher emotion regulation is not always a solitary act. The participants found great emotional benefit when sharing and cooperating with colleagues. Finally, while the investigation revealed that emotion regulation was often performed for the benefit of students, they raised an important point that teachers cannot be in a position to help students unless they themselves are in an emotionally healthy condition. Gkonou and Miller's study is important in highlighting the interpersonal nature of emotion regulation actions and motives.

A third important study is that of Bielak and Mystkowska-Wiertelak (2020). In this work, the authors conducted vignette-led surveys with students, and combined these with testimony from semi-structured interviews with nine teachers in Poland to investigate the interpersonal emotion regulation strategies that were used. Interpersonal emotion regulation strategies, in this case, referred to those strategies which were purposefully used to regulate students' emotions. In other words, the study attempted to understand how teachers manage students' experiences of emotions (both positive and negative) relating to language learning rather than how they manage their own emotions.

Firstly, Bielak and Mystkowska-Wiertelak found that teachers employed all categories of emotion regulation strategy to regulate student emotions. Situational strategies focused on the creation of a relaxed classroom atmosphere, while attention deployment strategies involved directing the students' attention away from difficult tasks at hand. Cognitive change strategies involved reassuring the students and helping them to accept the negative parts of the learning process, while response modulation strategies included using music, meditation and breathing to influence students' emotional states. The study showed that teachers reported interpersonal emotion regulation more commonly than learners were able to remember. This, the authors noted, wasn't surprising since students might not always be able to interpret teachers' behaviours as emotion regulation, even if that was what the teachers were intending, and even if such actions were successful. That being said, the authors stated that more training could help to improve this situation and increase the use of underreported strategies, such as response modulation strategies.

In this brief review I have attempted to highlight some of the key research directions that have been studied to date in applied linguistics. The qualitative studies of emotion regulation have revealed some very important points regarding the hedonic, instrumental and relational uses of emotion regulation behaviours. They have also begun to comment on the contextual nature of emotion regulation strategy choices. One thing that can be gleamed from this review is that the studies have each focused narrowly on one particular motive of emotion regulation. In other words, the studies have tended to focus on either hedonic, or instrumental or relational uses of motivation. This is not meant as a criticism of the work, since these studies have not purported to explore emotion regulation on such a wide-reaching basis; however, it does illustrate a clear need for an all-encompassing study, the kind of which I offer in the second half of this book.

3.5.3 Emotion regulation studies within the Japanese context

As may be clear from the direction of this chapter, my focus has been gradually narrowing and I now arrive at an important juncture. Since the study in the second half of this book will focus on the Japanese context, have there been any studies conducted there already? In fact, two minor studies have directly targeted the emotion regulation of teachers in the Japanese context. Firstly, Littleton (2021) investigated the emotion regulation of four kindergarten EFL teachers working for a private language school in the Japanese context. Although this study was small in nature, Littleton uncovered an important contextual stressor which may be relevant to the Japanese tertiary context: the fact that a teacher's limited second language ability might create communication difficulties with Japanese students and staff.

Jim King and I also conducted a small exploratory study of emotion regulation that led to two papers. The first paper (Morris & King, 2018) focused on the regulation of the specific emotion of frustration, and reported on four emotional stressors experienced by teachers in the Japanese tertiary context: student apathy, classroom silence, misbehaviour and working conditions. The second paper (Morris & King, 2020) took a broader approach to understanding emotion regulation, exploring the general motivations and strategies that were reported in the data. This second paper also considered the complex interdependence between context and emotion regulation behaviour, focusing on four specific areas: the use of situational strategies as a form of pre-emptive emotional control, the use of attention deployment strategies in varying social relationships, the use of cognitive change across multiple temporal timelines, and the use of response modulation strategies to meet epistemic responsibilities as language teachers.

Although I am, of course, biased, I believe that we have made some relevant points in these papers regarding the dynamic and contextually informed nature of emotion regulation. For example, in our first paper, one participant's regulation of their frustration towards classroom silence was directly related to their in-moment interpretation of the reasons underlying the silent behaviour. When interpreting her students' silence as being caused by poor behaviour, the participant employed hedonically motivated response modulation and cognitive change strategies; yet, when interpreting her students' silence as being caused by language anxiety, the participant employed instrumentally motivated situational strategies. Meanwhile, in our second paper (Morris & King, 2020), we wrote about a teacher who employed cognitive reappraisal across at least three different timelines: firstly, in the moment of emotions themselves when the participant dealt with in-class disappointment; secondly across the school year as the participant negotiated his relationship with a difficult student; and thirdly across the teacher's career as he became a more experienced teacher. Findings such as these highlight the dynamic temporal complexity of emotion regulation. This early exploratory study functioned as a strong proof of concept, reaffirming the need for the contextually valid investigation of language teacher emotion regulation motives and strategies that this book reports on.

3.6 Lessons Learned: The State of the Field

The above sections have explored the limited literature in general education and applied linguistics, highlighting the rapid growth of emotion regulation as a topic of interest in language teacher psychology, while equally revealing the many salient gaps that still remain. I hope that the chapter has been instructive not only in presenting an overview of the current field, but also in establishing the need to explore emotion regulation in thick contextual detail.

Many important general findings have been made. It is clear from these studies, for example, that language teachers regularly employ all five categories of emotion regulation strategy to regulate their emotions, and the studies have gone some way to unearthing such strategies. Moreover, the studies show support to the notion that language teachers employ emotion regulation in aid of diverse contextually specific goals. In other words, the central assumptions underlying this book have been shown to be fitting.

Within the field of applied linguistics, it has been seen that there are only very limited studies to date. These have tended to adopt narrow foci on well-being (Heydarnejad et al., 2021; Talbot & Mercer, 2018) or instrumental purposes (Bielak & Mystkowska-Wiertelak, 2020). There has been attendance to all forms of emotion regulation strategy but the literature is weighted particularly towards the use of cognitive change and response modulation, and there should be more attention paid to other forms of strategy to form a more holistic view of their use and impact.

The most prominent methodological approach that has been seen in these studies has been the semi-structured interview, which was employed in every qualitative study. Although some studies have adopted other data collection methods, such as the use of the vignette methodology with students in Bielak and Mystkowska-Wiertelak (2020), research has not adopted any form of introspective approach which can unearth teachers' thought processes during their teaching (with the exception my previous work with Jim King). Moreover, there has been little attempt to provide independent observation of teachers' emotional behaviours which, when combined with stimulated recall approaches, may help to reveal instances of emotional behaviour that are potentially hidden from participants (see e.g. Gkonou & Mercer, 2017). These methodological points will be returned to later when I discuss the data collection for the study that occupies the second half of this book.

4 The Non-Japanese Teacher in Japan

4.1 Introduction

In the second half of this book, I will present a study of the emotion regulation of a group of non-Japanese language teachers working at a university in Japan. To set the scene for this, a few questions seem pertinent: Who is the non-Japanese teacher in Japan? What role do they play in English education? What are the emotional responsibilities and pressures that they face? In this chapter I aim to answer these questions.

There are numerous reasons why I focus on non-Japanese teachers. On the one hand, there is the fact that this is a group to which I belong. Though originally from the UK, I have been living and teaching in Japan for more than 15 years and working in universities for nine years. Undertaking this study is, to some degree, driven by a desire to understand my own experiences and practices with more nuance. A second reason is that non-Japanese teachers are frequently positioned in a somewhat differentiated role to their Japanese counterparts. For various historical and sociocultural reasons, Japanese and non-Japanese teachers have different expectations placed upon them, and these expectations influence the work that they do and the conditions under which they do it (see, for example Geluso, 2013; Hayes, 2013; McVeigh, 2002; Nagatomo, 2016; Rivers, 2013; Seargeant, 2009; Tajino & Tajino, 2000). I am sure that this is the case in many different teaching contexts around the world, and it seems crucial to understand the impact that racial and cultural expectations have on the emotional experiences of teachers.

In this chapter, I discuss three main topics. I first give a broad overview of English education in Japan, including its scale and purpose. I then explore the role of higher education in Japan. Although the Japanese tertiary education system has many similarities to those in other countries, it also has a number of idiosyncrasies. In the final third of the chapter, I turn my attention to the non-Japanese teacher. I consider their role in English education and discuss the pressures that influence their emotions.

Before beginning, I would like to make two important points for those unfamiliar with the Japanese context. The first point is about generalisability. The Japanese university system is large and diverse, and readers should understand that there will usually be localised differences in each institution. The second point is about terminology. In this chapter, I use and differentiate between the terms 'native speaker' and 'non-Japanese teacher'. I believe that 'non-Japanese teacher' is a more inclusive term, and agree that the term 'native speaker teacher' can be problematic (e.g. Cook, 1999; Nayer, 1994); however, within Japan, 'native speaker teacher' is a widely used phrase, usually referring specifically to Kachruvian inner circle speakers of English. Native-speakerism is pervasive in the Japanese context, often affording status to inner circle nationalities and diminishing the standing of teachers born elsewhere. A significant amount of important work continues to address this issue (e.g. Lawrence & Nagashima, 2020; Lowe, 2015; Matikainen, 2019).

4.2 English in Japan

In this opening section I discuss English education in Japan on a macro-level scale. I begin with an overview of the English education system, along with its reported successes and failures, and then describe two sociopolitical reasons why English education is provided in the public educational domain.

4.2.1 English education in Japan

This study takes place in Japan, a country with a long history of language education. Traditionally, foreign languages have served as a gateway for the Japanese to access international culture, and in the modern era, English is by far the most widely studied language, remaining as an important medium through which Japan interacts with the world. English has been a compulsory subject in secondary education since the 1950s and is now compulsory in elementary education too. In addition to their classes at school, many young people also study English at preparatory cram schools and at private English conversation schools, and some will also study overseas for short intensive periods. Students who enter university in 2025 have therefore studied English for at least eight years, with many having a great deal more experience than what is officially provided.

The Japanese English education system has reported many successes. For example, Neustupný and Tanaka (2004) observe that the system has instilled a survival level of English competence in a large percentage of the population, supplied many qualified translators and given the insular Japanese an everyday sense of contact with the outside world. There are also, of course, a large number of Japanese who have achieved a very high proficiency in English, and the Japanese ELT system as a whole has created a population who have a desire to learn English as a means of communication, a fact underscored by the 91 billion yen (£600 million) spent on private language education in 2018 (Ministry of Economy, Trade & Industry, 2019).

Despite these successes, English education in Japan is often painted as a failure and weaknesses in the system have been attributed to a range of factors including incohesive government policies, archaic teaching methods, entrenched examination systems, poor teacher training and inhibiting teaching and learning cultures (see, for example, Aspinall, 2006; Hino, 1988; Horiguchi *et al.*, 2015; Koby, 2015; McVeigh, 2002; Nagatomo, 2012; Oda & Takada, 2005; Sakui, 2004; Tahira, 2012). The deficiency of English education is so embedded in the Japanese public consciousness that its failure has been termed 'a cultural perception, an image, and an ideology' (Horiguchi *et al.*, 2015: 7). Teachers working in Japan must therefore negotiate a discourse of failure which fuels government rhetoric, policy decisions and reforms.

4.2.2 Why does Japan study English?

Two often cited factors said to account for low English abilities in Japan are that the majority of Japanese citizens remain without an actual use for English in their daily lives (e.g. Matsuda, 2011; Oda & Takada, 2005; Tsuneyoshi, 2013; Yano, 2001), and that young people lack any clear purpose for studying the language (McVeigh, 2002; Neustupný & Tanaka, 2004). This raises the question of why Japan troubles itself to coordinate and pay for English education on a nationwide scale. While it is true that English provides Japan with a tool through which citizens may interact with the outside world (Neustupný & Tanaka, 2004), a role that dominates the conversation in business and politics, another important perspective is that English in Japan might serve symbolic and ideological functions within Japanese culture. Such arguments were first proposed more than 20 years ago, but despite the many political, social and technological advancements within Japanese society, they remain very relevant to English education today.

Firstly, it has often been argued that English study functions as a systemic tool for the ranking of students' intelligence. This purpose is tied to the way that English has historically been taught and examined through a unique form of the grammar translation method that is known in Japan as *yakudoku*. The goal of yakudoku is for learners to produce written Japanese translations of English texts (Hino, 1988) and the method has been widely critiqued for its failure to produce strong second language users (e.g. Aspinall, 2006; Hino, 1988; Horiguchi *et al.*, 2015; Koby, 2015; McVeigh, 2002; Oda & Takada, 2005; Sakui, 2004). While reforms to the yakudoku method have been in progress for at least two decades (see e.g. Ministry of Education, Culture, Sports, Science and Technology [MEXT], 2011a, 2011b, 2014), they have been held back by entrenched university entrance examinations which focus on objective grammatical knowledge and cause washback throughout pre-tertiary education (Aspinall, 2005; Horiguchi *et al.*, 2015).

An unfortunate side effect is that English study in secondary schools is very intensively focused on passing university entrance examinations rather than on acquiring communicative skills. This means that the kind of English taught in schools is frequently addressed by its own sobriquet of *juken eigo* (examination English) (e.g. Koby, 2015; Sakui, 2004), and it has been argued that juken eigo remains entrenched because it serves an important cultural function: it is useful as a tool with which to rank Japanese students' academic performance for entry into higher education and the workforce (McVeigh, 2002; Neustupný & Tanaka, 2004; Tsuneyoshi, 2013). This is exemplified by the fact that it is frequently knowledge of rare grammatical items that are tested for in Japanese entrance examinations (Aspinall, 2005; McVeigh, 2002). Success is therefore defined by how obscure your declarative knowledge of the English language is rather than your ability to use it communicatively.

A second role that English learning plays in Japanese society is ironically, in strengthening national identity (e.g. Hashimoto, 2000; Horiguchi *et al.*, 2015; Kubota, 2015; McVeigh, 2002; Seargeant, 2009; Yamagami & Tollefson, 2011). This view is predicated on the idea that while English offers Japan opportunities for economic and political success, it also presents threats to cultural homogeneity. In other words, while English may link Japan to the world, it should not come at the expense of giving up what it means to be Japanese. This 'outward–inward tension' (Kubota, 2015: ix) has been both catalysed and reinforced through two powerful political discourses since the 1970s and 80s: *kokusaika* and *nihonjinron*. Kokusaika is an insular interpretation of internationalisation which is concerned with how Japan can interact with foreign cultures while maintaining its own unique identity (Hashimoto, 2000), while nihonjinron refers to a large body of nationalist literature which has sought to establish and validate that the Japanese are a unique people (Dale, 1986). Both of these discourses have been widely criticised for their nationalist agendas (e.g. Dale, 1986; Kubota, 1999; Miyoshi & Harootunian, 1991), but they have had a powerful impact on second language education policy (Hashimoto, 2000).

4.3 The Japanese University

Having outlined some of the broader sociopolitical factors affecting English education, I want to now present an overview of the role that Japanese universities play within society, and the role of English education within these institutions. This section will set the scene for the proceeding one, which will consider the teaching work that non-Japanese teachers do and the conditions under which they do it.

4.3.1 Overview of Japanese universities

Like in many other developed countries, Japanese young people have many routes open to them when they finish high school at age 18. Those choosing to continue in education may choose from four-year universities, two-year universities, junior colleges, technical schools and vocational schools. The study in this book took place in an undergraduate programme at a four-year university, which in Japanese are called *daigaku*. The most recent statistics available indicate that more than 2.9 million students attend the 810 daigaku in Japan, of which 86 are national (created by the central government), 102 are public (established by regional governments to meet local needs) and 622 are private (owned and managed by private companies) (MEXT, 2023). Students at daigaku typically study for two 14-week semesters each year, with long breaks in the summer (July–Aug) and spring months (Feb–Mar). Undergraduate programmes follow a US system, such that students receive a general education for the first two years and a specialised education for the final two years. A consequence of this system is that the majority of undergraduates in Japan, no matter their major, receive at least two years of English language study as part of their courses.

4.3.2 The role of higher education in Japan

A rather unique point of education in Japan is that it has been called a 'selection process' (Nagatomo, 2012: 22), the goal of which is to help rank young people for their future employment and, by association, their life paths. Although it is undoubtedly a heuristic, Nagatomo (2012) describes a very useful three-tier differentiation to help us understand how education level corresponds with career success in Japan. Nagatomo notes that those attending elite and higher-level universities will be able to access the larger, more successful corporations; those attending lower-ranked institutions will be rewarded with white-collar jobs in smaller companies; and those not attending university at all will make up the lower-prestige blue-collar workforce. This means that entering a good university may profoundly influence a Japanese young person's life opportunities.

Traditionally in Japan, the name of the university that a student attends is more important than any grades they receive or subject they study (Bradley, 2009; McVeigh, 2002; Nagatomo, 2012). McVeigh suggests that this is because Japanese companies prefer graduates to be a blank slate, free of skills and preconceptions, that they may train into their own company culture (McVeigh, 2002). This is the first point that presents a potential emotional difficulty for teachers – while entering a good university is perceived as difficult, graduating is perceived as easy (Hale & Wadden, 2019). Consequently, it has been suggested that some teachers struggle to motivate students to attend or complete more than the minimal amount of work to graduate (McVeigh, 2002). Fortunately, this kind of situation is less likely at more highly regarded universities, and some have noted that universities are becoming stricter in their graduation requirements (Bradley, 2009; Hale & Wadden, 2019).

4.3.3 Issues facing Japanese higher education

The most significant social issue that Japan currently faces is its dramatically shrinking population, and it is impossible to overstate the significance of this for the higher education sector. Since the 1990s, the population of Japan has been decreasing rapidly owing to a low birth rate, and the number of 18-year-olds has dropped from approximately 2 million in 1990, to only 1,112,893 in 2022, a trend that is predicted to continue (Research Institute for Higher Education, 2022). This decline has led to many universities receiving insufficient applications to fill their student quotas (Hale & Wadden, 2019; Kinmouth, 2005; Nagatomo, 2016), and it has forced institutions to take recruitment and student satisfaction seriously under threat of financial ruin. It is increasingly common for universities in Japan to spend money on advertising and improved facilities in an effort to remain competitive within a shrinking market share, and the future of many institutions remains uncertain (Bradley, 2009; Kinmouth, 2005).

Because of this demographic crisis, since 2004 the Japanese government has continually made significant changes to Japanese higher education and its institutions. The changes have included the semi-privatisation of the 86 national universities, a merit-based distribution system of research funds, and the development of more rigorous assessment systems for the whole university sector (e.g. Eades *et al.*, 2005; MEXT, 2012; Poole & Ya-Chen, 2009). These changes have been compared to those made by Margaret Thatcher in the UK during the 1980s, in particular because of a move towards a neoliberal, league table-driven education system where commercial forces impact the future of institutions (Eades, 2009; Goodman, 2005).

The stress of the demographic crisis has already caused some universities to make major structural and directional changes which have had an impact on the work that university teachers are expected to do. Some universities, for example, have deemphasised productive language-focused classes in lieu of more marketable Test of English as a Foreign Language (TOEFL) and Test of English for International Communication (TOEIC) preparation classes (Bradley, 2009), while others have implemented vocationally oriented course and management structures which prioritise teaching at the expense of research, and result in increased workloads for poorer conditions (Eades, 2009).

4.4 The Non-Japanese University Teacher

Having given an overview of Japanese higher education, I will now turn my attention to the people at the heart of this book: non-Japanese teachers. The vast majority of non-Japanese EFL instructors are employed in three different contexts in Japan: in private language schools (known as *eikaiwa gakkou*); in elementary and secondary schools as assistant language teachers (ALTs); and in universities as lecturers and researchers, positions referred to as the 'pinnacle' (Nagatomo, 2016: 36) of ELT employment that many teachers aspire to, and which form the context for this study.

Securing employment at a Japanese university is not easy, and it typically requires a master's degree or PhD, experience teaching within Japan, three academic publications and some Japanese language ability (Larson-Hall & Stewart, 2018). Given these rigid requirements, it is very likely that non-Japanese teachers will work in one (or both) of the two other contexts (eikaiwa gakkou, ALT) before being employed in a university. These employment contexts undoubtedly have an effect on the teachers that they become, and subsequently on their emotion regulation decision-making. I begin this section by introducing ALT and eikaiwa gakkou contexts and then explore the work that non-Japanese teachers perform in the higher education sector.

4.4.1 Non-Japanese teachers in pre-tertiary education

Japanese young people attend six years at primary school (ages 6–12), three years at junior high school (ages 12–15) and virtually all (around 97% – MEXT, n.d.) attend three further non-compulsory years at high school (ages 15–18). In all of these pre-tertiary contexts, non-Japanese teachers most commonly work as ALTs supporting Japanese teachers in the classroom. ALTs may be employed by the government on the Japan Exchange and Teaching Programme (which has the best working conditions and highest prestige), by private companies who have acquired contracts with local boards of education, or less commonly, by schools themselves. It has been suggested that ALTs are often employed for their exoticism as non-Japanese, based on the expectation that their presence will motivate students to study English (Breckenridge & Erling, 2011).

Although the work of ALTs is nominally to support Japanese teachers in providing English education, what this means in practice varies widely. Reports suggest that some ALTs are given a great deal of responsibility, being asked to take a leading role in instruction and contributing to class planning and development, while others are side-lined in their lessons (Sakamoto, 2014; Tajino & Tajino, 2000). Furthermore, some ALTs find themselves working in only one location, while others find themselves shuffling from school to school, and this seemingly leads to much variation in the overall quality of the ALT experience (Breckenridge & Erling, 2011).

From an emotional perspective, working as an ALT for any length of time is clearly a job of intensive emotional labour. The orientation manuals condition ALTs to be energetic and positive, asking them to be a 'motivator' (MEXT & British Council, 2013: 11), and to 'keep a positive attitude' (Council of Local Authorities for International Relations, 2013: 53). I do not present this emotional labour as wholly negative – ALTS serve a very important role in Japan and many, many of these teachers have a positive and successful career in Japanese public schools.

4.4.2 Non-Japanese teachers in the private sector

An alternative path in Japan is to work in private language schools (eikaiwa gakkou). Such schools employ more than 10,000 instructors (Japanese and non-Japanese) across Japan, the majority of which work part time (7387) rather than full time (3359) (Ministry of Economy, Trade & Industry, 2019). Teachers in eikaiwa gakkou typically teach small group classes to children and adults, and possibly to a variety of student demographics (e.g. elementary school children, housewives, businessmen) in the same day. As such, teachers may have to adapt their personas quickly and often.

Eikaiwa gakkous frequently position the English language as something desirable, exotic and international (e.g. Hooper & Hashimoto, 2020; Kubota, 2011; Seargeant, 2009). This means that they tend to hire non-Japanese teachers who are young, attractive and foreign looking (e.g. Appleby, 2013a, 2013b; Kubota, 2011; Nagatomo, 2016). For this reason, eikaiwa gakkou have been criticised for propelling the myth that the only way to learn a language is through interactions with a native speaker (Seargeant, 2009).

From an emotional perspective, teachers seem to be aware that they are working for companies whose primary goal is profit. They have reported viewing students as customers that need to be satisfied (Appleby, 2013a; Yarwood, 2020) and have described being asked to sustain efforts to be energetic, outgoing and positive (Appleby, 2013a; Bailey, 2007). This emotional labour is not always easy for the teachers, who may feel a tension between their emotional responsibilities and pedagogical desires; however, recent publications have highlighted that there are many professional teachers within the private English school industry who lament the way that eikaiwa gakkou teachers are perceived in professional circles as non-serious (Hooper & Hashimoto, 2020; Hooper & Snyder, 2017). Indeed, I began my own career in an eikaiwa gakkou and found it immensely rewarding and enjoyable. I consider it a time of great growth which continues to inform the teacher I am today.

4.4.3 Non-Japanese teachers in Japanese universities

Recent statistics suggest there are 7735 non-Japanese teachers who work full-time at Japanese universities, and 13,021 who work part time. This represents 5.4% of the total number of teaching staff (MEXT, 2016); however, it is not known how many of these are teaching foreign languages. Employment conditions vary between and even within institutions, but of great significance is the form of employment contract a teacher is employed on. Some teachers are part time, and some are tenured, but many work on fixed-term full-time contracts. Under these contracts workers typically teach 8–12 courses at a single university and receive a comparatively good salary and benefits, but their contract is limited to a certain number of annual renewals (typically 3–8 years in total). After this point, a teacher is required to leave their university and seek work elsewhere.

Although non-Japanese teachers may often find themselves in precarious employment conditions, a factor which has been shown to cause emotional difficulties and stress (King, 2016b; Morris & King, 2018), I also think it is important to be reminded that universities offer far superior conditions to other forms of ELT employment in Japan. Many non-Japanese university teachers are very satisfied with their employment situation. For example, Butler (2019), in an autobiographical account, describes in detail her great joy of working on part-time university contracts, noting that she values the freedom these working conditions afford her from committee work and meetings. Indeed, the committee and administration work at Japanese universities has frequently been described in negative terms (Bradley, 2009; Minter, 2009).

4.4.4 The teaching work of university teachers

In the final section of this chapter, I discuss the practical teaching work that non-Japanese EFL teachers do. My goal here is to explore the responsibilities and potential emotional stressors that these teachers might face.

Firstly, the importance placed on English as an academic subject, along with the fact that students receive a general education for their first two years of undergraduate study, means that a great majority of university students take English classes (Larson-Hall & Stewart, 2018). English is routinely offered as a major subject in many universities, and students on these courses can be expected to earn credits in both communicative and theoretical language lessons throughout their degrees.

Earlier in this chapter I reported that in Japan there is a form of examination-focused English (juken eigo) in formal education taught through the yakudoku method. As was noted, this form of English prioritises the production of Japanese translations of English texts and is taught almost exclusively through Japanese explanations of grammar points (Hino, 1988). In other words, juken eigo teaches learners how to change the foreign language into Japanese as opposed to teaching them to productively use the foreign language. In practice, juken eigo represents one of the most salient examples of the Japanese/non-Japanese dichotomy in English education in Japan. This is because juken eigo is almost exclusively taught by Japanese teachers (Nagatomo, 2012, 2016). Non-Japanese teachers on the other hand, are responsible for the teaching of English for communicative and productive purposes, and this division remains true even in the tertiary sector. This tension has been referred to as *eigo vs eikaiwa* (English vs English communication) (e.g. McVeigh, 2002; Nagatomo, 2012, 2016).

In universities, non-Japanese teachers tend to focus on the eikaiwa form of instruction. They therefore teach speaking and listening skills or imported academic English skills (such as EAP-style presentation and writing skills), whereas Japanese teachers tend to teach English literature and linguistics (Nagatomo, 2016). This not only affects the methodologies that non-Japanese teachers are expected to use (typically forms of communicative language teaching), but also influences the teachers they are expected to be. While the Japanese-led eigo classes represent the serious form of English learning focusing on test success (the 'meat and potatoes of English-language teaching' – Nagatomo, 2016: 208), the non-Japanese-led eikaiwa classes represents the fun, expressive and interactive, but ultimately less serious form of learning (McVeigh, 2002; Nagatomo, 2012, 2016). Non-Japanese teachers may therefore be expected to provide more energetic and enjoyable classes than their Japanese counterparts, and this may in turn see them being viewed as less serious by colleagues (Poole, 2010).

In the eyes of students, both Japanese and non-Japanese teachers do seem to conform to their expected roles. For example, in terms of teaching abilities, Japanese students have reported that they prefer pronunciation (Kasai *et al.*, 2011; Walkinshaw & Oanh, 2014; Yazawa, 2017) and cultural instruction (Kasai *et al.*, 2011; Walkinshaw & Oanh, 2014) from non-Japanese teachers, and appreciate Japanese teachers for their ability to teach grammar (Walkinshaw & Oanh, 2014; Yazawa, 2017). Similar observations can be made about the emotional atmospheres that teachers cultivate in their classes. In a survey of 1088 Japanese college students, Shimizu (1995) found that 69% of students considered their non-Japanese teachers to be energetic, 71% to be humorous and 75% to be cheerful (vs 4%, 4% and 3%, respectively, for Japanese teachers). Conversely, the students considered 56% of Japanese teachers to be strict, 80% to be formal and 43% to be serious (vs 14%, 4% and 23% respectively for non-Japanese teachers). In these studies, students identify features that are in keeping with the eigo vs eikaiwa dichotomy of teaching work in Japan, in particular the notion that serious learning takes place in the Japanese-led eigo classroom and non-serious in the non-Japanese-led eikaiwa class. Although student perception is only one indicator of the realities of the classroom, it suggests that there is indeed a tangible difference between the work performed by non-Japanese and Japanese teachers.

Nagatomo (2016: 57) wrote simply that in Japan, 'Japanese and foreign teachers are different', and she commented that until the teaching styles of eigo and eikaiwa are reconciled, criticism of the English education system in Japan is unlikely to cease. What also remains true is that until eikaiwa and eigo are reconciled there are likely to be unique emotional responsibilities and difficulties for non-Japanese teachers to negotiate.

4.5 Lessons learned: Who is the Non-Japanese University EFL Teacher in Japan?

Who is the non-Japanese teacher working in Japan? In this chapter I have explored the political, social and historical factors that may influence the emotional experiences and work they do at universities. Although I have shown many salient facets of the Japanese tertiary education system, I think it is particularly useful to highlight three of the most important points about the non-Japanese University EFL teacher which will help to establish important context for the forthcoming chapters:

(1) The non-Japanese university EFL teacher has very likely worked in pre-tertiary education or private language schools before they began their university career. This means that they will have a degree of awareness of Japanese culture and learning styles.
(2) The non-Japanese university EFL teacher is most often not employed on a tenured contract. They are more likely to work in a part-time or limited term position which may be somewhat precarious.
(3) The non-Japanese university EFL teacher may have different expectations placed on them in comparison to their Japanese counterparts. They may be asked to focus on conversational-style classes rather than technical classes, and from an emotional perspective, they may be perceived by students to be more cheerful, positive and lenient than their Japanese counterparts.

5 A Study of Emotion Regulation

5.1 Introduction

So far in this book, emotion regulation has been a very theoretical affair, observed from a distance, thought about, commented on, but not yet experienced firsthand. This chapter marks the turning point, for it is here where I begin the process of my own inquiry into language teacher emotion regulation. The study I detail took place between 2018 and 2022, with data collected during the 2019–2020 academic school year in Japan.[1] It focused on three questions.

(1) What emotion regulation strategies do a group of non-Japanese EFL teachers working at a Japanese university use to regulate their emotions?
(2) What emotion regulation motives do they employ these strategies in aid of?
(3) What contextual factors influence their choices of emotion regulation strategies and motives?

At the heart of these questions was my desire to understand both why and how. Why, in their subjective opinions, do language teachers attempt to regulate their emotions in their work? And how do they do this? I very quickly reasoned that satisfactory answers to these questions required me to decipher the complex and dynamic interplay between language teachers' intentions, actions and contexts. Of course, the complexity of this interplay defied a positivist, reductionist approach, which would have condensed many of the individual and unique facets of emotion regulation decision-making. I knew then that this study required a relativist ontology and interpretivist epistemology, with the collected data being qualitative in nature. Such research brings with it several important assumptions. It assumes that there are differences in the way that individuals perceive their world, and that individuals construct subjective sense and knowledge through their interactions with others. Moreover, it assumes that these subjective accounts can be accessed by individuals and subsequently articulated to researchers.

In this chapter I give a detailed explanation of the study, focusing on important details such as the participants, the study design, the data collection and the analysis. As in all good descriptions of qualitative research, I endeavour to be as open and honest as possible. To this end, I have scattered a number of reflections throughout the chapter to illustrate my thought processes.

5.2 People and Places

I begin by giving a description of the research site and the participants that took part in the study.

5.2.1 The research site

In my exploration of language teacher emotion regulation, I spent 1 year collecting data at *Fukuzaki University* (a pseudonym), a private four-year daigaku located on Japan's main island of Honshu. Fukuzaki University serves approximately 5000 students, both at undergraduate and postgraduate levels, who major in various liberal arts subjects. The campus is located in the suburbs of a major city, approximately 30 minutes' walk from nearby train stations and is self-contained at one location. The main buildings of the campus encircle outdoor relaxation areas, gardens and sports facilities, and the university has a very spacious feeling in comparison to many inner-city universities in Japan. There are numerous areas on campus for students to study independently, buy lunch and meet friends, and the facilities are modern, with a number of the buildings less than 10 years old. Fukuzaki University has a high degree of focus on language-related subjects (European and Asian languages), and while students at the university are required to take English language lessons for their first two years, the majority of the students will take English language classes, or content and language integrated learning (CLIL) classes (in English), for the full four years of their degree.

I conducted the research within the International Languages Department (also a pseudonym) at the university. The primary purpose of this department is to provide all students with a foundation in English language skills, no matter their major. As such, the courses function horizontally across the university. The faculty in the International Languages Department teach two forms of courses. The majority of their work is teaching required English language courses to first- and second-year students in all majors. Such courses cover all four skills and serve general and academic forms of English. These courses meet for two 90-minute classes per week, with the exception of the 1st year Communication class, which meets four times per week.

In addition to the required courses, some of the faculty also have responsibilities for teaching elective CLIL courses to third- and fourth-year students. These courses also meet twice a week, though only for one semester, and focus on a diverse range of topics pertaining to history, culture and sociology. CLIL courses are optional for faculty in the International Languages Department, with teachers receiving an additional salary.

Approximately 70 teachers are employed within the International Languages Department. They all work on fixed-term contracts for a period of no more than six years. The great majority (90%+) of the teachers in the department can be considered to be English L1 speakers, primarily from inner circle countries, with only a minority (fewer than 10%) being English L2 speakers (inclusive of Japanese L1 and non-Japanese L1 speakers). The international-leaning demographic of the department is unique to the International Languages Department within the university.

5.2.2 The participants

I chose the International Languages Department at Fukuzaki University for reasons of convenience – The site was commutable from my home and place of work, and I was able to secure access through professional connections. Although this kind of sampling is not the most preferable choice from the perspective of objectivity, It afforded me an intimate perspective and allowed me to conduct extensive data collection around my responsibilities at the time as a full-time lecturer.

I recruited participants through purposive sampling using two criteria. The first criterion was that the participants should have a minimum of six years' English teaching experience (in any context). This was because the emotions of newly qualified teachers are qualitatively different to those of experienced teachers (see e.g. Lemarchand-Chauvin & Tardieu, 2018), and I desired to learn from experienced teachers who would potentially employ emotion regulation actions more stably. The second criterion was that the participants should have taught in Japan (in any setting) for at least three years. This was because Japanese societal factors were important to the investigation, and I desired that the participants have a degree of experience so that they could articulate such features deeply.

The participants were all English L1 speakers who had grown up in inner circle countries, with the exception of one participant, Catherine, an English L1 speaker who group up as a third culture individual in various countries in South and North America. The participants had been teaching for between 6 and 20 years (mean 11.9 years) and had worked in the Japanese context for 3–19 years (mean 8.9 years). I have included

Table 5.1 Demographic information about the participants

Pseudonym and gender	Country (s) of formal education	Qualifications	Teaching (years)	Teaching in Japan (years)	Reported Japanese language ability
Catherine (F)	Various countries	MA[a]	16–20	6–10	Upper intermediate
Eleanor (F)	Australia	MA TESOL Certificate QTS Secondary[b]	16–20	6–10	Beginner
Gina (F)	USA	MA	16–20	16–20	Intermediate
Jamie (M)	NZ	MA BA[c]	6–10	6–10	Lower intermediate
Jessica (F)	UK	MA BA CELTA	6–10	6–10	Lower intermediate
Luke (M)	USA / UK	MA	6–10	3–5	Intermediate
Millie (F)	USA, UK, Japan	MA	11.5	6–10	Intermediate
Nathan (M)	UK	MA MA other[d] TESOL Certificate	6–10	6–10	Intermediate
Peter (M)	Australia	MA QTS secondary BA Japanese	11–15	11–15	Advanced
Richard (M)	USA	MA	6–10	6–10	Upper intermediate / advanced
Stewart (M)	UK	MA TESOL Certificate	19	19	Intermediate
Tom (M)	UK	MA	11–15	11–15	Lower intermediate
Vivienne (F)	USA	MA	6–10	3–5	Intermediate
Wendy (F)	USA	MA	6–10	3–5	Lower intermediate
Zoe (F)	USA	MA	6–10	3–5	Upper intermediate

Notes
[a] Refers to a master's degree in TESOL, applied linguistics, education or similar.
[b] Refers to qualified teacher status within secondary school contexts.
[c] Refers to a bachelor's degree in TESOL, applied linguistics, education or similar.
[d] Refers to a master's degree in a subject outside language education.

detailed demographic information about the participants in Table 5.1, with some elements generalised to protect participant anonymity.

5.2.3 Reflection 1: The participants and me

Before I move on to consider the particulars of the study itself, I would like to offer a reflection on my own position in the study and my relationships with the participants. Since I am also a teacher with experience in the Japanese tertiary sector, I consider myself to very much be an insider in the research. Researchers can have insider status in relation to shared knowledge, pre-existing relationships (Mann, 2016), or innate features such as gender and age (Mercer, 2007). Moreover, insider positions are dynamic and changing, with researchers occupying simultaneous insider/outsider positions at different times (see e.g. Breen, 2007; Greene, 2014; Heigham & Sakui, 2009; Mercer, 2007). My own insider/outsider status fluctuated continually while I was working with different participants. I shared, for example, Britishness with four participants (Jessica, Nathan, Stewart and Tom), being a parent with seven participants (Gina, Vivienne, Tom, Jamie, Nathan, Eleanor and Stewart), and similar career paths with six participants (Tom, Jessica, Nathan, Eleanor, Peter and Stewart). In practice, this meant that I needed to be continually reflective of the potential dangers of my insider status with each participant independently.

Insider status has been called a 'double-edged sword' (Mercer, 2007: 7) since it brings both benefits and risks to research. It can afford comparatively easy access to institutions and participants (Greene, 2014; Mercer, 2007; Thorne, 2016) and can reduce practical barriers (e.g. travel time) when collecting data (Mercer, 2007). It can also result in more natural interactions since there is likely to be more rapport (Breen, 2007; Mercer, 2007) and fewer cultural misunderstandings with the participants (Breen, 2007; Greene, 2014; Mann, 2016; McDermid et al., 2014; Mercer, 2007). Certainly, my insider status conferred all of these benefits.

By contrast, insider status brings risks to data quality. I had to be careful that familiarity did not lead me to project my own opinions onto participants (Greene, 2014; Mercer, 2007) and reflect regularly on my pre-held biases about language teaching in Japan to ensure that I did not make assumptions that my participants did not share (Breen, 2007; McDermid et al., 2014). By considering these points, it became clear to me that issues of shared status were most salient with five participants: Tom, Jamie, Nathan, Peter and Stewart. These five participants all shared similar attributes with me: they were male, had a long history of working in Japan, had Japanese partners, and in the cases of Nathan, Tom, Jamie and Stewart, were parents to young children. Our shared similarities meant that rapport was easy to forge, but I tried to take special care with my interactions, being aware that our similarities meant that there was greater potential for me to have unshared assumptions with the participants' experiences.

5.3 Designing a Study of Emotion Regulation

As I mentioned at the beginning of this chapter, my goals in this study were to explore the how and why of the participants' emotion regulation through a qualitative approach. Rather than following a pre-determined qualitative methodology I characterise this study as an interpretive description. Interpretive description is not a discrete method, but an approach to planning whereby researchers focus on the principled mixing of research techniques (Thorne, 2016). In this case, I used interviews, observations and stimulated recall methods to collect data, and I took key tenets from grounded theory and complex dynamic systems theory (CDST) to implement the procedures. In the following section I explain these choices in detail.

5.3.1 Data collection choices: Interviews, observations and stimulated recall

I collected data through three different methods: semi-structured interviews, classroom observations and stimulated recall interviews, and in this section, I want to explain my reasons for choosing these methods.

Firstly, semi structured interviews were chosen because I desired to access the participants' subjective thoughts and understandings on emotion regulation to form a general picture of their background. I needed such a picture because it would reveal emotion regulation decision-making and habits, uncover underlying personal factors impacting the participants and set the scene for data collected through the subsequent observations and stimulated recall interviews.

Very early on in the planning process, I also recognised the need to include an observational component. This was because emotions are, by nature, visible and performative. Teachers display emotions both deliberately and automatically. Equally, they frequently hide, or try to hide, their emotions from classes. By including an observational component, I could triangulate the teachers' testimony on their teaching and have a more detailed contextual understanding of their decision-making.

I also felt that the participants' introspective thoughts would be critical to me understanding the things that I observed. Thus, I decided to employ stimulated recall interviews. Stimulated recall is a retrospective form of introspection that asks a participant to recall their thought processes about an event that has happened in the recent past. The methodology is well tested (see Sanchez & Grimshaw, 2020), and has been used to investigate, among other things, students' interpretations of their silent behaviours (King, 2013a, 2013b), the impact of content familiarity on learner engagement (Qiu & Lo, 2016) and triggers of student anxiety (Gregersen *et al.*, 2014). Among studies of language teachers, Gkonou and Mercer (2017) employed a version of the methodology within their study of social and emotional intelligence and concluded that the methodology was highly effective for emotion-directed research.

5.3.2 Conducting a stimulated recall

Although many readers may be familiar with interview and observation protocols, some may be unaware of the processes and objectives of stimulated recall; therefore, I would like to give a few explanatory paragraphs about this methodology, its purpose and the benefits it conferred on this study.

When conducting a stimulated recall, two stages take place. Firstly, an individual is observed completing a task. The researcher takes detailed notes and makes a recording of the task. Secondly, the researcher interviews the participant. During this follow-up interview (which I will call *the stimulated recall interview*), the notes and recording are used as recall stimuli, supporting the participant to remember and report on what had happened during the task (see Gass & Mackey, 2017, for an excellent overview of the method). Researchers must prepare well and implement the method with care. The most important considerations are the potency of the recall stimuli, the time lapse between the task and the interview, and the nature of the questions being asked (Borg, 2006; Gass & Mackey, 2017; Sanchez & Grimshaw, 2020).

In the case of my study, the task in question was the teaching of a class. Participants were observed, and recall stimuli later supported them to report on their thought processes in relation to their emotion regulation during salient classroom events. By using this process, I was able to achieve four important aims.

(1) I accessed real-life examples of emotion regulation to support the semi-structured interview testimony.
(2) I was provided with detailed accounts of the emotion regulation motives and strategies that were employed in event-specific uses of emotion regulation.
(3) I was able to explore multiple instances of emotion regulation within the same 90-minute period, enabling an image to be formed of the dynamic nature of emotion regulation.
(4) I was able to triangulate the participants' testimonies through my independent observations.

Given the above benefits, I am a strong advocate for the use of stimulated recall when investigating classroom-based emotion research. The method provided very rich data that I feel sure I would not have been able to access using other methods, and like Gkonou and Mercer (2017) reported, there were occasions where the method helped to reveal new insights for the participants themselves.

5.3.3 The influence of grounded theory methodology

At the beginning of this section, I mentioned that this study was informed by both grounded theory and complexity theories, and here I want to explain in more detail what I mean by the verb 'inform'.

Summarily speaking, grounded theory is a methodology that eschews hypothesis testing and prioritises the construction of theory through the data analysis procedures (Bryant & Charmaz, 2011; Charmaz, 2014; Creswell & Creswell, 2018; Hadley, 2017). Although this study was not a full grounded theory in its formal sense, I adhered strongly to three core tenets from the tradition. These tenets were the iterative collection and analysis of data; the constant comparison of data, codes and literature; and the use of inductive and abductive reasoning (see Charmaz, 2014, and Hadley, 2017, for excellent overviews of grounded theory). These tenets were crucial in affording a flexible, principled and dependable study.

The first tenet, iteration, refers to the fact that within grounded theory data is collected and analysed as it becomes available. In the inquiry I applied an iterative data collection process where I simultaneously collected and analysed data as I moved from participant to participant. This allowed me to remain open to following where the data led and helped emerging ideas to remain embedded in the data.

The second tenet was the constant comparative method. This approach suggests that researchers make continual comparisons of their data as they analyse it – across participants, across time, and with extant literature (Bryant & Charmaz, 2011; Charmaz, 2014). Within the analysis, I employed constant comparison to make sense of the data by examining the participants' words in interviews and actions in observations, by considering similarities and differences between each participants' responses, and by continually moving between the data set and the existing literature on emotion and emotion regulation.

The final tenet referred to the use of induction and abduction, forms of logic that are applied within the grounded theory methodology to ensure the conclusions remain embedded within the data (Charmaz, 2014; Hadley, 2017). Inductive reasoning refers to the notion that theoretical conclusions be derived from data rather than from pre-existing beliefs, while abductive reasoning is a pragmatic approach that encourages researchers to make inferences and probable guesses using observations about what they have seen and their own existing knowledge. In my study, I employed both forms of logic: my theoretical conclusions were informed directly from the data I collected, yet I remained conscious of any data which was unexpected and potentially challenged existing theory and literature.

5.3.4 The influence of complex dynamics systems theory

Numerous times throughout this book I have commented on the complex and dynamic nature of emotion regulation. Teachers regulate their emotions through decision-making that is dependent on their interpretations of classroom events, which are themselves filtered through their past experiences and shaped by the range of outside pressures that are placed upon them. In order to investigate the way that these many contextual factors intersected with the participants' emotion regulation, I approached the research wearing a lens that was informed by CDST. By 'lens' here, I mean to say that the tenets of CDST guided the way that I recognised and attended to the role of context in the study. This lens was worn both during the initial design, as well as in the data collection and analysis.

CDST is an increasingly popular approach to research in applied linguistics (see e.g. Sampson & Pinner, 2021), and its central premise occupies a polar position to reductionism: rather than viewing contextual factors as problematic issues that need to be controlled or removed, CDST intentionally accepts the existence of a multitude of contextual factors as having influence over the phenomena under study (Larsen-Freeman & Cameron, 2008). CDST therefore recognises that teacher behaviours and actions are not independent of interpersonal narratives, relationships and larger sociopolitical structures (King, 2016a), but rather, exist because of them. It also recognises that these behaviours and actions change dynamically, occasionally stabilising into repeating patterns at particular moments in time.

An appreciation of time is one of the most important strengths of CDST (MacIntyre *et al.*, 2021), and for a study adopting a CDST lens, it is the interaction of contextual factors across different time frames which becomes important as researchers attempt to ascertain how particular behaviours and phenomena came into being (de Bot *et al.*, 2007; King, 2016a; Larsen-Freeman & Cameron, 2008). Consequently, researchers adopting a CDST lens have three primary goals: to identify which contextual components are affecting the participants, to select which are important, and then to describe how these interact across time (King, 2016a).

Practically speaking, the CDST lens had an impact on three areas of my inquiry: the research design, the data collection and the data analysis. Firstly, with regards to the research design, the CDST lens influenced my choice to employ multiple data collection procedures to attend to different dimensions of emotion regulation behaviour (as recommended by Gilmore, 2016). This approach enabled me to have a greater understanding of how a teacher's perceptions and experiences interacted with classroom- and institutional-level factors to inform emotion regulation. Secondly, with regards to the data collection, the CDST lens had a guiding influence on my interview and stimulated recall survey designs. These instruments attended to the ways in which the participants' emotion regulation behaviours had changed across numerous timelines, including locally moment-to-moment within the classroom, more widely across the semester they were teaching in, and also ontogenetically across their careers. Thirdly, with regards to the data analysis, the CDST lens had a visible impact on my coding practices. When coding, I placed a high degree of focus on the contextual factors emerging in the data and the ways that they were interacting to afford and constrain emotion regulation. Within the early data analyses, for example, I took a conscious decision to assume that all contextual factors might be relevant; consequently, the initial pass through the data produced a set of 238 codes relating to context. This enabled a fine-grained and nuanced understanding of the data as these codes were refined during secondary and tertiary analysis phases.

5.3.5 Mapping the study

At this point of the chapter, I believe it is useful to offer a map of the study to illustrate how the data collection methods were combined to answer the research questions (see Figure 5.1). As can be seen in the diagram, the participants each completed a single semi-structured interview, which was then followed by two observations and two subsequent stimulated recall interviews. The data was collected iteratively from participant to participant, and primary analysis took place as data continued to be collected in accordance with the principles of the grounded theory method.

The data from the interviews and stimulated recall sessions were not treated independently but combined together to answer the research questions. The combination of data in this way helped me to achieve what Bryman (2006: 106) has called 'completeness', referring to a more extensive account of the phenomena being studied than which could be achieved by a single data collection method alone.

5.3.6 Reflection 2: My philosophical crisis

To conclude this section on the study design, I include a short reflection on my philosophical approach to this research, which I think offers insight on my decision-making throughout the project.

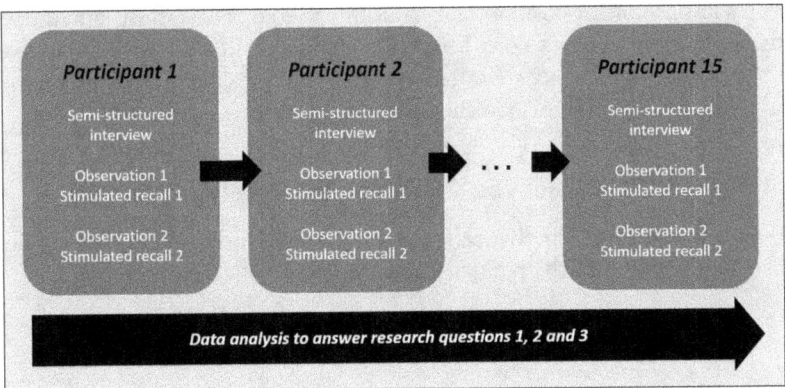

Figure 5.1 Map of the study

At the point I began this study, I had spent a lot of time reading about research and thinking about research, and I had moved through something of a philosophical crisis. I have an educational background in mathematics, and I strongly identify with rationality. Certainly if you had asked me in my 20s, words like 'constructivist', 'interpretation' and 'subjective' would have been entirely alien. But in 2015, as I moved between my master's degree and my doctorate, I found myself more and more drawn to emerging qualitative studies of the psychological experiences of language teachers and students. These studies were fascinating, exciting, enthralling, surprising and rich. As a practicing teacher myself, I found that I was gaining far more from reading such papers than I did from the statistical analyses of surveys and questionnaires – I could finally see myself and my own experiences in academic papers.

The philosophical crisis I faced was ultimately one about research itself – What is research and why is it important for education? On these matters, I found Richard Pring's *Philosophy of Educational Research* (2004, 2015) to be very useful. Pring rightly points out that the definition of a 'good' education is not universally agreed upon. Governments, teachers and citizens hold various opinions on, for example, the holistic outcomes that formal education should provide, and the kind of knowledge, skills and training that young people need to acquire. Language education in Japan does not escape this trap, for there exists strong disagreement on the role of English within education and the country at large. Pring suggests that educational inquiry aimed at prescriptive rule forming cannot be successful in every circumstance and that there is significant value in inquiry which focuses on educator informing.

I share Pring's position, and it has root in the philosophical school of pragmatism. Therein, the goal of research can be viewed as a way to make 'educational action more intelligent' (Biesta & Burbules, 2003: 80) and to 'provide resources that enable educators to see new problems or see problems in a new light, to guide their observations and to help them with interpreting the problematic situations they encounter' (Biesta & Burbules, 2003: 80). From a philosophical standpoint, therefore, the goal of this study (and indeed this book) is very clear to me: I hope that readers will recognise themselves in the participants' voices, empathise with the data and conclusions, and leave with newly transformed thoughts about their own classrooms.

5.4 Rolling Up My Sleeves: Collecting and Analysing the Data

Having explored the theoretical details of the study, in this final section I give an overview of the particulars of the data collection and analysis

5.4.1 Collecting data 1: The semi-structured interviews

The first interview that I conducted with each participant was a semi-structured interview. These each lasted between 40 and 76 minutes (mean = 54 minutes), and were audio recorded. For each of the semi-structured interviews I used an interview protocol, and a copy of this can be found in Appendix A.

The interview protocol was widely tested, and there are three points worth highlighting that made the interviews successful. The first was the opening content question which changed dramatically between the pilot study and the main study. When I first began broaching the subject of emotion regulation with teachers, I found that it was not always easy for them to discuss their emotion regulation habits. This was almost certainly because, with few exceptions, the teachers I investigated had not had much opportunity to formally reflect on their emotion regulation. One of the first interviews in the pilot study was particularly telling, because in 75 minutes it produced only one or two usable data points. Clearly, I had improvements to make! At this point, I investigated how other researchers dealt with this issue and realised that there was a better way forward. Rather than beginning with a general opening question, I adapted a narratively informed question that Gross and Richards (2006) had used in a study of emotion regulation. The opening question became:

> I would like you to think of a time in the past week or two when you tried to alter your emotions in the classroom. Go ahead and take a few moments to think of a time when you tried to alter your emotions. When you're ready, I'd like you to describe this to me in as much detail as you can.

This new question saw immediate benefits – participants reached a very clear understanding of the notion of emotion regulation and the direction of the interview. For other researchers wishing to investigate emotion regulation, I highly recommend this kind of starting point.

The second feature of the interviews that I wish to highlight was the fact that the questions on the protocol did not follow a numbered order, but instead were grouped into categories. Four categories of question were chosen. The first three related to the potential motives of emotion regulation. They were grouped as questions about emotional labour/epistemic motives, performance/social motives and well-being motives. The fourth category was labelled 'general questions', and was a flexible grouping that allowed me to add questions to the protocol as themes emerged. Again, I saw many benefits from this practice. The opening narratives provided by the participants were rich and involved, and extended sometimes to 15–20 minutes of the interview. These opening narratives enabled a natural move into discussions of more general areas of emotion regulation depending on their content. For example, if a participant's opening narrative dealt with issues related to stress, then I could follow this up with questions from the well-being motives category. Alternatively, if a participant's opening narrative dealt with issues related to emotional responsibility, I could follow up with questions from the emotional labour category. The fact that the questions were organised in this way on the protocol allowed me a great deal of flexibility and lent a natural progression to the flow of the interviews.

The third feature I want to highlight is that I used a printed list of emotions to support the participants in their interviews. This was a simple piece of paper with a list of 15 emotion words. Such a list was originally employed by Sutton (2004), but I extended the list used in that study by including extra emotions words that were commonly discussed during the pilot study (e.g. frustration, guilt). I was somewhat worried that the participants would be led to believe that the emotions on the list were the only emotions I was interested in, so I was sure to explain that the list was not indicative or presumptuous but designed simply to help participants to gather their thoughts. Numerous participants commented positively on the emotion lists, observing that they were supportive in helping them look more deeply at their teaching practice.

5.4.2 Collecting data 2: The classroom observations

What is good practice when observing emotion regulation in a language classroom? One of the difficulties, of course, is that emotions are both internally experienced and externally presented. The purpose of the observation was to record the latter, and I took great care in my actions before, during and after the observations so that I would not unduly influence the teacher and students.

In each observation, I arrived shortly before the class began, greeted the teacher and students, and positioned myself at a desk at the side of the room. I chose the side of the room, rather than the back, because in doing so, I was in a position to observe both the teacher's emotional expressions, and also the responses of the students. During each class, I made an audio recording to be used as a recall stimulus. Although video recordings are liable to be stronger stimuli than audio recordings (Gass & Mackey, 2017), I was conscious that participants and students would feel nervous being video recorded, leading to a less natural lesson.

In addition to the recording, I took extensive notes on a pre-prepared observation scheme (a copy of which can be seen in Appendix B). The scheme was relatively free form, giving me a flexible space in which to write. In principle, I took notes on the following four things:

(1) Classroom stages: I took general notes on classroom activities and what the teacher/students were doing.
(2) Highly visual emotional events: When incidents occurred where a teacher had visibly expressed an emotion, I took notes on what was happening in the class at the time, on facial expressions, on who was interacting and on what was being said.
(3) Potential emotional events: Since the participating teachers might have suppressed emotions during the lesson, I took notes on events which

had the potential to elicit emotions. Such incidents were varied in nature but included students' actions (such as when students were chatting or disengaged) and teacher–student interactional behaviours (such as when teachers interacted warmly with a particular student).

(4) Classroom layout: I made diagrams of the classroom layout, including table numbers, to aid discussions and recall.

My observations for a single class frequently extended to four or more pages, and I worked under the general principle that it was better to over record rather than under record notes. In other words, I took notes even when it was perhaps unlikely that the teacher might have experienced any form of emotional response. Generally speaking, more notes were taken during the first half of classes, when teachers had more front-of-class instruction, then during the second half of classes, when students were often working on assigned tasks.

5.4.3 Collecting data 3: The stimulated recall interviews

Gass and Mackey (2017) suggest that the time interval between the event and the stimulated recall interview is a crucial factor in ensuring the validity of data. In my case, I conducted all of the stimulated recall interviews within 24 hours of the observation with the exception of two interviews (Luke's first stimulated recall interview, and Jamie's second stimulated recall interview) which had to be rescheduled because of illness. In these cases, the stimulated recall sessions instead took place within 48 hours of the class being conducted. The stimulated recall interviews each lasted between 19 and 51 minutes (mean = 38 minutes). In line with best practice, I employed detailed protocols during the stimulated recall interviews (see Appendix C) which were adapted from Gass and Mackey (2017).

An important principle for reducing the interviewer's impact on testimony in stimulated recall sessions is to allow participants to select their own events of interest that they wish to speak about (Gass & Mackey, 2017). To do this, the first content question I asked in each stimulated recall interview was for the participants to write a list of any strong emotions that they had felt during their class. Participants typically produced a list of three or four emotions that they could recall, though sometimes this list was significantly longer. Luke, for example, produced a list of 17 emotions following his first observation! These lists formed the starting point for discussions in the interviews. I asked about the emotions in question, at what point in the class they were experienced, the causes of the emotions, how the emotions were regulated, and the participants' opinions on any contextual factors that might have been influencing their emotions and behaviours. I also prepared a list of important events from the class that I wished to discuss. During the interviews, I used my notes and classroom diagrams as recall stimuli to support the discussions.

Occasionally, I also used the audio recordings to supplement the notes; however, given the short time between the classes and interviews, the participants almost always had a very clear and strong recall of emotional events, and the audio recordings were used only a handful of times.

5.4.4 Analysing data: Coding

I created full transcriptions of each interview using an orthographic system adapted from Wray and Bloomer (2006) (see Appendix D). This system recognised non-vocal and paralinguistic features such as pauses, volume and laughter, and reported on unfinished ideas and unclear speech. Transcription of both the semi-structured and stimulated recall interviews resulted in a very large corpus of 305,000 words, an amount of data that I found, quite honestly, intimidating. Consequently, I spent a lot of time early in the coding process familiarising myself with the data, exploring different coding methods, and following threads into dead ends. In the end, I formulated an effective four-stage coding procedure.

5.4.4.1 Coding stage 1: Tape analysis of the data

I first conducted a tape analysis, listening to each interview within a week of it being conducted and making notes in my research journal of emerging themes, ideas and reflections. At this stage, I didn't use formal codes but jotted down ideas and thoughts. Throughout this early stage of the analysis, my adoption of a complexity lens meant that I was actively trying to recognise how contextual factors underlay the participants' explanations of their emotion regulation, and this was reflected in many of my journal entries.

5.4.4.2 Coding stage 2: Structural and descriptive coding

Because I had such a large amount of data, my first formal task was to make the dataset more manageable. I did this by applying structural and descriptive codes using NVivo 12. Structural codes label data according to their relevance to a particular research question or subtopic within the conceptual framework, while descriptive codes summarise data using descriptive language (Saldaña, 2016). I coded the data in large sections, each typically representing a single incident or narrative from the testimony, and my structural codes related to four main categories.

(1) Emotion regulation strategy: I coded data according to the kind of emotion regulation strategies that were being discussed.
(2) Factors influencing behaviours and emotions: I coded data according to the contextual factors that were being discussed.
(3) Emotion regulation motives: I coded data according to the emotion regulation motives that the participants regulated their emotions in aid of.

(4) Specific emotions: I coded data according to the specific emotion words (e.g. anger, sadness, joy) that were used by the participants. Where no emotion words were used, the excerpts were coded as 'general negativity' or 'general positivity'.

In all, this coding cycle elicited more than 400 structural and descriptive codes.

5.4.4.3 Coding stage 3: Axial coding

Following the structural and descriptive coding, I used axial coding cycles to assess the relevancy of existing codes, categorise groups of codes together and delete unnecessary codes. In practical terms, during the second coding cycle I worked through the codebook, my memos and the transcripts, applying comparisons and grouping/deleting codes as necessary. At the end of this coding cycle, the 400 codes were subsumed into 88 higher-order categories.

5.4.4.4 Coding stage 4: Theoretical coding and presentation decisions

At this stage of the analysis, I was ready to formulate the final direction of the analysis – the 'story' (Holliday, 2007: 91). It is appropriate here to comment on the presentation of my data and my structural choices in the proceeding chapters of this book. This is because with qualitative data, theoretical coding is inherently related to both the research questions that were posed, and also to how the data is presented in final written texts (e.g. Holliday, 2007). In practice, given the research questions that I was exploring, there were multiple ways for me to present my data analysis, and these different ways would have taken my writing in different directions.

As a reminder, my research questions targeted the strategies, motives and contextual factors that emerged in consideration of the participants' emotion regulation. As readers continue to move through the proceeding four chapters, they will observe that each chapter deals with a specific category of emotion regulation strategy. In Chapter 6, I discuss the use of situational strategies of emotion regulation. In Chapter 7, I discuss attention deployment strategies. In Chapter 8, I discuss cognitive change strategies, and in Chapter 9, I discuss response modulation strategies. In other words, the decision that I have taken is to organise my results and discussion according to my first research question (emotion regulation strategies), with discussion of my second and third research questions (motives and contextual factors) integrated within this text. This decision was made after a great deal of consideration and experimentation.

To justify this decision, I think it is useful to describe two other directions that I explored. The first direction was to focus on each of my three research foci separately. In other words, to organise my text by presenting firstly, a discussion of emotion regulation strategies; secondly, a discussion of motives; and thirdly, a discussion of contextual factors. A second route that I travelled was to organise my chapters in relation to emotion regulation motive. In fact, I wrote a full draft of three chapters – one chapter focusing on well-being, one focusing on emotional labour, and one focusing on instrumental purposes. When I took these two routes, however, I found that my discussion was rather dry. In particular, much of the complexity regarding how emotion regulation strategies interacted with motives and contextual features was lost. The writing did not illustrate clearly how, for example, a particularly emotion regulation strategy might be applied successfully by one teacher and unsuccessfully by another teacher. Nor did it adequately explain how one strategy might be used to achieve two different motives simultaneously. When I organised my discussion around emotion regulation strategies, however, these rich complex details emerged vividly. This was the primary reason for organising my text in this way.

Having made the decision to organise my discussion around emotion regulation strategies, I was able to move forward with theoretical coding. The final coding cycle therefore focused only on one structural coding group: emotion regulation strategies. I printed groups of excerpts under each axial coding category (situational strategies, attention deployment strategies, cognitive change strategies and response modulation strategies), read them multiple times and compared them with other testimony and the extant literature. This process led to refinement of the codes into the categories that were employed in the final written form.

What I hope to have highlighted in this section is that my decision on the final presentation of my results was taken after a significant amount of exploratory work. By integrating my discussions of motive and contextual factors under higher-order headings relating to emotion regulation strategy, I believe that I have been able to successfully illustrate the complex interweaving of these three features of the data.

5.4.4.5 Member checking

Perhaps what might be considered the final stage of the data analysis was the verification of the testimony and interpretations by the participants themselves. Member checking is widely posited as one of the most important practices for ensuring the credibility of qualitative data (e.g. Cho & Trent, 2016; Creswell & Creswell, 2018; Creswell & Miller, 2020; Dörnyei, 2007); however, despite this stated importance, it was very surprising for me to learn that few guidelines exist on how to perform member checking in a structured and principled manner. (See also Hallett, 2013, who discusses this issue.) Consequently, I detail here my own interpretation of best practice, and I provide a copy of the instructions I used with participants in Appendix E.

There are four potential traps that need to be avoided when member checking: participants may be surprised by how their testimony reads owing to the nature of the transcription process (Carlson, 2010); participants may provide researchers with too little or too much feedback (Carlson, 2010); participants may disagree with the researcher's interpretations or be offended (Candela, 2019); and participants may be distressed if asked to relive potentially distressing testimony (Hallett, 2013). To mitigate these issues, I followed three principles when member checking:

(1) to be upfront with participants about the nature of the reports I was sending them (with regards to length and content);
(2) to provide clear expectations on the feedback I was seeking;
(3) to consider the participant's needs on an individual basis.

I conducted member checking in June and July of 2021. I contacted the participants by email, and upon agreement sent them copies of the relevant sections of the analysis to review. The participants were given detailed instructions of what was expected of them: specifically, that they should read the extracts, and comment on their agreement or disagreement with the testimony. Participants were asked not to elaborate on any points with further thoughts, but to focus on their agreement and reasons so.

All 15 participants opted to take part in the member checking process, and completed checks were received from 12 participants (Tom, Gina, Jessica, Jamie, Millie, Luke, Catherine, Zoe, Richard, Eleanor, Peter, Stewart). No disagreement was seen on behalf of the participants, which is reassuring with regards to the credibility of the study.

5.4.5 Ethical considerations

Before finishing this chapter, I want to briefly address the ethics of the study. Throughout all stages of the research, consent was informed. The participants were made aware of the direction and goals of the study through plain language statements and consent forms at the outset. Participating teachers were also reminded of their rights at the beginning of each interview.

Since the stimulated recall stage of the data collection involved audio recording classes, I also obtained informed consent from each student attending those lessons. To gain this consent, I visited each class the week before their first observation, introduced myself, explained the study and provided written forms of consent. Students who were absent from these meetings were followed up with by the participating teachers.

Since the teacher participants would be describing the potentially sensitive emotional dimensions of their work, which may have included denigrating remarks about colleagues or students, all participants were given full confidentiality throughout the study. In practical terms, numerous steps were taken to ensure this. When transcribing interview data, names were recorded as pseudonyms and I followed a blanket policy not to discuss any aspects of the research while at the research site.

5.4.6 Reflection 3: Interview demeanour and the need for rapport

My final reflection, which ends this chapter, focuses on my demeanour during the interviews that I conducted. Instructional texts (and common sense) iterate that interviewers remain aware of their impact on the participants and their testimonies. As such, when interviewing I followed the general recommendations of many experienced researchers (e.g. Dörnyei, 2007; King *et al.*, 2019). That is to say, I attempted to facilitate strong rapport while minimising my impact on the participants by limiting disclosure of my own opinions, by maintaining a professional distance and by remaining conscious not to lead participants.

What I found very quickly though, was that an overtly strict interview style was inhibiting rather than facilitating the participants' testimonies. I was particularly struck by the notion that an ideal interview space was one where participants felt able to share stories that did not always portray themselves in an ideal light, and that hiding my bias was not simply enough to achieve this (Dörnyei, 2007). I came to the conclusion that a higher degree of rapport and mutual sharing was needed than I had initially anticipated in order to create a safe environment for the participants to disclose their emotional stories. In short – I think I needed to relax a little.

In recognition of the fact that interviews are co-constructions between interviewers and interviewees, I found Mann's 'parameters of sensitivity' (Mann, 2016: 157) to be highly informative. Rather than being dogmatic about the way an interviewer conducts themselves, Mann suggests developing a sensitivity to core issues, such as the interviewer's use of disclosure and empathy. I came to recognise that Mann was correct – by disclosing some of my own personal experiences I could generate dialogue, and by indicating empathy for participants' circumstances I could help them to feel more able to open themselves up.

Dörnyei (2007) gives useful practical tips on how to balance interviewer neutrality with empathy and sharing. Some of the methods that I adopted included sharing my own negative emotional experiences with participants, adopting a questioning style which reinforced that the participants' experiences were commonly shared, creating a relatively casual air and displaying enthusiasm. Of course, I had to be careful about the use of these strategies, and when reviewing the testimony later, there were some occasions where I felt that my sharing had possibly led the participants. In these cases, I made a judgement call on whether I felt the testimony was problematic, and in cases where I had any doubt, I removed them from the analysis process.

5.5 Lessons Learned: Studying Emotion Regulation

In this chapter I have tried to be as open and honest as possible about the difficulties of studying language teachers' emotion regulation while also giving a series of practical steps that future researchers can follow. To end, I want to draw attention to two particularly important lessons that I have learned from my investigations of teacher emotion regulation.

(1) Teachers are not always aware of their emotion regulation. This is not only because of the automatic nature of some emotion regulation, but also because most of us rarely consider emotion regulation in our daily lives. What I found in this study was that teachers were not always cognisant of their emotion regulation decision-making. This led to some interesting 'aha' moments as the participants occasionally reached new insight, but also highlighted a further important point. Namely, that it was when discussing the most highly emotional of experiences that teachers were truly aware of their emotion regulation actions. When discussing intensely emotional situations (both positive and negative), participants were able to describe their thoughts, memories, impressions and regulation vividly. Unsurprising, there is much to be learnt from the most painful and euphoric of classroom experiences.

(2) What teachers say may not be what the researcher thinks they mean. One of the difficulties of being a teacher who researches other teachers is that we have different shared assumptions of our practice. There were numerous times in the study where the ways that the teachers described their emotional practice gave me an image which was not born out in the observations. When a teacher describes themselves as 'fun', or 'serious', or 'jokey' or 'strict', it pays to remember that these words are not universally understood. Challenging interviewees to define their descriptions is excellent practice moving forward, but I would strongly argue that the stimulated recall method is one of the best ways for researchers to interrogate participants about the intersection between their words and behaviour. This is something that my colleagues and I have previously explored in detail (Morris *et al.*, 2023).

Note

(1) The academic year in Japan runs from April to March; thus, the data was collected between April of 2019 and March of 2020.

6 Environment

'Imagine your job,' I sometimes tell my classes. 'Now imagine that you could change one thing about your job to make your work more enjoyable or less stressful. What would you change?' My 21-year-old students typically work as serving staff in cafes or as private tutors in preparatory cram schools. Some want less frustration from the technology in their lives ('buy a new air conditioner', 'fix the vacuum cleaner', 'the computer is so slow'), others wish for more comfort ('buy a coffee machine', 'give me a nice chair', 'change the uniform') and a few make rather optimistic pleas ('let me be late sometimes', 'double my wages', 'fire my boss'). Although this activity paints a hypothetical scenario, at its heart lies an important truth – employees in any context can and do manipulate their working environments to manage the emotions they experience. These actions may be small and simple, such as when they organise their desks with pictures and personal items, or may be large and complex, such as when they rearrange their schedules so that they have enough time to adequately prepare. These kinds of actions, which target both positive and negative emotions, belong to a category of emotion regulation known as *situational strategies*. Situational strategies target the external world we live in, and they are employed in advance of an emotion occurring to generate it into being or prevent it from ever starting.

6.1 Introduction: Teachers Moulding Their Environment

In this chapter, I discuss both forms of situational strategy – situation selection, which refers to when individuals create or avoid environmental opportunities for emotions, and situation modification, which refers to when individuals make environmental changes to manage emerging emotions. I combine these strategies for two reasons. The first reason is because they both target the same feature of the emotional context – the external world the individual finds themselves in. The second reason is because the complexity of real-world decision-making means that the boundaries of any particular 'situation' are often arbitrary, and differences between what might be considered situation 'selection' and what might be considered situation 'modification' are not always discernible. Precedent for combining situational strategies in this way exists in the literature within general psychology (Gross, 2015).

A suitable subtitle for this chapter might be 'teachers moulding their environment', because this is a useful summary of the way that situational strategies were used by the teachers at Fukuzaki University. The participants reported taking regular active steps to manage their external circumstances, which helped them to increase their positive emotions, to attenuate their negative emotions and to manage the behaviours of their students. The overall picture painted by the data was that situational strategies were extremely common – all 15 of the teachers regularly employed this form of emotion regulation.

This is the first of four data-led chapters, and each one follows the same three-part structure. I begin each chapter by exploring *characteristic strategies*. Here, I detail some of the most common emotion regulation strategies that emerged in the data and, where applicable, discuss the motives that lay behind the participants' decision-making. These sections make excellent reading for those who are new to the topic of emotion regulation, and for those who wish to understand the strategies that teachers use and the reasons underlying their strategy choices. In the second section of each chapter, I then consider *contextual factors*. Here, I discuss the most important affording and inhibiting contextual points. These sections are useful for those who wish to understand the broader issues affecting teachers and their emotion regulation choices. Finally, in the third section of each chapter I explore what I have called *complex considerations*. By complex here, I refer to those examples of emotion regulation which were particularly unique, often involving the interaction of multiple contextual factors, strategies, motives or goals. These sections are the most nuanced, offering readers much food for thought as they reflect on emotion regulation in their own teaching and research.

6.2 Characteristic Situational Strategies and Motives

To begin my discussion of the use of situational strategies, I illuminate on what were the most common examples of this kind of emotion regulation used by the participants and I consider some of the motivations underlying their uses of situational strategies.

6.2.1 Job crafting

One of the most common ways that the participants used their environment to impact their emotions was through a collection of actions known summarily as *job crafting*. These are the steps that individuals take to 'shape, mould, and redefine their jobs' (Wrzesniewski & Dutton, 2001: 180), and they refer to the ways that teachers might make changes to their working practices within the remits of the expectations placed on them by managers and institutions. From the perspective of motive, the use of job crafting regularly served prohedonic desires as the participants sought and took opportunities to engineer more positive emotions in their day-to-day work. Prohedonic emotion regulation, as was discussed in Chapter 2, refers to when someone wants to increase the intensity of their positive emotions for the simple reason that doing so increases their subjective well-being.

There are different types of job crafting, and one common form used by the participants was *relationship crafting*. Relationship crafting relates specifically to actions individuals take to organise their social experiences (see Falout & Murphey, 2018). A clear example of this was the case of Vivienne. Appreciating the unstructured time she had with students before the beginning of lessons, Vivienne would actively arrive early to her classes so that she could engage with the students, learn about their lives and join in their jokes. This choice brought her a great deal of positive emotion: 'I really enjoy that moment of sort of understanding a little bit extra about their daily life and I'm always smiling and laughing'. Gina too, found ways to engage with students on a more personal level by beginning her classes with 'coffee time', a student-led activity inspired by a skit from the TV Show *Saturday Night Live*. During the activity, Gina asked her students to discuss a chosen topic and later share ideas with the whole class group. Gina enjoyed coffee time for the chance it gave her to learn about the full richness of her students' lives. She explained:

> It's a great way to get to know the students because sometimes their topics are like, you know, what-, what are you planning to do this summer? … So, I get to know what their plans are. What their lives are like outside of class…. I get to make jokes, and make them laugh…. I get to hear them speaking English…. But mostly, *it's just fun for me to hear their reports*, you know? So that's for me. That's the fun. [emphasis added]

As can be seen, although Gina's activity has pedagogic goals, it simultaneously has emotional goals, supporting her to feel closer to her students and to increase the intensity of her positive emotions.

A second form of job crafting, *task crafting*, relates to the way that teachers adapt their approaches to classroom pedagogy (see Falout & Murphey, 2018), and this was also very common in the data. When the participants described how they increased their levels of joy in their work, all 15 spoke of continual efforts to tailor the whole spectrum of syllabi-, material- and activity-level features of their courses. They spoke of creating energy in their lessons using competitive and physical activities to 'liven things up' (Tom) and planning classes that were 'very interactive' (Wendy). They employed activities that they personally favoured, such as 'random games' (Millie), enjoyable apps (Catherine) and meditative exercises (Wendy). And they reported designing classes around topics that they themselves were interested in: 'selfishly I probably just choose the unit topics that I like' (Eleanor), or those they thought would get a good reaction from students: 'I've tried to find some interesting questions to ask them and um interesting trivia' (Richard). This behaviour is prototypical task crafting because the participants made these decisions autonomously within the boundaries of their positions, and they are prototypical emotion regulation because they were performed with the express purpose of generating positive emotional states within themselves.

At the heart of this task crafting appeared to be the pursuit of creativity. Peter, for example, had created an original multimodal vocabulary system that he had implemented within the boundaries of the unified course assessment. By employing a popular social media platform as a database for new words, he felt proud that he had created something new for the students, 'another, you know, string in the bow', that they could use to more creatively learn vocabulary. Similarly, Wendy had made the decision to introduce poetry into her writing classes, taking great joy in the expressive and inventive output her students were able to produce. She remarked that the positive emotions poetry generated in her was palpable, and also noticed by others: her close colleagues remarked that 'every time you come back from teaching [poetry], you are just so excited and like wanting to show "this is what my kids did today".'

It was Stewart, however, for whom creativity had come to play the most striking role in his pedagogy. Stewart reported creativity as a central feature of his classroom, noting that 'the things I've enjoyed the most about teaching- things in which the students are being creative and having creativity at the centre of- the centre of teaching', and he tied the pursuit of creativity to his interpretation of his institutional responsibility to increase student autonomy: 'I mean it's just implicit in [students] taking or take over their own design, their own control and putting it in their hands.' Most strikingly, Stewart cited creativity as a leading factor when selecting courses to teach each academic year: 'I chose to have double [first year communication course], and if I wasn't able to have that, to have [second year communication course]. Both of them are very creative courses.' The notion that the creativity teachers employ in their work has an emotional facet is, of course, not a new idea. For example, creativity has previously been regarded as 'a source of ongoing professional renewal and satisfaction' (Richards, 2013: 42). But when viewing creativity from the perspective of emotion regulation, it appears to function not only as a 'source' of positivity, but also as an emotional tool, one through which teachers may, with deliberate and skilful application, generate and strengthen their positive experiences in the classroom.

6.2.2 Proactive coping

The job crafting reported on in the previous section was employed to generate positive emotions, but situational strategies were also used by the participants at Fukuzaki University to prepare for and deal with potential negative emotions during their teaching. In these cases, the situational actions they employed were rooted in the field of coping, the study of how individuals deal with stressors. In particular, the participants engaged in acts of *proactive coping*. The meaning is in the name here – these are efforts taken in advance to prepare for potential, yet general and undefined, future stressors (Aspinwall & Taylor, 1997; Greenglass & Fiksenbaum, 2009).

For the participants at Fukuzaki University, proactive coping was relatively common, with examples found in the data of 11 of the participants. A broad range of actions were reported, including one participant who consciously provided all instructions in a slow and controlled manner to reduce stressful misunderstandings (Jessica); another who physically changed the classroom desk layout because 'you sort of lose control of it when it's not- the space is not in the right- (2) as it- as it should be' (Stewart); and another who made deliberate efforts to ensure that grading guidelines were transparent and easily understood, a strategy which allowed her to mark more objectively and reduce opportunities for contention: 'the more I can be prepared to, to explain [grades], the happier I am' (Vivienne).

For five participants (Wendy, Gina, Vivienne, Stewart, Peter), the development of strong routines was an important form of proactive coping that helped them to reduce the potential for stress. Typically, these routines helped them get into the headspace of the workday by, for example, habitually arriving to school early (Peter), and making sure that technology was set up and working properly (Peter, Vivienne), but they were also important in the private lives of the participants too, ensuring that sufficient time was made for exercise and family (Stewart). Some teachers also employed strong classroom routines with students to reduce stress. Gina, for example employed a rigid classroom management system that encouraged students to take charge of different roles within the room. Some members of the class were responsible for taking attendance, others for handing out work and others for feeding back their group's ideas to peers. Gina reported that her classroom management had helped her to reduce the frustration that she felt with regards to her students being unwilling to contribute ideas and speak out in class. She explained that:

> Whoever the leader of the group is... they know that they're going to be called on many times in that class period, and they're going to have to be ready with something. So, they're prepared.... I think it does play a part in helping me stay- stay calm.

Gina's system, therefore, was 'quietly playing in the background', acting as a crutch that she could 'depend on' when dealing with the particularly common problem of student reticence that exists within some Japanese classrooms (King, 2013a, 2013b). Since she no longer had to worry about the potentially frustrating situation where students might be unwilling to contribute, she was able to 'stay calm' and focus on other areas of her teaching. Gina's classroom management system is noteworthy as a potentially successful emotion regulation strategy for dealing with the issue of silence, complementing other solutions such as the notion of an extended wait time (King, 2016b; Smith & King, 2018).

Serving a similar purpose to routines, proactive coping was also performed through effective class preparation. Seven of the participants (Tom, Gina, Catherine, Vivienne, Catherine, Eleanor and Peter) reported that they saw thorough advanced lesson preparation as an important step in the management of their emotions, and this was highly visible in the testimony of Tom:

> I always know there's a chance of [a busy morning] happening so everything is on my desk. You know, my folder is there with all the work in there, with the notes on top, so I know I can just pick it up and go straight to class.… I don't want to feel, like, stressed, and I don't want to feel, like, kind of uncomfortable and incompetent. So, to avoid that I kind of do all of- yeah, I take these kind of pre-emptive steps I guess.

As this testimony demonstrates, for Tom, preparation was a practical affair. Aware that as a parent of a young child he may be rushed in the morning, and equally aware of the added stress that a lack of readiness might cause for him, Tom took conscious and proactive steps to ensure everything was ready to go. Tom reported that his preparation was important, since there were occasions where he might have family problems in the morning, meaning that he might have to 'walk in there blind', and other teachers also reported that this thought terrified them:

> Yeah, the thought of someone like five minutes- coming up to me saying 'you got to give a class in five minutes', that would be a nightmare. Like, I spend hours on each- and this is, I mean- this is something- I've been teaching this course for- this is my last- sixth year right…But I'm still spending an hour or two hours preparing each class. Like going through it and checking it in my head 'how's that gonna flow?'

As can be seen here, Peter, despite having more than 11 years' experience at the chalkface, and also despite having taught the same course six times, still reported a substantial amount of time getting ready for each class to manage his emotions. Effective preparation, then, is not a strategy limited to new or inexperienced teachers.

Tom and Peter both employed effective preparation in order to prevent emotional uncertainty at the lesson-level; however, effective preparation was also reported as a useful way to manage larger course-level anxieties too. Vivienne for example, reported feeling what she called a significant 'broad, curriculum-anxiety' every time she started a new position. This was driven by worries that she may be failing to hit some of the institutional goals, worries that were themselves arising because of a desire to 'be excellent in reality at what I do'. Vivienne went on to explain how she dealt with these negative emotions:

> I know what my boss expects of me, I know what everyone else in my professional sphere expects of me, and finally, I know what the paperwork says I need to do. I need to check off a, b, and c and you mix all that together to be sure that you're satisfying everyone. And then you take that plan to the students. And when you meet the students for the first time you see if your plan is actually feasible or not, and then you can draft things that might make sense. So, coming into a new job, that- that anxiety is just so high, and I plan the crap out of it.

Highly aware of her personality and desire to please, and the negative emotions that this personality feature brings with it, Vivienne's planning was a proactive response to deal with anticipated negative emotions. Proactive coping is, by definition, a strategy of resource and skill management, of which the ability to plan and organise effectively is a defining feature (Aspinwall & Taylor, 1997); thus, as is exemplified by the testimonies of Tom, Peter and Vivienne here, the most salient contextual factors influencing the participants' use of planning appeared to be a highly attuned awareness and recognition of what causes them to feel negative emotions in the classroom.

6.2.3 Problem-directed action and problem avoidance

A third set of characteristic strategies related to how the participants tackled the many classroom and relationship difficulties that they encountered. Broadly speaking, teachers have two ways to act when they encounter a problem: they may face the issue head on and try to resolve it, or they may withdraw from the stressor to the point that it no longer causes them to feel the emotion. These two actions conform to what is known as *approach* and *avoidance* behaviour (Roth & Cohen, 1986), and two situational strategies which are applicable to these orientations are *problem-directed action* and *problem avoidance*, respectively.

Problem-directed actions are attempts to resolve the causes of negative emotions so that such problems (and resulting emotions) do not arise in the future (Aspinwall & Taylor, 1997; Larsen & Prizmic, 2007). In accordance, many of the problem-directed actions taken by the participants were behavioural and classroom management practises designed to resolve negative and stressful situations involving students. In total, 11 participants were found to employ problem-directed action to deal with relatively low-level stressors such as off-task and disruptive behaviours, talking over the teacher, chatting in the L1 and using smartphones (Jamie, Stewart, Wendy, Eleanor, Peter), as well as to manage a pronounced student reluctance to contribute to class discussions (Tom, Catherine, Vivienne, Richard, Eleanor) (see also Morris & King, 2023). One of the most common ways that teachers can perform problem-directed action is by actively addressing classroom issues. A prototypical illustration of this can be seen in testimony from Peter, who, when discussing experiences of frustration, described how he directly approached a student who often failed to actively participate in classes:

> One class she just fell asleep.... She was always on the phone sending [social media] messages and stuff. So after class one day I said 'oh you know those days where you slept in class the whole time? Well they will count as an absence because you weren't in the class and you weren't participating. And you know when you're on your phone and stuff? You know, that's going to affect your participation and stuff.' And she actually (0.5) for me after that she was fine.

To fully understand how Peter applied problem-directed action in this instance, it is also important to understand the nature of absences and participation at Fukuzaki University. Like many institutions in Japan, Fukuzaki University places a premium on attendance, meaning that students need to be physically present and actively participate in classes to receive credit for courses. Moreover, students at Fukuzaki University are liable to fail a course if they are absent on too many occasions. Peter's problem-directed action here then is two-fold: he raises the issue he is facing with the student directly by speaking to her about the issue, and also issues warnings of punishment in the form of a reduced grade. Fortunately, in this case Peter reported success from his use of problem-directed action, but success is by no means guaranteed, and teachers do not always feel they are able to resolve complex behavioural issues, particularly if control of the issue is hard to maintain (Morris & King, 2018).

Of course, interventions are not the only way that a teacher may deal with negative classroom behaviour and the participants also avoided problems, both emotionally and physically. Four of the participants employed emotional distancing to protect themselves. Like the teachers in King (2016b), the participants' motivations for distancing were multifaceted. For Wendy and Millie, their choice to distance was hedonically motivated, with Wendy noting simply that 'I don't need necessarily a deep relationship with (students)', but for Luke and Jessica the choice was more complexly related to their notions of duty, and this is illustrated in the following excerpt from Jessica:

> When there's like deadlines or they have to do something. I'm quite firm about it. Um, like, you know, this is- it's your responsibility, not mine, and quite clear. So even though we are- we do have a good relationship, like, they're not my friend [Laughs]. We are not best mates basically.

Jessica's use of emotional distancing here takes the form of clearly marked boundaries between the students' obligations and her own. This distancing is not only protective of her well-being, but her refusal to describe her students as 'friends' also suggests that she is aware of the potential danger of becoming too close to students, lest her position as 'teacher' be compromised.

At Fukuzaki University, three participants reported distancing themselves physically from problems. Luke, for example, had a student who he felt couldn't 'pick up on certain social cues'. He reported physically avoiding this student but felt he was not always aware of this behaviour: 'I don't notice that I'm actively avoiding, but then after the fact I'll kind of think "oh, maybe I should have, you know, maybe I didn't engage with him"'. For Luke, it was, in fact, his own emotions which alerted him to his distancing behaviour:

> I think that I must [avoid him], because I feel guilty sometimes…. If I'm doing group to group stuff, and he's at a certain table, and I go to that table… it's going to be dragged out a little longer, and then I'm not going to be able to monitor tables A, B, C…. I might feel like 'oh, I just realized I skipped his table.' And then I might feel the guilt of 'am I giving him and his group as much attention as they deserve?'

Luke's avoidance actions here are hedonically motivated, since they reduce his negative feelings of 'frustration', but also instrumentally motivated, since he reported a need to ensure sufficient time to work with all the tables in the room. However, we can also interpret that Luke's hedonically and instrumentally motivated emotion regulation actions were in discordance with his epistemically motivated desires to treat the student fairly. Thus, while Luke's physical distancing benefited his immediate emotional state, this was not an ideal solution since it brought with it another negative emotion (guilt) that he would later need to contend with. The conclusion arising here, therefore, is that physical distancing from students may be emotionally taxing if it interferes with a teacher's other classroom responsibilities.

6.3 Contextual Factors Affording and Shaping Situational Strategies

In this chapter so far, I have exemplified those common situational strategies that the teachers at Fukuzaki University employed, but in order to more deeply understand situational emotion regulation, I want to consider the underlying contextual forces that influenced the participants' decision-making. Analysis of the data revealed that the participants were responding to a wealth of societal, institutional and personal pressures that guided their situational emotion regulation in effective and ineffective ways.

6.3.1 Student responses and situational strategies: Emotional contagion

Within the interviews, a great deal was made of the fact that teachers' situational actions often generated positive emotions in students, and that these positive emotions could then feed back to the teacher as a form of emotional contagion (see Hatfield *et al.*, 1994). On this point Stewart remarked: 'if [students] make something that's very creative and well done, I get a lot of joy out of their joy.... Pride in helping them create something which I can genuinely see that they are proud of.' This was particularly true for the use of task crafting, and a trend seen among all of the participants was that pedagogic decisions were often made with students' emotions in mind: 'You make something (1) and it works, then yeah you feel good about it, but mostly it's the students. If the students have enjoyed it, then it's like- yeah it's better' (Tom).

Much has been written of the dynamic bidirectional nature of student–teacher interplay (de Bot *et al.*, 2007; King, 2016a; Larsen-Freeman & Cameron, 2008), by which it is meant that both teachers and their learners continually impact each other in their historically and relationally situated interactions, and this interplay was visible throughout the data. The teachers' choices to implement creative and enjoyable activities subsequently led to student positivity, which subsequently led to teacher positivity. Positive emotions then, were something that participants like Stewart tried to generate consciously in the students, so that they would later see that joy returned back to them (see also Morris, 2022).

6.3.2 Identity and situational strategies: The teacher I want to be

Job crafting was not only performed in a casual manner. It also served as a manifestation of identity and was employed to meet epistemic higher-order emotion regulation motives (see also Morris, 2022). This was visible in testimony from Nathan. It was clear at multiple points in Nathan's interviews that within his remit of being a language teacher at Fukuzaki University he placed a high priority on impacting students' critical faculties and providing pastoral care. He spoke on more than one occasion about the pride he felt for materials he had created for a second-year reading course. These texts, he suggested, contained content that was 'useful and important information for [students] and their lives', and the 'absolute joy' he experienced was clearly displayed during his first stimulated recall interview where, unprompted, he spoke of how the text he had created for the class that morning had had a powerful impact on him:

> The paper that they were studying was something that I wrote. It's basically a summary of some of the most robust findings in cross-cultural psychology.... I think I'm telling them something important. Um, I think that it's- they can learn from it.... I think it gives- uh give me meaning in what I'm doing, you know what I mean? It gives it- it gives it a purpose.

I interpret from Nathan's use of the words 'important' and 'meaning' here that he believes the content of his lessons hold real value for his students, and that perhaps this value is more worthwhile than the vocabulary and grammar they may learn alongside. In that sense, he appeared to have become, in the words of Falout and Murphey (2018: 221), a 'teacher of more than language' those who consider themselves 'teachers of practical life skills' (2018: 221).

Nathan's notions of his teaching self strongly influenced the interactions he sought and the relationships he built. He reported making a considerable effort to support students with both in-class and out-of-class issues: 'I am there for those kids… I will do my absolute best', and he had a particularly strong desire to help students with mental health issues, 'standing up for them, or helping them out'. From an emotion regulation perspective, it became clear that Nathan had crafted his position in his relationships with students so that his interactions were of an intensely caring nature, which stemmed from his own (largely negative) primary school learning experiences:

> I was mischaracterised and put in special needs classes and so on and so forth and- (0.5) um, which is why I never really wanted to be a teacher because I didn't like teachers. Um, I don't just wanna be alright, I wanna really be a powerful force for good in those students' lives.

Much can be learned here in consideration of how a teachers' identity formation influences their emotion regulation choices. Nathan's description of himself as 'a powerful force for good' suggests an intense engagement that is reminiscent of the potentially resource-taxing emotional labour that comes with education's ethic of care (Gkonou & Miller, 2017; Miller & Gkonou, 2018). Indeed, Nathan reported that 'there are times when I get home and I just crash', but equally he did not report a sense of extreme stress. This may be because his behaviours were in line with his epistemic notions of teaching: of his job he explained that 'it's a vocation. It's a career. It's something that (0.5) in a way you kind of feel a calling to'. Nathan saw the goal of teaching as requiring an intrinsic promise not unlike those found in other caring professions: 'if the Hippocratic oath for the doctor says "do no harm" (0.5), you know, for a teacher I think I have to go beyond that. I think you have to be "trying to do good"'. What Nathan is describing here can be characterised as a form of positive emotional labour (Humphrey *et al.*, 2015), and similar to participants in Miller and Gkonou (2018), it appears that by meeting his perceived responsibilities of teaching he is able to interpret experiences in an adaptable manner, despite those experiences themselves being emotionally taxing. Indeed, the only times he reported negative emotions were when issues with students went unresolved: when he felt that he had failed in his responsibilities as a caring teacher. The consequences of this may be that when teachers are able to successfully perform relationship crafting in accordance with the role that they see themselves as occupying within the classroom, they could negate the potentially negative impact of their emotional work.

6.3.3 Relationships and situational strategies: Avoiding students

In any classroom, the most important relationships may well be those between the teacher and each student. Unsurprisingly, therefore, students lay at the centre of many of the participants' situational actions, particularly those involving avoidance. In the case of physical avoidance, three remarkably similar cases emerged. In each case, personality clashes between the teacher and a student caused the participants to withdraw and actively avoid interacting with the students. Eleanor, for example, had a student who was highly intelligent, with English ability far above the average level of the class, but for whom she reported as having 'the kind of personality that I- (3) I'm a little bit intimidated by'. When I asked how she dealt with the emotions that arose from this student, she reported 'I just kind of avoid her to be honest'.

Problem avoidance, when used selectively, can be a potent way for an individual to reduce stress, but avoidance is most successful when it is used only temporarily as a means to prepare for a problem-directed action (Roth & Cohen, 1986). It was highly positive to observe, therefore, that over time all three of the participants had reflected and found ways to engage and interact positively with the students they were avoiding. To exemplify with Eleanor, it was the realisation that there were areas that she was able to offer teacherly support. Eleanor explained:

> There are some things that I found that I can help her with. Not with speaking per se, but anytime there's writing. I'll give her feedback on her writing. And she's always, 'oh my gosh, I'm terrible at writing', even though there's not many mistakes, but they're the same kind of mistakes. So, it- we're talking about trying to focus on those a bit more. So now I feel a little less anxious because I feel like I do have a bit of a role with teaching her.

Here then, Eleanor has found a purpose in her interactions by recognising a topic through which she can engage with the student. As was posited by Roth and Cohen (1986), then, physical problem avoidance may well be a viable strategy for dealing with students with whom the teacher has a strained relationship, providing that it is used as a temporary means for finding more direct solutions.

6.3.4 Notions of professional responsibility and situational strategies: Avoiding topics

Distancing was not only related to the relationships that existed between students and teachers, but also to the kinds of topics that the teachers felt professionally able to engage with. Luke, for example, displayed a high level of awareness of his status as a '32-year-old male' with '80% young Japanese women', as well as of the discourse surrounding the 'romantic occidental desire' (Appleby, 2013a: 127). This discourse positions Western men as archetypes of romance and sophistication in Japan, particularly in the private English language industry (Appleby, 2013a; Kubota, 2011). Luke's awareness of 'the problems with (0.5) the exotic *gaijin* [foreigner]', led him to distance himself from some topics in class, as becomes clear in the following excerpt from his first interview:

> Luke: What will often happen is at the beginning of the class, when I meet them, there'll be a handful of them who will say- who will kind of give me the googly eyes, kind of 'oh'.
> R: This is semester, day one?
> Luke: Semester, day one. It's like, 'oh, this teacher. Oh, this young teacher we have. Wow'. And I work very hard to move into a space that's kind of like (0.5) a friendly, nice person who listens and cares. And that's it [emphatic]. And when I get questions about 'do you have a girlfriend?' 'Do you have a wife?' Duh duh duh. I speak very openly. I'm honest with them. I want to show them that I'm not trying to hide or be private, but I'm also not interested in those topics.

As can be seen here, Luke employs situational behaviour, acknowledging and responding to the students' questions, but also swiftly moving the focus of the discussion onto other more neutral topics. Similar to the distancing performed by the participants in Gkonou and Miller (2021), Luke's actions were driven heavily by internal notions of professionalism. Luke explained further:

> Partially. I don't feel like I can get close to students. I feel like even if we share culture and language, and more in common, I still wouldn't, because I think it's in violation of the teacher's role to be too friendly to students. So, when the emotions come up like that, I push them aside. And I chalk it off to hard work and that's- that's part of the job. (3) Because I don't know, that's just the way I think teachers should be.

It is a known fact that individuals often employ multiple emotion regulation strategies concurrently to deal with any given emotion (Heiy & Cheavens, 2014), and Luke exemplifies this here through his report of how he enforces his epistemic notion of teacher responsibility. Thus, in addition to his situational strategy to move students away from unwanted topics, he simultaneously uses attention deployment ('I just push them aside') and cognitive change ('I chalk it off to hard work and that's- that's part of the job'). Luke's overall use of emotional distancing therefore emerged as a highly complex combination of emotion regulation actions which were used together to great effect.

6.3.5 Institutions and situational strategies: Freedom vs control

Since situational strategies are built on the premise that control of external environments affords adaptive regulation, perhaps the most salient contextual factor that emerged as influencing the participants' ability to apply situational strategies was the level of freedom and autonomy that they were provided within their institution. Although teachers at Fukuzaki University are responsible for achieving departmental-wide outcomes within a prescribed curriculum, the participants reported an admirable degree of freedom, being allowed to choose unit topics, class texts, in-class activities and the directions of projects and assessments. This level of independence within the classroom is not unusual in Japan, (e.g. Butler, 2019), and a useful side effect of this lack of micromanagement is the affordance it offered the participants to apply situational strategies.

While on the one hand, a lesson that can be taken here for institutions is to offer their faculty independence, a balance must be struck. Too much control could lead to the constraint of creativity (Jones & Richards, 2016; Richards, 2013) and the potential for stressful emotional work (Benesch, 2017; De Costa et al., 2020), but too much freedom could cause anxiety owing to a lack of direction (Humphries, 2020). Gina appeared aware of this issue and reported positive experiences at Fukuzaki University in comparison to her previous University in Japan: 'I would say we had too much [autonomy] at my old school and no one knew what to do. Whereas here, there is a certain amount of autonomy, but there's always people to talk to, and get input from.' Peter shared similar thoughts to Gina, but he also spoke of how he felt disappointed that the level of autonomy he was offered had become more restricted over time. 'Compared to when I started and compared to now there was a lot more freedom…I understand why the whole curriculum is trying to get pinned down. But, doing that might take away the freedom to (0.5) to grow.' Peter recognised however, that the level of freedom he was offered when he started was only emboldening to him because he had extensive previous experience in Japan. He vividly recalled that when he began at Fukuzaki University he was told:

> 'Here's an example syllabus (0.5) but you don't have to do that'. Like, (2) and I felt like sink or swim. I was- (1) it was super exciting to me because I was like 'okay. I got this many years' experience and I got good ideas and this is that' right. I'm really comfortable with (0.5) the level they're gonna be. I've taught in a high school for four years (0.5) and I- (0.5) and I understand a lot about Japanese culture.

It appears for Peter that the confidence and excitement he felt for negotiating the institutional freedom were highly dependent upon his self-efficacy, which was itself built upon his experience not only working with Japanese students in the public education system, but also because of his extensive knowledge of Japan. While the evidence in this study is limited, from the perspective of emotion regulation the ideal balance between institutional autonomy and control may be dependent upon the experiences and confidence of each individual teacher within the department. Managers, therefore, may do well to adopt an inquiring and flexible approach when considering how to apply this balance.

6.4 Complex Considerations

So far in my discussion I have reported on the most common situational strategies the participants employed, the motives they were employed for and the contextual factors constraining their use, but in this final section I would like to touch on some of the more uncommon but highly sophisticated ways that situational strategies were used. I discuss two topics in particular: the use of dynamic emotional distancing, and cases where situational strategies were combined with other forms of emotion regulation.

6.4.1 Dynamic emotional distancing

Previous studies on emotional distancing have tended to present this strategy as a relatively stable feature of a teacher's personality (King, 2016b), an unquestioned cultural feature (Yin, 2016), an inevitable outcome of classroom experience (Hagenauer & Volet, 2014), or as an automatic momentary practice (Miller & Gkonou, 2018). These studies have not considered the fact that emotional distancing may be a fluctuating process, with teachers increasing and decreasing their distance from their students and work in response to external stressors. Yet, for two of the participants at Fukuzaki University this indeed emerged as being the case. In the first example, Jessica reported how a temporary busyness in her personal life had pulled her attention away from her work and left her emotionally drained: 'I've got (1) lots of people coming to stay with me this weekend. They're all gonna want to do stuff all the time. I've got loads of grading to do and that's stressing me out a little bit.' As a consequence, during her first stimulated recall session she reported employing emotional distancing as a temporary form of stress relief. To do so, in her observed class she had chosen to review a topic the students had already studied. This decision meant that she was able to avoid engaging with students: 'It wasn't really much of me talking to them. It was more like them talking to each other.' Furthermore, she reported that she felt a disengagement from the class owing to the fact that her attention and emotional energy were being drawn elsewhere: 'I just didn't really feel that bothered if it, you know, I didn't really feel stressed about things not going to plan today.' The distancing Jessica is describing here is clearly a support mechanism that she employed to protect against negative emotions which might have arisen in class. Unfortunately, though, Jessica's distancing was problematic, and she reported that her choice brought with it a certain degree of 'guilt' that she had let down her students.

Emotional distancing as a process was even more pronounced in data from Richard, who reported that the emotional closeness of his relationships with students had fluctuated throughout his career at Fukuzaki University. His confusion appears highly explicit in the following extended extract where he described how he had continually renegotiated the boundaries for how closely he should form relationships with his students.

> It's something that- something that I struggled with sometimes. Like, there have been times when I've like taken students out to go to like, like *Saizeriya* [Saizeriya is a famous Japanese chain restaurant], like a Saizeriya day where a bunch of students came together. I didn't pay for them. But still we did some events like that. And I was just like trying to feel out- how to- how to balance it, because some teachers like [Teacher A]. I don't know how she manages it. She's always going out with her students. Like, they're her best friends and I- for me, I can't. To me that's too much. I can't cross that line and just take them out all the time and invite them over to my apartment and stuff. I just can't. So, so- that was last semester that I tried to- I tried to occasionally do other events outside of class. Like, we went last semester, no not last semester, last year, the year before I did a little bit too, but, um, (2) or doing like coffee talks like [Teacher B] does, I did some of those as well. But I see, I don't know, how do I say- how do I? I guess for me I was- those things are kind of like experiments that I was trying to figure out how close or how far away to treat students.

Here, Richard appears entirely unresolved about the degree to which he can, or should, become close to his students. He reports attempting to negotiate his relationships through different 'experiments', and even compares himself to a peer who he felt had, perhaps unprofessionally, developed extremely close relationships with students. On the surface, Richard's confusion may appear somewhat surprising, since the professional boundary between teachers and students is highly explicit in most working contexts. However, in the Japanese educational context the role of the non-Japanese EFL teacher has often been positioned as lying somewhere between Japanese teachers and students. Indeed, it is not uncommon for teachers in the language teaching industry to be sought for their energetic and positive nature (Appleby, 2013a, 2013b; Kubota, 2011; Nagatomo, 2016), and private language school teachers have reported being actively encouraged to spend time with their students outside of the classroom (Nuske, 2020). It may be that Richard, whose formative teaching experiences were in a Japanese high school, has received mixed messages or a lack of explicit guidance, causing him to feel unsure about where to place himself in relation to his students. This uncertainty meant that he has been largely unsuccessful in negotiating his emotions on the subject.

In another stage of his emotional distancing, Richard also reported that he had recently tried to 'step back' from the closeness of his relationships with students. When I asked him why this was, he reported that he was making himself increasingly distanced from the students because his six-year contract at Fukuzaki University was coming to an end: 'I feel like there's this sort of psychological disengagement a little bit because I know I'm not going to be here that much longer.' When I asked Richard about the emotions he was experiencing at the prospect of leaving, he reported 'elements of frustration or disappointment or um (3) helplessness' and he lamented:

> The (3) teacher mill that they have at [Fukuzaki University], like this idea that you just come in and you're here for a little bit and then you have to go, kind of makes you cynical a little. I think like, like, why? Why? Why do they have this? I'm not saying that they should hire me forever. But it just seems to me like a poor system. For at least from an educational standpoint, because people are always coming in. They're always- they're only partially engaged because they know they're only going to be here for- for a few years, and then they- new people are trained and it just- it just feels (3) a little artificial or a little (2) cynical.

Richard's testimony here mirrors a participant in King (2016b), who felt a similar inability to connect with his students as his contract came to an end, and much like participants discussed in Morris and King (2018), Richard is employing emotional distancing to protect his well-being as a direct consequence of the stress caused by his working conditions. Such findings suggest that emotional detachment is a very real, and highly detrimental outcome of the precarious nature of language teacher employment. It is something that is likely to result in profoundly negative emotional experiences for some teachers.

6.4.2 Powerful in tandem: Situational strategies and response modulation

In the final section of this chapter, I want to bring attention to the fact that situational strategies were not always employed in isolation from other forms of emotion regulation. Situational strategies were most often performed in tandem with response modulation, particularly when the participants responded in real time to classroom behavioural issues. As a reminder, response modulation refers to emotion regulation actions that target the symptoms and expressions of emotions. Speaking in general terms, when the participants dealt with behavioural issues, they seemed to have more success when they were able to suppress or control their outer emotional displays. This success was related both to their ability to reduce their own experiences of stressful emotions as well as to affect positive change in the students (see also Morris, 2022). We can observe this in the testimonies of Tom and Jamie as they dealt with classroom difficulties.

In Tom's case, he reported 'frustration' with a class who were not fully engaging with discussion tasks in a communicative-focused course, despite the fact that students had chosen to take the course knowing that interaction was a major component. Tom reported that he had felt the students would 'just do anything to finish the conversation as soon as possible'. He also felt disappointed that the students were not taking more control over their learning, asking himself in the interview, somewhat facetiously, 'why you studying [foreign language communication] if you don't want to talk to each other?' Tom reported using problem-directed action by raising the issue with the class directly in a pointed and highly controlled manner, which he explains in the following excerpt:

> R: Would you have said you lost control at that point?
> Tom: No. No. It was very controlled. It wasn't- (1) and I thought about it as well. And I sat there when they were doing the activity and I thought about what I was going to say because I don't want to- yeah (0.5) you don't know what you will say if you just [clicks fingers], you know, if you just do it. It's better to plan these things. So, I sat there listening to them and I let them just sit there in silence for a few minutes as well. Just to give them a chance to-, you know, to make sure I was making a fair point kind of thing.... Very clear. No wasted words because I wanted them to understand the message.... So, it was just concept check questions (0.5) like 'what's your major?' '[foreign language communication.]' 'What does communication mean?' 'Talking to each other.' 'Were you talking to each other?' 'No.' 'Okay. What can we do to-' you know? And then- and then just like talk with them, like, 'okay you need to, you know, expand your answers. Ask for reasons and things'.

As can be seen here, Tom intervened with students by raising awareness of their problematic behaviour, but this was done in a highly controlled manner. He spoke slowly and clearly, with 'no wasted words'. Furthermore, Tom's self-control was formed through careful planning: as described, he sat and thought carefully about his actions prior to interjecting, and he ascribes this control as key to the success of the intervention. It is useful to compare Tom's response to testimony from Jamie, who reported employing problem-directed action in a less controlled manner (see also Morris, 2022). Jamie noted that he had a class of male students who had not been paying attention in recent classes: '[they] are just always talking and they're like, they're always the last ones to figure out what's going on and things like that', and he recalled an incident in a recent class where he attempted to apply problem-directed action but was unable to maintain control over his emotions:

> I had been shuffling the students, um, around doing a speaking fluency task.... Instead of actually moving seats, which takes very little effort, they start trying to talk diagonally to each other. And I'm like, you can't communicate like that, you know, you've got people like talking in your ear, you know? And so, I saw this, and I just sort of said, like, 'what are you guys doing?' [claps hands] Right, and I actually clapped like, pretty loudly like and, and one of the girls- on different table got a little bit of a fright.

Here in this testimony, we see that Jamie was unable to maintain control, resulting in an outburst of emotion, and a loud clap. In fact, one of the potential benefits of problem-directed action is that it allows for the healthy ventilation of emotions through emotional expression (Roth & Cohen, 1986) but, owing to Jamie's lack of controlled articulation of his feelings, he felt remorse over this incident. This negative emotion was compounded by a sense that he had contradicted his own values:

> I lost control…. It doesn't reflect well on the teacher. The students will probably, you know, it'll- it'll low- lower the students' opinion of you. I generally think of myself as being quite composed. Yeah, so it was, yeah, a little bit unlike me. And I think I haven't done anything like that with that class.

It appears that the lack of self-control behind Jamie's problem-directed action increased his negative emotions rather than diminishing them, leading to feelings of guilt and self-reproach. Thus, the dynamic nature of emotions is once again revealed as Jamie's interaction with his student has resulted in a new emotion that needs to be regulated. One of the dangers of any problem-directed action towards student behavioural issues therefore is that it may not be successful, particularly if the actions are driven by a lack of emotional control.

6.5 Lessons Learned: Power Over Our Environment

This chapter has shown that situational strategies are an extremely important tool for teachers to manage their classroom emotions. Situational strategies seemed to most primarily serve hedonic higher-order motives, but equally, they also were able to simultaneously achieve epistemic and instrumental goals on many occasions.

Situational strategies were used to generate positive emotions, pre-empt negativity and deal with classroom stressors as they arose. Positive emotions were generated through job crafting strategies, which were employed by all participants in two forms: task crafting and relationship crafting. The use of these strategies involved agentive changes to task, material and syllabus-level features of the participants' classrooms. They were heavily driven by notions of creativity and afforded by the high-level of institutional autonomy afforded by Fukuzaki University. Emotions were pre-empted through actions that fell under the umbrella of proactive coping, and which included well-established preparation routines and the use of emotional distancing. Emotional distancing was performed both as a relatively stable personality trait by some of the participants, and as a dynamic process by others. Finally negative classroom emotions were offset at the point of arousal through approach and avoidance techniques. Problem-directed actions were most commonly performed as classroom management actions when students were misbehaving or off task, and these were more likely to be successful when the participants were able to maintain control over their actions and emotions. The teachers performed physical problem avoidance from students who they had difficulties connecting with, though they also reported success in reaching those students over time.

As I explored earlier in this book, if we consider emotions to be generated along a timeline, then situational strategies can be considered the earliest strategies that individuals employ. Of course, however, there are many times when teachers may be unable to take such actions, and in these cases other emotion regulation strategies might be more appropriate. In the proceeding chapter, I investigate the teachers' attention, and show how this too was a powerful tool through which they could regulate their emotions.

7 Attention

Attention is one of a language teachers' most important teaching tools. Teachers pay attention to how fast and complexly they speak, to where they look and to where they place their hands. They pay attention to where they are in the lesson plan, to what has been achieved and to what is coming next. They pay attention to whether the students are listening, to what difficulties they are having, to the words the students are using, to the pronunciation of their speech and to how much more time they need to complete the task. They pay attention to the students' facial expressions and moods, and pay attention to how they might respond to any unfolding events.

Attention is of course a difficult muscle to flex. It can easily be drawn away by things happening elsewhere – by movement, lights, sounds, memories and thoughts – and it is something that is influenced by our energy levels, by the time of day and by the time in the semester. Yet, attention is how teachers actually participate in the lesson, and it is perhaps unsurprising that the agentive actions language teachers take to move their attention can have a powerful impact on their emotions. Such actions are known as attention deployment strategies.

7.1 Introduction: Teachers' Points of Focus

Attention deployment strategies are essentially movements of focus, and they are based on a simple premise: Emotions occur when our attention is drawn to a subject; thus, by moving our attention towards or away from that subject, we are able to manipulate emerging emotions. The target of a teacher's attention can be something external and physical. For example, studies have shown that teachers move their attention away from behavioural issues to reduce negative emotions such as anger (Sutton, 2004; Yin, 2016). Alternatively, the target of a teacher's attention can be something internal and intangible, and studies have also shown that teachers may move their attention towards memories of positive experiences (Talbot & Mercer, 2018). Overall, language teachers' uses of attention deployment strategies have received relatively little scrutiny in comparison to other kinds of emotion regulation strategies, and discussion of the role of context in affording and constraining the use of attention deployment is virtually non-existent.

In this chapter, I explore the use of attentional strategies by the participants at Fukuzaki University. Although they were quantitatively the least discussed category of strategy, their use emerged in 14 of the participants' testimonies. As I did with situational strategies in the previous chapter, I begin by exploring the characteristic strategies that were utilised, and then consider the contextual factors that influenced their use. Following this is an exploration of the more nuanced uses of attentional strategies. There I will discuss the automatisation of attention deployment, consider how attentional strategies emerged as important tools for achieving multiple emotion regulation motives simultaneously, and discuss how one participant used attention deployment to empower their future growth.

7.2 Characteristic Attentional Strategies and Motives

Three attention deployment strategies were particularly common in the data: distraction, concentration and mental time travel.

7.2.1 Distraction and concentration

Distraction and *concentration* are quintessential attention deployment strategies. They define those situations when a teacher chooses to direct their attention away from a source of emotion (distraction), or alternatively move it towards a source of emotion (concentration). Such sources may be located in the teacher's immediate environment, but they may also be thoughts, memories or potential futures. They are important strategies because there are many times in the classroom when an emotion a teacher is experiencing needs to be deprioritised to other classroom concerns. Twelve of the teachers at Fukuzaki University reported applying distraction and concentration in their work.

A typical example of concentration and distraction can be seen in the following excerpt from Vivienne discussing how she dealt with feelings of frustration caused by the poor time-management skills of a colleague she was co-teaching with: 'I walked around. Um, I graded a couple of students' work. I decided to hand back some work.... I jumped in and tried to help students with a question.' In this excerpt, Vivienne describes multiple attentional actions. She is moving her attention away from her colleague, a source of negative emotion, and towards other classroom features, such as her students and their work. She is therefore simultaneously distracting herself from frustration while also concentrating on other less negatively valenced emotional stimuli. The participants frequently applied distraction and concentration concurrently in this manner, and I wasn't always able to differentiate which was the primary strategy being used.

Generally speaking, distraction and concentration were used in the pursuit of hedonic motives, and for five teachers this was to attenuate relatively low-intensity negative emotions that arose from the participants' unfavourable appraisals of their own teaching behaviours. Catherine, for example, applied distraction to deal with a minor level of anxiety that appeared as she acted out the meaning of the word 'bullying' in class by pretending to punch one of the students:

> Other people might think this is terrible. Like holy cow! And [student A] is not reacting like she normally would.... How did I recover? Um, I went on to the next word.... Let's just move on. It's not worth getting anxious over.

Here then, Catherine again moves her attention away from the source of negative emotion (her actions) and concentrates on something else (the next part of the class). There were a wide range of other emotional circumstances which led to the use of concentration and distraction; thus, in addition to Vivienne's frustrating colleague and Catherine's anxiety regulation, the participants applied the strategies to manage irritation arising from students failing to follow instructions (Eleanor), frustration arising from classroom technology issues (Peter), and sadness arising from personal circumstances, such as the death of a pet (Zoe) (see also Morris, 2022). Nine of the participants employed the strategies to in-class issues, while three participants applied the strategies to out-of-class issues.

7.2.3 Mental time travel

Mental time travel refers to when an individual directs their attention to events from the past, present, or future, to reminisce, savour, or anticipate emotions respectively. Unlike distraction and concentration, which were primarily employed to regulate immediately experienced negative emotional states during classroom teaching, mental time travel was used by the participants to regulate emotions over longer periods, particularly in advance of classes taking place.

In all, eight of the participants reported using this strategy for prohedonic and instrumental purposes. In other words, they used mental time travel to increase their quality and quantity of positive emotions, which subsequently improved their everyday teaching performance and class enjoyment. This was done through a form of forward-looking anticipation. The participants routinely and actively imagined how future classes might unfurl, leading to a range of positive emotional states including curiosity (Stewart), and 'eagerness.... Sort of a forward-looking sense of excitement' (Vivienne). Put simply, the teachers built up positive emotions for lessons in the days and hours leading up to them, and they anticipated the students' excitement too.

The participants' attitudes to class preparation were one of the crucial mediating factors underlying these positive feelings, with teachers reporting that when they had spent a significant amount of time planning, they felt stronger anticipatory emotions. Vivienne, for example, explained that she planned her lessons meticulously, and became 'really, really eager to see how they respond to stuff that I prepare, and I'm eager to see if my idea of what they will do in response will be seen out- will be fulfilled.' The high level of autonomy provided by Fukuzaki University was thus at the heart of the use of anticipatory mental time travel, allowing the participants to prepare classes freely in ways which generated excitement.

Positive anticipatory emotions were not only felt in the hours leading up to classes, but also during the lessons themselves at particularly opportune moments. Peter, for example, explained how he used a lot of prepared humour in his classes, with the anticipation of such moments in class inducing positive emotions. This can be illustrated by an event I witnessed in Peter's second observed class. Peter was teaching the students to remember the spelling of the word 'frying' (as opposed to flying) by using a humorous image of the singer Rhianna wearing a yellow dress resembling a fried egg. Peter pointed out that Rhianna began with the letter 'R', so when they needed to remember the spelling, they just needed to imagine her dress. The moment in class was very well received, with students erupting in laughter, and when I asked about his emotions during this incident, he reported strong anticipatory attention deployment behaviours: 'I try to keep a straight face. I'm like this is gonna be, hopefully, pretty cool.... It takes a long time to make that- to make all that, but it's worth it.' Here then, Peter's deliberate decision to put prepared humour into his class afforded him the opportunity to use anticipatory mental time travel to generate positive emotions, and his choice of 'it's worth it' suggests that he felt prepared humour was important from the perspective of his own well-being. The lesson here seems to be that when teachers are afforded the agency and time to plan interesting lessons, their attention and forethought provides them and their students with emotional rewards.

The use of mental time travel discussed in this section was somewhat distinct from previous work on this strategy. Most prominently, Talbot and Mercer (2018) found that mental time travel was a regular practice for their language teacher participants. Rather than looking forward, however, Talbot and Mercer's participants used mental time travel to return to events from their past. By thinking about and reflecting on positive student feedback, their participants experienced feelings of pride and satisfaction with their achievements. If we consider the current findings in compliment with Talbot and Mercer's it seems possible to understand that mental time travel can be used as a potent and holistic tool for increasing teacher positivity.

7.3 Contextual Factors Affording and Shaping Attention Deployment

In the discussion so far, I have shown that classroom incidents and a teacher's orientation towards planning (along with the agency afforded by an institution) can give rise to positive attention deployment, but two other contextual points are worthy of discussion, and both are related to the teachers' personality. I address these here in turn.

7.3.1 Personality and attention deployment: Being 'fairly unconfrontational'

One of the most important tenets from general literature on attention deployment is that using this form of emotion regulation to resolve negative emotions can be very effective over the short term (McRae & Gross, 2020). However, since these strategies do not resolve the underlying issues at hand, a reliance on attention deployment for dealing with stress can cause negative long-term consequences (Morris & King, 2020; Roth & Cohen, 1986). Indeed, for one participant, Jamie, the overuse of distraction was having a negative impact on his stress and health. In Jamie's second observation, I noted that one student in the room seemed particularly disruptive, failing to bring homework and standing up in the middle of a group discussion to move to the corner of the room to plug his phone charger into the wall. When I asked Jamie about his emotions in this case, he reported that he had been feeling a degree of frustration with this student in recent weeks, and that he had been distracting his attention away because of his perceived responsibilities to the other students:

> How I deal with it in the moment? I guess um (2) I tend to, I tend to, (3) you know, try and just shrug it off and, and not let it, you know, sour my mood for the whole lesson or anything like that. Of course, I've got, you know, a whole bunch of other students that I need to be, you know, paying attention to as well. And (2) yeah, so (4) I don't know if I (2) deal with it at all actually.

Here, Jamie demonstrates his distraction by his use of 'shrug it off', and he alludes to the fact that he concentrates on other students. As the discussion continued, it became clear that Jamie was highly stressed by his problematic student. He reported that his frustration was at a level 'eight' (out of ten), and most alarmingly, that he was having sleeping issues owing to his emotional distress:

> This morning I woke up at three o'clock, right, and I'm trying to get back to sleep and you know, when you're trying to go back to sleep, and things are going through your mind [laughs]. Actually, there were a couple of students that popped into my head and of course, like, [the student in question] was the one that sort of first popped into my head.

It has been previously shown in laboratory studies that continual distraction can have a negative impact on well-being (Quoidbach *et al.*, 2010), the reason being that it may interfere with one's ability to actively deal with a stressor in an appropriate manner (Roth & Cohen, 1986). This appears to be the case for Jamie too. His testimony illustrates how distraction can be effective if used sparingly, or in combination with other strategies, but that it should not be relied upon as a panacea for emotional issues in class. It also shows the importance of educating teachers on appropriate emotion regulation strategies so that they have the psychological resources needed to deal with emotions arising from disruptive student behaviours. Any person's orientation towards approaching or avoiding an emotional stressor is tied to personality traits, with extroverted, more positively oriented individuals liable to use approach forms of problem-solving and neurotic, more negatively oriented individuals liable to use avoidance (Elliot & Thrash, 2002). Jamie appeared aware of these features of his own character, describing himself in his first interview as 'cautious' and 'fairly unconfrontational'. Fortunately, Jamie had begun to recognise the potential danger that he was in and had already made plans to tackle his classroom issues more directly by talking to the student in question: 'I have actually decided to have a word with the group that he normally sits with.... I have been thinking about it, and it's affecting me and it- and you know, it's not acceptable.'

7.3.2 Personality and attention deployment: Being 'the friendly type'

Personality also appeared to be a persuading factor with regards to the participants' use of mental time travel, with Peter, perhaps more than any other participant, reporting a huge degree of positive emotions driven by his anticipation and savouring of classroom experiences. Peter described his personality as being 'the friendly type', and said he was 'always really excited' for classes. Regarding his teaching, Peter placed positive emotion high on his list of desires: 'having good vibes in the classroom might be the key to enjoying teaching', and in his first stimulated recall interview he observed that 'there were moments when I was just having the best time in that class. Stuff was flowing'. Peter reported to me on more than one occasion that he had a very long commute to work (a total of three hours per day), and that the excitement he experienced when teaching was what meant he did not burn out. He reported his feelings with an interesting metaphor:

> I remember at university taking services marketing and they were saying, like, an aeroplane seat (0.5) if you're not on the seat you can never get that seat back. You know, that chance to be on that seat is gone- it- once it's gone. So that's my- that stuck with me as far as teaching. I put in a lot of preparation. That's all the training and this is the game- game day right. So, I'm excited to go and see how the class- see my ideas work and see the interaction and stuff.

It is indicative that Peter chose to use the term 'game day' to describe the performative nature of his classroom teaching. This choice, alongside his notion that 'once it's gone it's gone' suggests that he views the classroom as a one-chance performance that can be either a success or failure depending on his actions. Lying underneath Peter's excitement, therefore, appears to be a tinge of anxiety and danger over the potential for things to go wrong. Indeed, the anticipatory excitement generated by the use of mental time travel appeared to be experienced alongside and perhaps even driven by the potential for failure in a number of testimonies. Nathan, for example, reported that 'background fear… keeps me on my toes', while anxieties over whether an activity 'will either bomb hard or… be fine' lay underneath Millie's feelings of excitement. In other words, it appeared that negative emotions often came hand in hand with positive emotions, highlighting, as others have before, that teachers' emotions may not be separated into neatly valenced categorisations (e.g. Hofstadler *et al.*, 2020; King *et al.*, 2020; Talbot & Mercer, 2018).

7.4 Complex Considerations

As with the use of other strategies, I observed a great deal of complexity in the participants' attentional decision-making. This was particularly true in the ways that attentional strategies were used to achieve multiple emotion regulation motives simultaneously, in the ways that the actions had become autonomised, and in the ways that attentional strategies could support teacher growth.

7.4.1 Concentration and distraction to achieve multiple regulation motives

While some of the participants told me that they used distraction and concentration for hedonic motives: 'If I were to dwell on it, um, it would just get more and more awkward and harder to get out of like a, like a pit' (Vivienne), the participants were also likely to employ these strategies for instrumental and epistemic reasons. Millie, for example, saw it as part of her duty as a teacher to deal with negative out-of-class emotions by concentrating on the goals that the students needed to achieve, commenting that 'I would put myself second. My- (0.5) what is more important is that students are learning something'. It also became clear that multiple higher-order motives could be achieved simultaneously through the use of distraction and concentration, a particularly enlightening example of which emerged during Luke's first observed class.

After Luke's class, I asked him to prepare a short list of emotions that he had felt while teaching, one of which he recorded as 'email from other teacher'. When I saw this note, I had absolutely no idea what it referred to, but when I asked him about it, he revealed a highly salient incident of negative emotion that had emerged owing to the actions of a colleague. At Fukuzaki University, students in their first and second years of study typically remain in the same class group for all of their English language courses. This meant that the participants in this study often shared groups of students with other teachers. One teacher, for example, might teach reading, while another might teach writing. In the case in question, Luke reported that a colleague he shared a class with was having 'serious, I think what I'd call conflict' with the students, and he felt the colleague had 'let his emotions get the better of [him].... Invalidated his position as like a leader'. Luke explained that the issue between the students and his colleague had been continuing for multiple weeks with both management and administrative staff becoming involved, and he reported a rollercoaster of emotions from his position as a middleman in the conflict. He was simultaneously 'sympathetic' and 'protective' of the students, 'exhausted' from controlling his emotions, and angry towards his coworker: 'how do you manage another teacher (0.5) doing these things?'

At Fukuzaki University, all of the students work from tablet computers, and during Luke's observed class, his colleague had sent an email to the students. The email had been an apology for some kind of event that had occurred earlier in the day. The email had arrived at the students' computers during the middle of Luke's lesson (with a ping sounding from multiple tablets) at an inopportune moment while Luke was explaining the target point of the class. This brought Luke 'real frustration' because 'just when it's getting good, it feels like this- (0.5) this, you know, sudden crack, and it's like, "oh, we have to go back." Now there's all these- this reminder to them of all these problems that they're having.' When I asked how Luke responded to the email and his own emotions, Luke emphatically reported to employing distraction and concentration, and his use of this strategy served a wide range of higher-order motives that were revealed throughout the exchange that followed:

> R: What did you do then?
> Luke: I ignored it.
> R: You ignored it?
> Luke: I totally ignored it um (0.5) because if I amplify it, I think only a few students even noticed the email, and brought it up and then we're talking about it and it did have a ripple effect, but (0.5) maybe it was the wrong move to ignore it, but I wanted to show them that, I meant what I said when I was like, 'you leave it at the door. Even if that comes knocking on the door, we ignore it'. And we're just gonna- we're gonna finish this class, like, come hell or high water. I don't care. We're gonna finish. (3) It's just it's- ugh. Yeah.
> R: From emotions, what were you doing? Were you just ignoring your frustration? What did you do with your frustration?
> Luke: Um (2) I figured I gotta talk to that guy later. And I can't solve that problem now in the room. I don't want to show them my frustration because they're already angry with him. If I showed them that I'm also angry with him, (2) that could (2) increase their anger. (1.5) Legitimate or validate their anger and take away from what we're trying to do in the class, which is communication.

While previous studies have shown that teachers are able to employ emotion regulation strategies to distract learners away from negative experiences (Bielak & Mystkowska-Wiertelak, 2020), this exchange shows that such actions are emotionally complex. Luke's use of distraction in this situation accomplishes multiple motives, simultaneously reducing his own frustration ('I can't solve that problem now in the room'), keeping students calm ('If I showed them…that could increase their anger'), modelling professional behaviour to the students ('even if that comes knocking on the door, we ignore it') and keeping students on task ('If I amplify it… then we're talking about it'). In other words, Luke's use of distraction achieves hedonic, epistemic, and performance benefits simultaneously; thus, distraction could be a viable way for teachers to achieve a wide range of emotion regulation and classroom goals in emotionally complex situations.

The situation described by Luke above was undoubtedly affecting for him. This was driven in part by a personal promise not to become involved in the situation, with Luke seeing himself as in a 'horizontal position to another teacher…. I don't need to take a position'. Since it is very common to employ multiple emotion regulation strategies to deal with a single emotion (Heiy & Cheavens, 2014) it was no surprise to find that Luke reported numerous other emotion regulation actions to manage his emotions from the incident, including speaking to the teacher in question (situation selection) and venting his emotions into a journal (response modulation). Luke was not alone in reporting the use of multiple emotion regulation strategies alongside concentration and distraction, with five other participants reporting similar strategy combinations.

7.4.2 The automatisation of attention deployment

A second important facet of the attention deployment strategies that I saw in the participants of Fukuzaki University was the degree to which they had become automatised (see also Morris, 2022). Many emotion regulation strategies, if used repeatedly, may well become habitual (Gyurak *et al.*, 2011), and for three of the teachers at Fukuzaki University (Nathan, Richard, Stewart) it became apparent that their length of teaching service meant that their use of attentional deployment had become automatic. All three reported that when they entered the classroom, they were able to instantly forget about their out-of-class emotions and focus on the students they were teaching. For example, Nathan reported that: 'I see these people smiling at me and the negative emotion's just completely gone, and I'm cured. I'm better.' Equally Stewart explained that 'I'll have had a grotty morning… (but) the teacher sort of takes over…. I think it's just your attention. Your attention's took into a different way, which then sort of- which then it develops your mood'. As can be seen in these cases, the participants are reporting that when teaching their attention is seemingly automatically distracted from out-of-class worries as they concentrate on what is happening within the classroom. While this ability to place stresses at the back of the mind during important classroom tasks may appear unsurprising to some, it cannot be taken for granted. An individual's predisposition towards adaptive emotion regulation in times of stress is not in any way guaranteed (Koole & Fockenberg, 2011), but this ability is important because as emotion regulation actions become more implicit, fewer psychological resources are required for the regulatory processes (Koole & Rothermund, 2011). A factor that all the teachers here had in common was the degree to which they enjoyed being in the classroom: they received a 'jolt of energy' when class began (Richard) and felt 'like I'm more me than I am at sometimes any other time in my life' (Nathan). These results suggest that experienced teachers may be able to employ habitual attentional deployment to regulate unwanted emotions originating from outside the classroom, particularly if they enjoy their teaching.

7.4.3 Mental time travel and teacher growth

A final complex and nuanced finding concerned how one teacher employed mental time travel in a unique way to facilitate their own professional growth. The notion of mental time travel originated in the positive psychology tradition, and perhaps this is the reason why research in education has typically only considered this strategy in the regulation of positive emotional states (e.g. Haeussler, 2013; Talbot & Mercer, 2018). Within this study, however, Luke reported to deliberately using mental time travel to visit times of negative emotion. Luke's discussion concerned a stressful incident from a previous year involving a student of mixed Japanese and Korean heritage. Luke felt that his relationship with the student was strained, commenting that she was 'a very difficult person. I think interpersonally, we did not get along', but he also reported that fractures in the relationship were compounded after he had taught a class on the lives of ethnic minorities in Japan, which he explains in the following excerpt:

> We watched a documentary called *Hafu*, about mixed-race Japanese. And they were a lot- there's- one of the women they document in that film is Korean Japanese.... It's a very emotional story within this film, and you bring that into a classroom, and I think that this student was very uncomfortable with that. I didn't do a good job of (0.5) sort of framing those issues well. I don't know if she had any issue with other students, but her own identity as a Korean Japanese person seemed to play into her emotions. I didn't know how to respond well to it.

Japan perceives itself to be homogenous, and many multiethnic citizens have faced challenges for sticking out in the notoriously traditional and conservative society. Luke felt that he did not 'frame the issues well' in this class, which led to distress for his multiethnic student. He acknowledged that his own behaviour was at least partially to blame for the uncomfortable feelings that arose in the student, and this factor played into his emotions throughout the incident and beyond.

Following the teaching of this class, Luke reported that the student's classroom performance faltered, that she failed to submit homework and that she began to be increasingly absent. Since attendance in Fukuzaki University is highly regulated, Luke's emotions exploded one day when his student sent him an email asking about whether she would be able to leave a class early. Luke responded with a rash email:

> I wrote back. And I regret doing this. I wrote back. I said, you know, 'if you don't want to come to class, don't come' [spoken emphatically].... I thought that was not the way to do it. You're much older than this person... you've got to be a model for how to communicate in these difficult situations.

As can be seen here, Luke felt a strong sense of remorse for his behaviour, which appears to have come from a sense that his actions were not congruent with his notions of teacher responsibility. Luke's email damaged his relationship with the student beyond repair, but what is interesting from an emotion regulation perspective is how Luke has used his memories of this critical incident to make positive changes, which were revealed as his explanation of the incident continued:

> I still remember it on purpose. I keep it in my mind, because I don't want it to happen again. If I see something- if I see signs of that, again, like with this new kid [Luke was currently struggling with a new student in his class]... totally could happen again. If I- if I make it into a contest of wills, right, a battle of like, who can control the room better? Um, it could totally happen again.... So, I keep her in my mind as a reminder of like (0.5) this is- this can happen. It doesn't matter if Luke, you think you're a nice guy, easy-going guy. That doesn't matter. What matters is what you do. What you say to the kids, students.

Here then, attention deployment has not been employed to generate positive emotions, but negative. It is clear from the testimony that Luke thought that there was a realistic chance this kind of situation would happen again, even going so far as to identify a potential student; however, Luke's use of mental time travel allows him to return to the strong emotions associated with his previous failure, and his purposeful use of this strategy helps to prevent him from causing a similar incident (and emotions) again. While previous literature has warned that repeated mental time travel towards negative events may lead to possible negative side effects if it becomes extended rumination (Quoidbach *et al.*, 2010), that does not appear to be the case here, where Luke's mental time travel towards feelings of guilt and stress are facilitating future growth. While the potential facilitating power of negative emotion has been explored in previous studies (see, for example, Gkonou & Miller, 2020, 2021; Golombek, 2016; Golombek & Klager, 2015; Kostoulas & Lämmerer, 2018, 2020), this finding is important because it isolates attentional forms of emotion regulation as a psychological tool for affording teacher development.

7.5 Lessons Learned: Attention and Emotion

At the end of this chapter, I feel it is worth reiterating some of the key lessons that can be taken from the participants' use of attention deployment. Attention deployment was widely used, particularly to offset minor negative emotions experienced during the course of teaching, and the strategies were most adaptive with regards to well-being when they were employed in conjunction with other strategies. If attention deployment is overly relied upon, there is the potential for stressful classroom issues to become worse over time, and this was evident in the case of at least one participant.

Mental time travel is a particularly useful strategy to generate positive emotions. The primary activating source I uncovered was class preparation, but the emotional complexity of the performative nature of teaching was also revealed as the teachers reported a mixture of excitement tinged with fear and anxiety. Mental time travel was also revealed as an important mechanism through which one participant reflected on past failures, leading to positive future behavioural changes. It appears clear that mental time travel may be a potential mediating mechanism for understanding how negative emotional events inform teacher growth, and is a tool worth considering for teachers and trainers seeking to explore how critical incidents in the past can be used as a force for good.

8 Cognition

Once, when I was a relatively new teacher, a colleague had to make an emergency trip back to his home country and asked me to stand in for his class for a week. In many ways, this was an easy proposition – the lessons were pre-prepared, no grading was required and my only responsibility was to provide entertaining and low-stress classes. On the Monday, I entered the room energised about meeting the students, and things proceeded smoothly until about the 30-minute mark. During my introduction to the class, a student at the back of the room began talking. As I was presenting the main lesson point, the student continued talking. As I delivered the task instructions, the student at the back of the room did not stop talking. My blood boiled, and for some reason I decided that the best way to deal with this was to address the student by name, raise my voice, call them rude and essentially shame them in front of the class. Still to this day I cannot fathom why I responded in the way I did. Perhaps it was because I was tired. Perhaps it was because I was feeling disappointed that my good mood was being trampled on. Or perhaps it was because I was feeling annoyed that I was volunteering to teach the class and wasn't being respected. Whatever the reason, it was not my finest hour.

This incident marked a turning point for me, and I resolved not to respond in such visceral ways in future. I began a process of reflection on the role of anger in teaching, on the importance of maintaining strong relationships and on the fact that students have lives beyond my classes. Seven years on, I can confidently say that I rarely, if ever, get angry in the classroom. I have come to understand how profoundly negative this emotion can be if left unchecked. I have regulated my emotions through a kind of strategy known as cognitive change.

8.1 Introduction: Teachers Regulating Their Thoughts

Clearly, the nexus between cognition and emotions is important – how we think about things subsequently influences the emotions that we experience in their presence. The emotions that teachers experience in their practice are therefore inextricably linked to their thoughts and beliefs.

In this chapter I discuss cognitive change strategies, emotion regulation which targets the appraisal component of emotional experiences.

They are, as the name implies, cognitively oriented actions influencing an individual's thought processes over time to adjust how they respond to emotional stressors. Research within applied linguistics and education has taken great interest in the use of cognitive change strategies, and they are viewed as powerful mediating strategies for adaptive emotional growth. Cognitive change strategies were widely used by the participants at Fukuzaki University and every participant reported them. As I have done in Chapters 6 and 7 of this book, I begin by exploring the most common forms of cognitive change that were employed. I then discuss the contextual factors affording their use and finish by discussing some of the complexity of cognitive change.

8.2 Characteristic Cognitive Strategies and Motives

I identified four prototypical cognitive change strategies, which I will discuss in turn.

8.2.1 In-situ reappraisal and ontogenetic reappraisal

The first two characteristic strategies in the data were forms of reappraisal. Reappraisal is the archetypal form of cognitive change, and it refers to instances when individuals adjust the way that they think and respond to an emotional stressor (e.g. Gross, 1998, 2014). It has long been recognised as having significant positive implications for well-being in both general lives (e.g. Gross & John, 2003; McRae & Gross, 2020; Troy et al., 2013) and education (e.g. Gregersen et al., 2020; Maher, 2020).

Reappraisal is normally considered to be a single strategy, but during my investigation it became clear that it would be useful to differentiate reappraisal into two complementary forms. This is because the teachers at Fukuzaki University used reappraisal over two different timelines. Firstly, they used reappraisal in very immediate timelines as a way to manage and reduce emotions from appearing at their point of arousal, and secondly, they used reappraisal over career-length timelines as a mediating mechanism for long-term cognitive change. I refer to these two forms as *in-situ cognitive reappraisal* and *ontogenetic reappraisal*, respectively.

I start by explaining in-situ reappraisal. A representative example can be seen in the following testimony from Peter, who described a technical issue involving a flickering projector screen during his first observed class:

> I thought 'oh, I've never seen this before. I wonder what it is? But I don't have time right now to fix- to get to the cause of it. I just need to try and (1) find a workaround'.... I don't wanna be freaking out and then ruin the vibe.

Peter recalled this incident with a high level of clarity, and what is clear from this excerpt is that he was able to intercept potential negative emotions by consciously recognising that such feelings would not be productive in the given circumstances. Through this act of in-situ reappraisal he was therefore able to influence the path of his emotions and prevent negative emotions from appearing.

Eleven of the participants were found to employ this form of reappraisal, all instances of which were hedonically targeted towards reducing negative emotions that were arising during teaching work. In these cases, the in-situ reappraisal seemed to function as a form of self-talk, with participants in interviews reporting their in-moment thoughts as an internal monologue. Jessica, for example, reported on how she regulated emerging feelings of annoyance directed towards herself because of actions she took when students were failing to follow her instructions. The class in question were completing an activity which required them to turn over their worksheets so that they could not see the language printed on it, but many of the students had not done this. Consequently, Jessica took it upon herself to walk around the class and turn over the papers for the students. While doing this, Jessica explained that she was 'kind of like embarrassed about the fact that I'm being such a control freak', and she used very telling self-talk when explaining her thoughts:

> Part of me is like, just like (2), you know, 'stop controlling them'. (1.5) Like, 'they're not children. They're not children'.... 'Does it matter really?', Like part of me is thinking like 'does it really matter if they, if they're not looking at it?'

Jessica therefore reported self-talk directed towards her own behaviour ('stop controlling them'), while equally trying to tell herself that the students' actions were irrelevant ('does it really matter...'). Similar evidence of self-talk emerged in Millie's first interview as she discussed emerging feelings of 'frustration' when students in a recent class were not paying attention:

> I was sharing a personal story and/or giving directions and I just [claps hands] no response whatsoever. And like chit chatting in the back and they know how much that bothers me. So I just kind of stopped and like, 'okay. What do I need to do to get them (0.5) doing what I need them to do?'

Similar to Jessica's testimony, we see here that Millie's cognitive intervention could be recalled as an internal form of explanatory self-talk, focusing particularly on what the best move forward might be. When I asked her about whether her self-talk occurred at the time of the emotion emerging, or whether it was an interpretation from the present, Millie was resolute: 'it was at that moment. I'm like, "I need a response. I need to know that they are understanding what I am telling them."' An important point to note is that in cases of in-situ cognitive reappraisal, the participants did not always report complete success in their regulatory attempts, with Millie, for example, reporting that her 'sunny disposition' had probably 'fractured' in front of the class.

As was mentioned at the beginning of this section, it was observed that participants also applied a second form of reappraisal, which I have termed ontogenetic reappraisal. Ontogenetic reappraisal differed from in-situ reappraisal because the regulation did not occur at the moment of emotion itself. Instead, a gradual career-length adjustment was recalled by 13 participants, with ontogenetic reappraisal acting as a mediating mechanism for the prevention of future negative emotions. To exemplify this, the following excerpt details how increased experience as a language teacher had helped Eleanor to deal with early career frustration that she had felt towards students' lack of willingness to communicate in English:

> When I was a newer teacher [lack of communication] used to annoy me more because I didn't really- (0.5) like, I just- I wouldn't have expected it to happen. But it does happen, and I think- (3) I mean getting angry at them, I don't think it's going to do much good anyway. It's just going to put me in a worse mood. If that makes sense?

In this excerpt we can see that Eleanor's response to student reticence has changed over time. This is because her recognition of this behaviour has matured as she has become more exposed to it. Eleanor has applied ontogenetic reappraisal to regulate her anger, recognising it as an unproductive emotion that will have an overall negative impact on her well-being. Tom reported a similar case of cognitive change with regards to student reticence, but in his case ontogenetic reappraisal appeared to arise from reflection on his position as the only non-Japanese person in the room:

> R: Do you think your level of frustration [with reticent students] has gone up or down over time?
>
> Tom: Yeah down....You have to adapt to the- to the place you- (0.5) you are teaching.... If you are somewhere and like, yeah, a couple of people are behaving like that, then probably it's okay to be upset about it. But if you are in a place and everyone is doing the same thing, it's like, yeah, maybe you are the one that's (0.5) you know, out of place, not the 20 people all behaving in the same way [laughs].

In other words, while Tom began his teaching career in Japan with a certain degree of frustration, he has come to reappraise this emotional stressor by recognising that student reticence is relatively normal to the Japanese cultural context. This awareness encouraged him to develop his own approach to dealing with quiet students, and he reported employing situational behaviours such as an extended wait time (King, 2016b; Smith & King, 2018) and increased eye contact, which further helped him to regulate his emotions.

8.2.2 Rationalisation

Reappraisal was not the only kind of cognitive change that emerged in the data. Another form was the way that the participants rationalised the behaviours of themselves and their students in order to see negative actions in a new light. Eleanor, for example, reported being able to reduce the negative emotions she experienced when a student had wilfully failed to follow her instructions by reminding herself that the students were only young: 'I'm annoyed, but at the same time, I just think "they're kids."'

Although the use of such rationalisation practises has been reported before (Hagenauer & Volet, 2014; Morris & King, 2018), previously, rationalisation was only discussed in cases where teachers rationalised the actions of students. I found it useful to learn in this investigation, therefore, that teachers also rationalise their own actions. This seemed to be an important hedonically motivated cognitive change strategy for dealing with negative experiences.

I observed this rationalisation in three remarkably similar cases reported by Wendy, Millie and Nathan. In each case, the participants felt a degree of negative emotions over choices they had made for classroom activities which they felt would not be well received. Wendy, for example, experienced negative emotions over the fact that her chosen activities were uninteresting: 'it was kind of a boring assignment because they had- it was read something and answer questions about it.... I think a bit (0.5) frustrated/annoyed because I knew at the time like it's not an exciting activity.' Millie similarly felt a degree of guilt because she had given homework with a short completion deadline: 'It honestly is unrealistic to give students homework on a fifth *koma* [period] class.... Over weekends occasionally I give them homework. They hate that, but they have more time to do it.' Both Wendy and Millie, reported to cognitively rationalising their actions by reminding themselves of the pedagogic benefits of their activity choices:

> I guess I just kind of justified, like sometimes we do more interesting things, sometimes we have to do more boring things. (Wendy)
> I think I justified it being as like 'you have today and tomorrow'. (Millie)

In these cases, then, the participants found ways to rationalise their choices so that they were positively aligned with their perceptions of their responsibilities as language teachers. Although they may view their activity choices as uninteresting, by reminding themselves that their decisions were in the students' best interests, they were able to relieve some of the negative emotions they experienced.

One of the important observations that I noted in these three cases was that the participants' decisions to rationalise boring activities was not driven by student complaints, but by the potential for complaints. The emotion regulation was performed because the teachers' perceived that the students might feel negative emotions and they wanted to pre-emptively intercept these experiences. On this matter, Nathan's was a particularly interesting case. He reported that when teaching something he felt was uninteresting, that he would often verbally apologise to students, telling them: 'I am really sorry. This is not as entertaining as it would normally be.' At the same time, he had a strong recognition that his feelings of guilt were not necessary, or even fair to himself. He explained:

> I think that- that guilt is kind of like an illegitimate emotional response. I don't necessarily agree with myself that I should feel guilty [laughs]. And I don't necessarily think that the students think that I should feel guilty either. Um (0.5) In fact I'm pretty confident they don't. Um, but I still feel things that your rational side would reject as ridiculous. They have to practice writing an essay. That might not be the most entertaining thing, but I will nevertheless try to make those classes as entertaining as I possibly can.

As can be seen in the excerpt, Nathan not only rationalises his decision to employ 'uninteresting' activities as pedagogically appropriate, but he also rationalises his own emotional response (guilt) as unwarranted. In other words, Nathan's use of cognitive rationalisation targets not only his behaviour, but also his emotional responses to his behaviour. In releasing his need to feel guilt, Nathan's actions are a form of self-compassion, which is very compatible with the adaptive management of psychological health (Mercer & Gregersen, 2020; Neff, 2011). Despite this, Nathan also reports an important discord: while he views guilt as 'illegitimate'; nevertheless, he still tries to make his classes 'as entertaining as I possibly can'. It appears as though Nathan's guilt and subsequent emotion regulation may relate to perceived epistemic pressures. In other words, they are driven by a thought, however tacit, that good teaching means ensuring that students experience positive emotions during classes.

It is perhaps important to be reminded here that the notion of an 'entertaining' teacher carries a significant amount of weight for non-Japanese teachers in the Japanese context. In universities, Japanese and non-Japanese teachers often have different responsibilities – non-Japanese lecturers teach speaking and listening skills or imported academic English skills, while Japanese lecturers teach English literature and linguistics (Nagatomo, 2016). This not only affects the methodologies that non-Japanese teachers are expected to use (typically forms of communicative language teaching), but also influences the teachers they are expected to be. Non-Japanese teachers may therefore be expected to provide more energetic and enjoyable classes than their Japanese counterparts, and there is ample evidence that both Japanese and non-Japanese teachers seem to conform to their expected role (see e.g. Kasai *et al.*, 2011; Walkinshaw & Oanh, 2014; Yazawa, 2017).

Nathan's testimony here is reminiscent of the 'motivational burden' (Acheson *et al.*, 2016; King, 2016b) that language teachers face, and it suggests that a potential side effect of this burden is negative feelings of guilt when employing an activity, no matter how useful or pedagogically effective, if the activity does not provide a positive emotional experience for learners.

8.2.3 Shifting the onus of responsibility

A fourth and final form of cognitive change was that seven participants consciously *shifted the onus of responsibility* for learning away from themselves and onto their students. Such emotion regulation was hedonically motivated – when they shifted responsibility, the teachers were able to relieve themselves of an emotional burden that came with their position as teachers. One of the major stressors underpinning this strategy was the subjective nature of grading. Five teachers reported being able to deflect negative worries and emotions arising when grading by consciously reminding themselves that students are responsible for the grades they receive. As Gina noted when discussing how she felt about grading written work: 'I feel like they- it's their responsibility to write a good essay and put time and effort into it. And if they get a C or an F, they clearly did not.... I don't really feel the pressure.'

It is important to remember that language teachers in a variety of studies have indicated a substantial amount of emotional distress over grading. Loh and Liew (2016), in particular, described in detail the stress and fatigue that can impact teachers when they need to grade written texts in a way that ensures their subjectivity is not called into question. Unsurprisingly, therefore, the design of objective grading criteria emerged as an important tool for supporting the participants in their cognitive change. Vivienne, for example, reported that the use of rubrics had been instrumental in affording her an ability to lay responsibility at the feet of the students without guilt. In her case, the grading in question was not written work, but was related to the use of the students' L1 in class. While limits on the use of L1 have continually been questioned (see e.g. Auerbach, 1993; Butzkamm, 2003), attempts to limit L1 in the (often monolingual) Japanese university classroom are not uncommon, and there was a strong tacit push reported at Fukuzaki University in some speaking courses to restrict the use of Japanese. From her point of view, Vivienne felt that the students in her first-year communication class were often 'rude' about their use of Japanese, using it to chat idly about personal matters and suffering from 'carelessness' when code switching. She also explained that it was her 'true professional opinion they would benefit from an English-only environment'. Vivienne reported a high level of stress over having to constantly deal with this matter though, feeling 'exhausted being the police. The person who would come in and shame the student'. This stress was only alleviated once she had found a more objective management system through which she was able to place the onus of responsibility onto students. She noted:

> What I realized was, um, I needed an emotional tool to help me, um, differentiate by grading differently, because I warned them 'if you use Japanese, your grade will go down'. And that's why I log it every day. Because, to me, it's punitive.

Vivienne had begun to record her students' use of L1 using a rubric and inform the students of the number of times that they had used Japanese each class. Through this more objective recording of students' Japanese use, Vivienne had been able to shift responsibility onto the students. This, she reported, helped her to attenuate negative emotions because it prevented her from feeling responsible for the students' actions while also being fairer to the class as a whole:

> I find that when I mark down 'ahh [Student M]. Japanese on July 1' I feel better. Because [Student M] is having a bad effect on the students around her and I'm giving her grade down in order to help them. Like I kind of feel like- like justice has been done.

Vivienne's words here, particularly regarding the notion of 'justice', highlight the emotional importance of maintaining a fair classroom. What this suggests is that when grading, rubrics and other forms of criteria can become more than simply 'sorting machines or... useful instructional tools' (Turley & Gallagher, 2008: 87), but rather, as Vivienne describes, 'emotional tools' that can help teachers to regulate negative emotions through cognitive change by allowing them to move the responsibility for the quality of grades to some degree away from themselves and onto students.

8.3 Contextual Factors Affording and Shaping Cognitive Change

Although the use of cognitive change has previously been cited as a common form of emotion regulation employed by educators, few past studies have adequately considered how contextual factors afford and influence cognitive change. For the teachers at Fukuzaki University, however, three important contextual factors emerged as being critical to the use of this strategy, and I discuss these three contextual factors in turn.

8.3.1 Relationships and cognitive change: 'Lovely' students

Many teachers would not deny that the relationships they form with students are an important and motivating part of their job. An interesting and important finding, therefore, was that the quality of the relationships that teachers were able to maintain with students was a major affording contextual factor with regards to the use of cognitive change. This was especially true for instances where participants employed in-situ reappraisal to manage their unfurling emotions in moment-to-moment interactions while teaching, which is illustrated well in the extract below where Jessica describes her emotional reaction to a student who had arrived late and was holding up the class:

> [The student]'s come in late but then [the student is] having a drink of water when I've said 'can you do something?'.... That just made me flare up quickly. But then, actually she's really lovely. So, it doesn't actually bother me deeply.

As can be seen in the excerpt, Jessica was initially unhappy that her student was both late, and also failing to follow instructions, but her positive perception of the student as 'lovely' allowed her to more easily reappraise the frustration she was experiencing. Including Jessica, five participants appeared more able to apply in-situ reappraisal like this when they had a positive working relationship with the student causing them a negative emotion. Undoubtedly, this finding has important implications for teachers in relation to how they may negotiate what Gkonou and Mercer (2017: 23) have termed 'the teacher paradox', the tension between treating students as individuals and treating them fairly. In this investigation it was found that, even on a hypothetical basis, differences in the quality of relationships may mean that teachers are unable to reappraise situations equivalently with two different students. Wendy, for example, offered such an awareness during an unprompted reflection in her first interview on her actions in a recent class. Wendy had a very positive relationship with a student (who I have called Student A), and she explained how that impacted a decision she had made in class:

> Okay, um, (3) so [Student A] that I have talked with a couple of times on the way to class, today she was like 'I'm really tired because I had practice at midnight last night', and so in the last third of the class they had- had a discussion, and they were supposed to be filling out their reflections. I was kind of like 'I know some of you had a late night and people running late and stuff. Some of you are really tired. So, if you want to just take a break and take a nap, that's fine. Just know that this is due Thursday and you can do it later.' And if another student had said the same thing, I'm not sure I would have had that same reaction.

In playing devil's advocate, I asked her what her response would have been had the same situation occurred with a different student (who I have called Student B), one that she had reported earlier in the interview to having difficulties with:

> R: So, if it was [Student B]?
> Wendy: I would have just been like 'suck it up dude [laughs]. You are not trying in this class anyway.'

What we can see here is that Wendy recognises that her ability, or perhaps willingness, to reappraise may be tied to the warmth with which she holds the student. Although she was able to treat her favoured student kindlier in recognition of their busy schedule, she admits that she would find this more difficult with a problematic student.

I think it is useful here to remember that any social interplay is bound by the actors' perceptions of each other (Hall, 1995); therefore, it may be a natural outcome for teachers to reappraise negative emotions with greater ease in interactions within relationships where the teachers consider there to be mutual respect. That being said, in previous studies, Jim King and I found that ethical tensions over preferential student treatment have the potential to cause stress (Morris & King, 2020), meaning that if teachers apply in-situ reappraisal without equity, it is possible it may cause harm for their own well-being.

8.3.2 Personal histories and cognitive change: Who we are now

Whereas in-situ reappraisal was dependent upon relationships, ontogenetic reappraisal was a much more personal affair. The major affording factors for this career-length form of reappraisal were the increased knowledge and experiences that the participants had accrued over time, particularly within the specific context of Japanese education (see also, Morris & King, 2023). Such resources enabled 11 participants to more ably understand their learners' circumstances, which in turn empowered a more pronounced ability to regulate negative emotions caused by classroom stressors.

In many ways, the fact that increased experience affords ontogenetic cognitive reappraisal is unsurprising because teachers have previously been found to feel fewer insecurities as they become more experienced (Gkonou & Miller, 2021; Mevarech & Maskit, 2015; Miller & Gkonou, 2018; Sutton, 2004); however, it was also important to learn that ontogenetic reappraisal could be kickstarted by formative critical incidents, which was the case for six participants. Millie and Nathan, for example, discussed critical incidents concerning their own displays of anger in the classroom which had helped them to more effectively regulate this emotion in future. I exhibit with Millie, whose ontogenetic reappraisal was initiated by an incident at her previous job involving an abusive student. Millie explained the background to what had happened:

> The first year I taught at the high school, there was this soccer kid that was picking on a part-time teacher, and [the teacher] was just taking it, and I could understand what [the student] was saying in Eng- in Japanese to her... and I couldn't handle it, because I'm like, 'how dare he say something like that to his teacher?'

Millie's reaction to witnessing this student's behaviour was very direct and involved strong displays of emotion, which became clear as she continued:

> So, I yelled at him in English in the class.... I could not understand why the teacher was taking that from this child. And I was like, 'he's outright being rude to you'. And she wasn't going to do anything about it. I think it was because she was part time.... I think [part-time teachers] just like to keep the peace. But I'm sorry, there is a respect issue. So, I yelled at this teacher- this- not the teacher, the kid. He sat down. He was quiet. And then after class, I'm like, 'you're going to report him to the disciplinary office, right?' And she wasn't going to, and I'm like 'if you don't, I will.' And so, she did. And he was given a punishment because he was being really rude.

Here then, it is clear that Millie reacted with very visible displays of anger towards a student inside the classroom. In Japan, however, these kinds of strong displays of emotion are actually very uncommon and discouraged (Matsumoto *et al.*, 2008; Safdar *et al.*, 2009). As Millie reflected on this incident and her behaviour afterwards, it caused changes to how she regulated her emotions in future situations:

> I know better to do that now. I know that doesn't get anything done. It just makes everybody scared of you.... That situation was a younger Millie.... So, I think I learned from this experience because the kid was not comfortable. The- the teacher was not comfortable the- I looked at the situation and went 'I should not do that again.' So now I know, kids causing trouble? Invite them to leave (2) or pull them aside and say, 'okay, what's the problem? Let's talk. Let's actually work this out.'

This testimony reveals that through mechanisms of ontogenetic reappraisal, which were themselves catalysed by her critical incident, Millie has been able to reappraise the way she responds to problematic students. Whereas before, she may have displayed visible anger, she now responds with attenuated emotional output. It is important to remember that critical incidents do not simply occur to individuals, but are 'produced' (Tripp, 2012: 8) through ongoing reflection; therefore, Millie's ontogenetic reappraisal is not mediated by the event itself, but by her subjective memory of the event. This means that guided reflection is likely to be an important instructional tool for teacher trainers in informing the kind of ontogenetic reappraisal that Millie utilised. The data thus far also suggests that it is effective for teachers to adopt an approach to teaching that recognises the distinct culture of the students, institution and classroom. While such approaches have previously been recognised as having pedagogic benefits (Sowden, 2007), the testimonies here reveal that it is also likely to be useful for emotion regulation. Such approaches may help teachers to manage and reduce their experiences of stressful emotions.

It was not only classroom experiences and critical incidents that informed ontogenetic reappraisal: Six participants linked their actions to generalised age-and-stage changes in their lives. For example, Peter, in email correspondence received following the completion of his interviews, described in great detail how his perception of unsuccessful classes had changed over time:

> When I was starting out teaching, I think I used to blame the students a lot if a class didn't go as expected, and I would get frustrated with the students, but over the years I have come to realise that it's usually something that I did (or didn't do) that made the class not go as I'd hoped.

When I asked Peter what had brought him to the realisation that it was his own actions that contributed to classroom failure, Peter reported that he didn't 'remember any one big event or anything that happened', but instead spoke of 'a general change in the way I approach the world in general', and he gave two important metaphorical anecdotes:

> (a) I used to get really frustrated when I was driving if I was running late and it would seem that I would always get red lights and stuck behind old people driving slow, and this would just make things worse. But now I (generally) try to flip that situation and just laugh and enjoy the scenery and think that I must be forcing things too much. So if I just slow down, everything will fall back into place.

> (b) I remember going to this old Japanese massage dude when I had a bad back (couldn't walk) and he kept trying to get me to undertsand [sic] this supposed Japanese proverb about everyone 'carrying their own *bento* [lunchbox] and injuries', and I just didn't get it. I didn't realise that I had caused my sore back, and it wasn't until much later that I finally got what he was talking about. I was responsible for what was happening to me.

For Peter then, a general change in his approach to how he viewed stressful incidents in his non-working life appears to have contributed to his ontogenetic reappraisal of his students' actions. His anecdotes explain how he has come to both be more accepting of things outside of his control, but equally more accepting of his own responsibilities. In his case, he has come to be more self-critical and receptive of his own failures as a teacher, while perhaps also realising that emotions such as frustration are not productive outside the classroom nor in.

Throughout this section we have seen how long-term changes mediated through ontogenetic reappraisal have given teachers a greater ability to negotiate classroom stresses, and such changes appear to correlate with notions of language teacher resilience (see Kostoulas & Lämmerer, 2018, 2020). These theories posit that teacher resilience is a form of growth that is informed by inner strengths and learned strategies. Peter's worldview and the testimonies of Millie and Tom in this section are reminiscent of such strengths and strategies, suggesting that ontogenetic cognitive reappraisal may support the building of resilience in addition to improving general well-being.

8.3.3 Roles and cognitive change: Teachers are 'guides', students are 'not active at all'

Earlier in this chapter I explained that one of the important ways the participants used cognitive change was to shift responsibility from themselves onto their students. An important affording factor for this use of cognitive change appeared to be the participants' interpretations of their responsibilities as language teachers. This finding was particularly acute with regards to the social responsibilities of the students themselves. I would like to compare similar testimonies from Jamie and Millie here. Both of these participants reported that they were feeling stress because of fractured student–student peer relationships in their classrooms, but each of them had very different behavioural and emotional responses.

When being asked about the incident this year that had caused him the most stress, Jamie described an anecdote about two students who were having conflict. A female student had come to him after class one day reporting that a classmate had been purposefully ignoring her. The student asked to no longer be paired with her classmate, and being a teacher who 'often empathises' with students, Jamie told the student that he would accommodate this request. Unfortunately, when establishing groups for final projects at the end of the semester, Jamie accidentally placed the two students together. This caused him to experience very negative emotions, and Jamie remained unsure about whether his accommodation of the student's request was the best action:

> I've been in classes with, as you know we all have, where there's (1.5) some students don't get on with others, and it's kind of clear. (2) Yeah, sometimes I, yeah, sometimes I sort of think like, you know, they can just sort that amongst- amongst themselves and they have to get through it. Yeah, I don't know. I'm not sure what's different in those sorts of cases.

An important part of Jamie's testimony here is his assertion that sometimes he feels students 'can just sort that amongst themselves'. This suggests that when two students have a social issue in class, Jamie has a desire to shift responsibility to those individuals to resolve their problems, but equally his testimony suggests he isn't sure about when and how to apply this cognitive strategy. In contrast to Jamie, Millie exhibited a great deal of confidence in her decision-making. She vividly recalled a student who had been having a similar peer conflict earlier in the year. She explained: 'I have a student called [Student A], and a student called [Student B]. [Student B] was convinced, convinced to the T, that [Student A] was just, like, hated her and wouldn't talk to her.' When I asked how Millie dealt with this problem, she reported that she intervened with the students, but also that she established a time-limit for her intervention to force the students to resolve the issue themselves: 'for two weeks, I will put you- make sure you guys are not in the same group. But after that, it's free game. So, um within two weeks, you need to go and talk to her.' In addition to this, she shifted the onus of responsibility for this situation away from herself and onto her student by reflecting on her role and its requirements:

> Teachers are more of a guider. I mean, we are teaching, teaching, teaching. But we are- we (2) are guides to knowledge and we are guides to relationships and we are guides to help build these things. Because once- once they're out in the real world, they have to figure out how to do it themselves. If we were holding their hands and are like, 'okay, now you're gonna be nice to her.' Yeah, it's not gonna do anything.

Here then, Millie positions herself, not just as a teacher of knowledge, but as a 'guide to relationships', and her clarity and confidence in this identity role appears to have afforded her an ability to cognitively shift responsibility, at least in part, to her students. This meant that the negative emotions she felt were reduced. It appears here, that a strong identity role awareness, when paired with a clear problem-directed approach to student/student relational issues, afforded effective cognitive change.

Relationship issues, of course, also exist between teachers and students, and positive teacher–student relationships require work and effort. Gina provided an enlightening use of cognitive change in relation to this when discussing her experiences of negative emotions owing to an inability to remember the names of some of her students:

> I have memorized every student's name in all my classes except for this high-tier [2nd year communication] class.... So sometimes I get caught, you know, not knowing a student's name... it's really embarrassing.... I think that in this high-tier [2nd year communication] class... some of them are not being interact- aren't- I'm not interacting with them at all because they never- because the other ones take up more time and energy and in a good way, but the other- the other ones just don't. They're not active at all.

Gina reported in her discussion of this incident that she felt 'a bit guilty', but it also seems that she believes the situation is not entirely her fault. This was made even clearer in the proceeding testimony as she elaborated on the role that students needed to play in ensuring a positive working relationship with teachers:

> But seriously, they should be interacting with me more if they want to be remembered. I feel like it's kind of on them too.... In my high-tier class, I kind of blame the students. I mean, come on, by now, if your teacher doesn't know your name, it's probably because you've never spoken to your teacher. Like, they never ask me any questions. They never come and talk to me.... So, I just was like, well, the onus is a little bit on you- just a little bit on you too you know.... If students want to be known by their teachers, they should probably interact with them a little more so that their face could be remembered.

Undoubtedly, positive classroom relationships are healthy and adaptive, benefiting teachers as well as students (Gkonou, 2022). Moreover, it makes sense that the teacher, as head of the class, should take a leading role in the development of warm and caring relationships which will bring this mutual benefit to both parties. However, it is also important from the perspective of well-being to remember that teachers should not martyr themselves to the job, and that the notion that 'everything depends on the teacher' is a myth (Britzman, 1986: 449); thus, while Gina's shifting of responsibility may be in contradiction to educational norms, it emerges as an important emotion regulation strategy for protecting herself from negative emotions. One of the difficulties that Gina undoubtedly faces, and that goes unacknowledged within her testimony, is the fact that Japanese pre-tertiary education is highly teacher centred; thus, Japanese students may be unwilling or perhaps even psychologically unable to communicate with their teachers proactively (Maher, 2020). This fact was highlighted strongly by King (2013a), who, in a 48-hour observational study with 900 students, recorded student-initiated interaction patterns only a mere seven times.

It is useful to be reminded here once again that teachers and students are bound in dynamically co-constructed relationships (King, 2016a), thus, both parties influence the course of the relationship over time. Gina's testimony therefore raises two interesting and relevant question for teachers to reflect upon. Firstly, to what degree should teachers and students share responsibility for the quality of the relationships that exist in the classroom, particularly in hierarchical societies such as Japan? And secondly, how can such responsibilities be actively conveyed and practised by both parties? Some authors have begun to explore these questions already (Gkonou, 2022; Gkonou & Mercer, 2017, 2018), but as Gkonou (2022) notes, these kinds of questions need to be centralised in research and explored in greater depth.

8.4 Complex Considerations

Once again, we come to the final section of this chapter where I detail some of the very complex and nuanced findings in the data. For cognitive change, I found complexity in the kinds of emotion regulation motives that were being sought by the strategies, and also in the ways that the participants actively generated empathy for their students.

8.4.1 Cognitive change and non-hedonic motives

Literature in language education has tended to consider cognitive reappraisal as an important strategy for the protection of a teachers' wellbeing (Morris & King, 2018, 2020; Talbot & Mercer, 2018), and indeed, the participants in this study also reported employing cognitive reappraisal (particularly, in-situ cognitive reappraisal) to tackle a wide range of stress-related emotions. This included irritation generated by late students (Jessica), embarrassment generated by the teacher's own spelling mistake (Zoe) and disappointment generated by beliefs that students were not able to perform as well as anticipated: 'It wasn't as fantastic as I was hoping…. Expectations not realised, let's lower the expectations' (Catherine). Previous studies have rarely, if ever, moved the discussion beyond teachers' psychological health, but I found it enlightening that in-situ reappraisal was also performed in aid of other motivations.

This is clearly visible in the following explanation from Jamie. Jamie described a particularly complex emotional event that had occurred to him recently where multiple higher-order motives were served by his use of cognitive reappraisal. Jamie had caught a student scribbling down notes on a piece of paper in the moments prior to a test, and he worried that the student's intentions were dishonest: 'my immediate reaction was "oh, she's trying to cheat."' Jamie reported that when he saw this, his first thought was to step in and address the behaviour firmly, but he stopped himself after reappraising the situation: 'I kind of had to... hold back and actually figure out what she was doing... I had to take my foot off the pedal a little bit.' When asked whether this was a conscious process, Jamie explained that it was, and that 'maybe in my mind I was jumping to a conclusion.... I'm pretty cautious about that kind of stuff in general'. Jamie continued:

> I think I tend to be like that, but of course there are cases where, you know, you are not always that disciplined, and I may have, like, jumped to the wrong conclusion.... Yeah, especially in that situation where I know the students, but I don't know them that well and obviously I don't want to- I don't want them to feel, um, you know, like I'm targeting them in any way. I would be cautious.

In this case then, Jamie appears to be performing in-situ cognitive reappraisal as a way to protect himself from negative emotions, but perhaps more importantly, it is also a way to prevent his actions from having a negative impact on his relationship with the student if he falsely accuses them of cheating. His emotion regulation therefore serves multiple motivated outcomes, hedonic, social and behavioural (towards himself), which were in concordance with each other. In all, six participants employed cognitive reappraisal in instances that included non-hedonic purposes, and in-situ cognitive reappraisal appears to have a range of uses for language teachers which reaches much wider than just for stress reduction. Any future investigations of the application of cognitive reappraisal to language teacher well-being should therefore remain conscious of the fact that the protection of well-being may be a secondary or even incidental outcome for teachers.

8.4.2 Empathy and cognitive change

As I noted above, many of the driving factors that informed the participants' uses of cognitive reappraisal were critical incidents in formative teaching and learning situations, and one of the defining features of these incidents was that they encouraged the development of empathy for Japanese students and their background circumstances. An example of this empathy can be seen in the following testimony, in which Peter describes his prior experience as an ALT in a Japanese high school and his surprise at the grammatically oriented nature of the classes he was involved in:

> I saw some of the stuff they were supposed to translate and it was like, uh, really high-level stuff.... It's almost like (English) is two different things... I mean that's a gross simplification and stereotype, but the idea that this

is- like a grammar exercise, and speaking English, are completely different things. So, there wasn't much emphasis placed on [speaking] and it was just when the [assistant language teacher] was in class, and the rest of the time the Japanese teacher would never speak English in class.

What Peter is describing here is the eigo vs eikaiwa dichotomy that I discussed earlier in Chapter 4. I would like to remind the reader that this concept posits that there are two forms of English taught in Japan: grammatically focused language study (known as eigo – literally 'English') which is used to support the ranking of students for university and the workplace, and a more conversational, supposedly less serious form of English (known as eikaiwa – literally 'English conversation'), which is used for building communicative proficiency (McVeigh, 2002; Nagatomo, 2012, 2016). Peter's experiences of this dichotomy appeared to support him to build empathy for his students: 'I am impressed that the students can speak (0.5) to the level that, you know, they can speak at', and this in turn enabled him to reduce negative emotions in classes: 'I don't feel like I get frustrated with actually them as (0.5) their English level is concerned.'

It was also an important finding to see that the empathy informed by ontogenetic reappraisal was often highly visible in teachers' interactions with students, suggesting that this form of cognitive change may bring relational benefits for teachers in addition to hedonic ones. Zoe, in particular, appeared to feel and display a significant amount of empathetic understanding when interacting with her students: 'with more experience you- it's easier to appreciate the student as like, a separate person with like, their own bullshit that they have to juggle and all the other things they have to do.' Zoe's description of students as a 'separate person' here is important. It suggests that she recognises that students have their own lives, joys, and stresses, and the impact of her empathy was visible in her second observed class when she dealt with a student who was sleeping rather than completing the required work. The observational notes that were recorded during this incident were highly indicative:

> The student opposite me is sleeping. Zoe comes over, and absolutely is not angry. She comes across as very warm and caring. She asks him how he is. How much did he sleep last night? She then explains to him about her own time management system and to-do lists. (Researcher's notes. Class Z2)

The important component in my observation was the fact that, rather than reproaching the student for sleeping, Zoe instead engaged him with a kind-hearted manner. When I asked her what was happening in her mind at this point, she reported a very empathetic understanding of the student's circumstances:

> I was thinking 'this is not normal for this student.' Like he's not a super, you know, chatty kind of person but, you know, normally he's, you know, fine at staying on task and doing, you know, at least the minimum and

sometimes a little bit more.... So, I asked him, like, does he get enough sleep? Does he spend a lot of time at work or something like super busy? And he said 'no' and I'm like 'okay, I don't know what's going on. But here, this is like a thing that I do that maybe can help you (0.5) get you know, (0.5) your things together' (2) as they looked- they were the one of the ones that looked super overwhelmed. But I dunno. Maybe they had like relationship issues or something personal that's what- like to me (0.5) if they don't wanna share then (0.5) I won't pry. But I can ask about- like I feel fine asking about like sleep and time management and that kind of thing.

In this excerpt we see that Zoe is not only able to feel empathy for the student, but to express it too. Rather than becoming angry or showing disappointment, she asks questions and considers the surrounding contextual factors that the student may be experiencing. As she notes, she is careful not to pry, but the fact that she is confidently aware of three areas she feels comfortable discussing with the student is indicative that this kind of interaction was not simply a one-off. When I asked her how her high degree of empathy for the student had developed, Zoe pointed to her own language learning as being a catalysing source of ontogenetic reappraisal:

Learning another language is so (0.5) God damn hard. (0.5) Like you think you make some progress and then- then the next lesson like you don't understand the thing at all and it's seriously so frustrating. Because I had that happen to me last night in Japanese class. And it was horrible (0.5) [sighs]. So, I understand. And (2) um (2) like it's really- it's so much more motivating for me when I can talk (0.5) to my Japanese teachers (0.5) and be like 'I don't understand this thing. And I don't get it. And I feel stupid and waaah!' And they're like 'it's okay. We'll figure this out.'

Here then, we see that empathy is a by-product of Zoe's own experiences learning Japanese. The fact that Zoe is emulating the kind of teacher that she herself prefers suggests that her ontogenetic reappraisal is performed, at least in part, in aid of her epistemic notions of good teaching. Mercer (2016b: 91) has previously argued that empathy is 'vital' to language education because of its 'centrality of relationships, social interaction, communication and intercultural competence' (2016b: 91), and, while Jim King and I have previously recognised that the development of empathy can benefit teachers' well-being (Morris & King, 2020), here we see that empathy also brings social and epistemic benefits too, impacting the way that teachers instruct and interact with their students.

Zoe was not alone in raising her own language learning experiences as informing ontogenetic reappraisal; Richard and Peter also spoke at length about how their language learning had provided them with a high degree of empathy for their students. The findings in this section appear to have very clear applications for language teachers: that the development of an empathetic understanding of learners' backgrounds and the difficulties of second language learning in general may well support teachers to regulate negative stresses and emotions through processes of ontogenetic reappraisal, and further enable them to support their students with a warmer, more caring emotional demeanour.

8.4.3 Teachers seeking empathy

The discussion above provides ample evidence that emotional experiences catalyse future teacher growth. This notion was previously introduced in Chapter 7, where I showed that by deliberately employing mental time travel, one teacher was able to use his memories of past emotions to inform his future actions. What the exploration in this chapter has revealed is that future changes are mediated through ontogenetic reappraisal. We have seen clear examples of what Kostoulas and Lämmerer (2020: 95) have termed *'adaptive adjustment'*, processes by which individuals are able to move through stressors to perform their teaching roles more effectively. In their model, emotion regulation strategies are seen as an important resource for teachers to build resilience to emotional stressors, and such strategies are defined as 'learned' (2020: 94) meaning that they can be developed across time. With this in mind, it is important for research to consider to what degree cognitive change may be encouraged and accelerated (see also, Morris & King, 2023).

Fortunately, a useful strategy emerged in two of the testimonies which detailed how teachers with a relatively small amount of experience in the Japanese context were able to develop an empathetic awareness of issues facing language learners in Japan. The general principle of the strategy was for teachers to take an active approach to learning more about their students. Vivienne did this through the use of individual consultations:

> In each semester, especially for the freshman, I may have one-on-one appointment time.… So, we have a chance to sit and talk and I asked them about 'how is life? How is their commute? Do they have a part-time job? What's their number one stress?' You know, 'how's the other class?' blah, blah, blah.

Vivienne went on to explain that these individual consultations helped her to develop knowledge of issues in her students' lives:

> I make notes about the kids who are in all the *saakuru* [university clubs and societies] and I make notes about uh, you know, a two-hour train ride every morning like- no wonder you're so late. No wonder you're so sleepy. So, it does help.

Through these excerpts we can see that Vivienne's engagement with the students on non-classroom matters gave her a greater understanding of their background circumstances. Empathy is commonly theorised as being formed of three components, *experience sharing*, referring to when individuals take on the emotions of others, *mentalising*, referring to when individuals visualise the emotional experiences of others, and *prosocial concern*, referring to when individuals want to help others (Zaki & Ochsner, 2016; Zaki *et al.*, 2012). Through her active approach to learning about students, Vivienne has come to mentalise her students' emotions and recognise that there may be issues in the students' personal lives which, while perhaps unrelated to language learning directly, nevertheless impact on their emotional states within her classroom. This empathy supports the accelerated processes of cognitive change that were initiated by her proactive approach. Luke reported a similar learned strategy to Vivienne, though in written rather than spoken form. He spoke in great depth about how learning logs – a weekly diary where students could talk to him about themselves and their learning (see e.g. Murphey, 1993; Woo & Murphey, 1999) – had enabled him to understand his students' lives in greater depth and thus regulate his emotions more effectively:

> [My colleague] observed my class and said, 'Oh, you know, do you have any questions about any issues you have?' And I said, 'I have trouble connecting to Japanese teenagers.' Like straight up. 'I just don't know what's going on in their lives, so when I talk about stuff, and I get a blank face, or I get a laugh, or I get a frown, I have no idea what any of those mean.' And he recommended the logs. 'Do the logs every week, or every month or whatever. And it's a way to talk with them.' And that just revolutionised my experience, like, talking to them and being like, 'Oh, what's this? What's that? What do you mean? What's your part-time job? Where do you work? How much do you make? What are your hours?' Knowing that they're commuting for two hours or they're working night shifts, like totally changed- because my university experience was, you live on the dorm. You live on the dorm. You live on the campus in the dorm, and you walk to class and you're barefoot, and you're- it was a very hippie college.[1]

Luke gives a powerful description here of how the use of shared diaries in this way have 'revolutionised' his teaching and interactions with students by giving him a greater insight into their lives. When I asked him how this connected to his emotions, Luke was able to give a clear response about its effect: 'they helped me see the students as people and not like customers, or units.... now I'm sitting down and I'm reading someone's journal, and it really individualises them.' In other words, like Zoe's testimony above, Luke has become able to recognise his students as having their own lives and stresses, and the logs were clearly a powerful source of support for him, not only in his ability to reappraise issues, but also bringing him greater satisfaction and positivity in his work:

> Now I'm starting to empathise and emotionally I have more room for them. Like, they make me laugh. It's funny, their lives are kind of- sometimes there's something sad or bad. I have more room. And in the classroom, I hope, and I try to bring that with me and be like, I know that you have, you have a really hard part-time job. I know that you have a really demanding club that you hate. So, when I talk with them, they know that I know that.

Learning logs have received some attention in literature as a tool for teacher development, with Hooper (2022), for example, describing the pedagogic benefits, and Miyake-Warkentin *et al.* (2019) reporting on resilience construction in relation to negative student feedback, but as Luke's testimony makes clear, the use of learning logs is also an important regulatory tool for emotions. Similar to Vivienne, social engagement through the learning logs have afforded Luke an empathetic mentalising of his students' lives, which in turn, has enabled him to employ ontogenetic cognitive reappraisal in a relatively short period of time. This ontogenetic reappraisal has thus provided him with powerful psychological resources for managing emotional stress.

8.5 Lessons Learned: Empathy at the Heart of Cognitive Change

In this chapter I have discussed the use of four kinds of cognitive change: In-situ reappraisal, ontogenetic reappraisal, rationalising and shifting accountability. These were used widely to manage negative emotions at the moment they occurred, and to mediate emotional change over longer timelines, serving a variety of higher-order emotion regulation motives.

Perhaps the most important conclusion I want to highlight at the end of this chapter is simply to say that cognitive change is clearly one of the most important categories of strategy for emotion regulation in teaching. It is a tool of great power, influencing the emotional lives of the participants in innumerable ways. It is something that teachers will do naturally, but equally it is something that can be improved or accelerated with support. At the centre of cognitive change appears to lie empathy: those teachers who had come to understand and empathise with their students' lives and classroom experiences were more deeply able to manage their emotions. Consequently, researchers, trainers and teachers themselves may find considerable benefit in taking a proactive approach. We can all benefit, I suppose, from learning more about the individual and collective circumstances that surround our students.

Note

(1) This excerpt has also been published in Morris and King (2023).

9 Response

Although the degree to which humans can accurately read the facial expressions of others is continually questioned, we only need to look at the many idiomatic expressions in English to understand that the face has a powerful impact on communication. In the UK, where I was born and raised, it is often said that we should try to 'keep a straight face' in serious situations, 'put on a brave face' in scary situations, or 'wear a poker face' when we want to hide something. Japan too has a wide range of idiomatic expressions relating to emotions on the *kao* (face). A person who can remain calm in a stressful situation might be described as having a *suzushii kao* (lit: a cool face), while someone who feels embarrassed might describe themselves as *awaseru kao ga nai* (too ashamed to show their face to another person), and in both the UK and Japan there will of course be times when we do something wrong and our guilt is *kao ni kaitearu* – 'written all over our face'. Clearly, the emotions we choose to hide and display in interactions have important consequences.

9.1 Introduction: Teachers Regulating Their Responses

Response modulation strategies are those actions that target the emerging symptoms of the emotions themselves, be those the facial expressions, bodily changes or the motivational components of emotions. Research within applied linguistics focusing on the response modulation of emotions has most notably been performed in the emotional labour tradition. This is an area of research which explores the tacit and explicit feeling rules that teachers follow. It is useful to be reminded that emotional labour is built on the premises that there are certain 'correct' emotions that teachers need to apply in specific situations, and that there are times when teachers feel the 'wrong' emotions and thus need to regulate them (Hochschild, 1983). Response modulation has some overlap here, but it is a broader construct than emotional labour, concerning itself not only with 'correct' emotional displays but also 'desired' ones. As will become clear throughout this chapter, response modulation was a universal constant of the participants' teaching work, being performed in aid of diverse emotion regulation motives and influenced by a range of contextual factors.

As always, I begin by outlining the characteristic response modulation strategies and motives used by the participants before exploring the contextual factors and complex, nuanced uses of this form of emotion regulation.

9.2 Characteristic Response Modulation Strategies and Motives

The response modulation performed by the teachers at Fukuzaki University generally concerned their emotional display choices, which I explore in two separate forms.

9.2.1 Expressional regulation

By far the most common and important response modulation strategies that the participants used were forms of expressional management, and this was most often for the students' benefit. The teachers at Fukuzaki University reported that they felt a strong desire to create and maintain positive classroom learning atmospheres, which in emotional terms meant simultaneously increasing the students' experiences of positive emotions while protecting them from exposure to negative ones. The teachers did this through a range of response modulation strategies targeting their own emotional output, including the *suppression* of negative emotions: 'I just kind of decided it would be better to hide my emotions' (Gina), the *genuine expression* of positive emotional states: 'I would never try to hide [excitement]' (Peter), and, when necessary, the *exaggeration* and *feigning* of emotions: 'I would make [my voice] excited sounding, and, like, higher pitched' (Zoe). The use of *humour* also featured extensively in the testimonies, with 11 of the participants reporting it as an important part of positive classroom learning environments: 'It just helps build a rapport. Connection. Loosens everyone up a bit' (Eleanor).

In addition to creating a positive atmosphere, a second relatively common motive behind the use of response modulation was for the instrumental management of student behaviours. For the most part, the negative student behaviours the participants described could be categorised as hassles – everyday irritating or frustrating issues that are specific to individual contexts (Kanner et al., 1981). For the participants at Fukuzaki University, these hassles included students chatting over the teacher (Jessica, Jamie, Wendy), being unresponsive (Richard, Millie, Tom), playing on phones (Stewart) and coming to class unprepared (Catherine, Eleanor). They were commonplace, and participants tended to report them as low-level stressors. Eleven of the participants were observed or reported to employ response modulation to address these issues, most frequently through the *modulated expression of negative emotion* (see also Morris & King, 2023). When using this strategy, participants chose to intentionally display relatively controlled expressions of disappointment or frustration towards students. An indicative example of this kind of emotion regulation was described by Eleanor, who stopped her class during the middle of a vocabulary activity to admonish them for failing to have studied. Eleanor expressed her anger somewhat directly. She asked the students rhetorically how they think they performed before explaining that they were 'very lucky' that the vocabulary activity was not a test. Eleanor's actions had a deliberate instructional motive: she explained that she had 'wanted to move on and sort of, in my angry way, tell them that they hadn't studied and therefore they hadn't succeeded' and she reported her behaviour as 'a teaching moment' that could be used to 'remind them how important it was to study.' The instances of modulated expressions of negative emotion like Eleanor's that were witnessed during classroom observation sessions were noted to be fleeting in duration and were generally successful in achieving the required instructional goal. Jessica, for example, was able to get a student to focus on class by calling on him by name and asking in a calm, though pointed manner, 'can you be quiet?'.

The instrumental use of response modulation strategies to address minor student misbehavioural issues such as those above has been previously reported both in general elementary (Hosotani & Imai-Matsumura, 2011) and secondary educational contexts (Yin, 2016; Yin & Lee, 2012), but the results here suggest that it clearly has a role to play at the tertiary level in Japan too, where apathetic and non-participatory behaviours have been reported on numerous occasions as frustrations for teachers (Cowie, 2011; King, 2016b; Morris & King, 2018, 2023).

9.2.2 Self-disclosure

Tangentially related to the participants' expression management was the use of very open and honest emotional displays which were delivered through *acts of self-disclosure*. Acts of self-disclosure refer to those instances where teachers share (often very personal) information about their lives that students would not be able to learn otherwise (Cayanus, 2004), and they arose in the testimonies of six participants. Within education, acts of self-disclosure have typically been framed as a relational practice (Elahi Shirvan & Taherian, 2021; Henry & Thorsen, 2018) but I position them here as an emotional practice, one that impacts the emotional output of teachers and consequently their instruction. Positioning acts of self-disclosure in this way is appropriate since the performance of disclosure, by definition, involves the sharing of personal stories about the teachers' histories, families and their lives outside the workplace, all of which have a clear emotional display component. This fact was recognised by the participants themselves, with Nathan commenting that: 'the more authentic story is the more emotionally resonant. It is- just with you and your voice and how you speak naturally because you're recounting your feelings.'

A prototypical example of an act of self-disclosure can be seen in the following extract from Tom's first observed class. At the time the self-disclosure was performed, Tom was eliciting different kinds of harassment from the students, and one of the groups had offered as an answer 'karaoke harassment',[1] which they defined as situations when a person is pressured to sing against their will during workplace parties. Tom responded to this suggestion of karaoke harassment with an act of self-disclosure:

Tom: Yeah, because my wife would- would definitely suffer from karaoke harassment, yeah.
Class: [laughs]
Tom: Terrible, terrible singer. Even when she sings to my son. Oh yeah terrible.
Class: [laughs]
Tom: Yeah, but I don't harass her. Don't worry.

Here in this extract, we see that Tom has chosen to bring his family life into the classroom for comic effect. In the proceeding stimulated recall interview, Tom reported that his choice to reveal the nature of his wife's singing ability was a socially motivated form of response modulation: 'That's deliberate because I feel like it makes me more relatable, and they can have fun with that you know.... it just makes you more relatable.' As can be seen, Tom's intentional choice to self-disclose was driven by the belief that sharing in this way would open a window to the teacher's personal life and give the students an insight that they could recognise and connect with.

Teachers also performed self-disclosure with instrumental motives in mind. This was most visible in the teaching of Nathan, who regularly used self-disclosure because of the emotional connection it afforded students to develop with the material being taught. During his second stimulated recall session, the text that Nathan was teaching from concerned the placebo effect in holistic medicine, and Nathan began his class by recounting a story of a friend at school whose mother had relied on holistic medicine following a cancer diagnosis, and who had later passed away. As I observed this class, I found the story to be highly affecting in its telling, and Nathan reported to feeling a whole range of emotions: 'sadness, tragedy... kind of goosebumps... guilt.' Equally though, he felt that the emotions that he exhibited in the story were the key to engaging the students, bringing material to life which might otherwise be rather flat: 'Statistics don't really communicate anything.... It's those narratives that- that persuade people. That persuade perhaps the irrational side of the human psyche that what you're saying is worth listening to.' The literature on self-disclosure agrees with Nathan: providing that self-disclosure is relevant to the topic being studied, students report greater levels of impact and interest in their learning (Cayanus & Martin, 2008; Cayanus et al., 2009; Elahi Shirvan & Taherian, 2021). What Nathan's testimony adds to this literature though is the potential for a teacher's act of self-disclosure to have a simultaneous positive influence on their own sense of classroom satisfaction. Nathan went on to describe the impact of his emotional self-disclosure as follows:

> This kind of an exhilaration, I think. You feel exhilarated. Exhilaration is the best way of describing it I think. (2) There is something to that. Adrenaline. Um (0.5) I don't plan- (2) a lot of what I do is unplanned, um, and impromptu, um, and that creates a sense of danger and exhilaration.

In other words, Nathan's use of self-disclosure had a salient impact on his own positive emotional states and well-being; thus, although his acts of self-disclosure were driven by instrumental higher-order motivations, 'I honestly believe that… the best way of teaching is to do things through stories', they brought with them inevitable hedonic benefits that should be recognised in future investigations of self-disclosure.

A third important motive that influenced the participants' uses of self-disclosure was their epistemic desire to be seen as both honest and human. Gina, for example, explained that she self-disclosed about her life because she wanted her students 'to get to know me a little bit more. Uh, think of me as human', and Millie reported that 'I like them to know that we are flawed. We aren't- don't have all the answers. We live our own lives. We have stuff going on outside'. The notion that teachers desire to be seen as human in the eyes of students is something that has been recognised before (Gkonou & Mercer, 2017; Sutton, 2004) but what was interesting in the data was the fact that 'being human' enabled the participants to teach life lessons alongside language content (see also Morris & King, 2023). I illustrate with Gina who interestingly reported to using self-disclosure alongside expressions of genuine emotions for reasons of empowerment. In particular, she wanted to model to her students that it was possible for females in Japan to balance a career with their family life. This line of thought emerged as Gina discussed the recounting of an anecdote to her class about a 'challenging time' she had spent at an event at her children's school:

> [The students] are just like, shocked that I had to go to an *undoukai* [school sports day] and make a family *bento* [lunchbox] for the entire family and spend the whole day at the undoukai and it was kind of miserable, but I went through it anyway, because my kids were happy…. I explained this to the students and they're like, 'wow! That's what you-' you know, they're kind of amazed that I lead this double life. So, I feel like it's kind of worth telling them those things because I want, especially the girls to know that it is possible to have- you know, be a mom and work. Be a mom and a worker. And that you can manage both. It's hard, but you can manage both.[2]

In this testimony we see that Gina felt her self-disclosure helped her to show her students that she was 'not just a teacher', and this in turn helped her to achieve her goal of acting as a role model for her female students.

Gina's testimony here is an example of how a teacher occupies multiple identities in the classroom that can be revealed through their interactions; thus, while to the students she may be seen as a teacher first, through her honest and emotional self-disclosure she shows her students that she is also a wife and mother. Recent research suggests that by revealing these kinds of 'master identities' (Tracy & Robles, 2013: 21), teachers can have a salient impact on students' classroom enjoyment levels as they come to see their teachers in a new light (Elahi Shirvan & Taherian, 2021). Gina's acts of self-disclosure here may therefore be particularly powerful for some of the female students that she hopes to reach.

9.3 Contextual Factors Affording and Shaping Response Modulation

So far in this chapter it has been seen that the participants' response modulation behaviours were most frequently aimed at influencing student emotions and behaviours. The contextual factors underlying this response modulation were, in fact, numerous, and I explore the most important of these here.

9.3.1 Responsibilities, identity and response modulation: Being a fun and caring teacher

One of the most powerful contextual influences over any person's emotions are the high-order expectations placed on them by institutions, culture and society, and this was absolutely true for many of the participants at Fukuzaki University. Within Japan, non-Japanese language teachers have long been positioned as being 'fun and energetic', with significant responsibilities to motivate learners and instil a love for the English language (e.g. Bailey, 2007; King, 2016b; Lawrence & Nagashima, 2020). This prescriptive form of emotional labour is predicated once again on the fact that in Japan there are two forms of English known as eigo (English) and eikaiwa (English conversation), with a status quo that positions Japanese teachers as responsible for the more serious examination-focused form of English, and non-Japanese teachers as responsible for the less serious conversation-focused form of English (Nagatomo, 2016). Given this positioning, it was not overall surprising that, like other recent work (e.g. King, 2016b; Morris & King, 2020), all of the participating teachers at Fukuzaki University regulated their emotions to routinely display mostly positive states to students (see also Morris, 2022; Morris & King, 2023). What was surprising, however, was that although a few teachers agreed that positive displays were occasionally required of them ('this is part of my job' – Luke), external institutional and sociocultural factors were not the primary driving forces. Instead, the participants' choices to display positive emotions were attributed to personality: 'I'm kind of like an a priori positive person' (Nathan), past learning experiences: 'there was one male teacher.... He didn't like children' (Jessica), and most saliently, by internal beliefs on good teaching practice, with 13 teachers reporting that positive emotional displays created atmospheres highly conducive to language learning. As Gina described: 'I want it to be a really positive atmosphere. And I want them to feel like they can talk freely. And I also don't want them to think that I'm, like, judging them.'

In addition to the pressure to be fun and motivating, a second form of sociopolitical pressure that teachers in Japan have reported is an expectation to present themselves as caring to students (King, 2016b). Although displays of caring did not feature as saliently in the interviews as discussions of being fun and motivating, they were still reported by more than half of the participants.

In previous work, King (2016b) showed that the degree to which caring is taken up within teachers' identities is highly variable, and indeed this was the case at Fukuzaki University too, where individual contextual situations meant that some of the participants were more driven to care for students than others. For some participants, caring emotions were only incidentally displayed, driven by interactional-level factors such as poor student health: 'I'm like, are you OK? We'll do (the activity) another time' (Vivienne), or relational-level factors such as the quality of the student–teacher dynamic: 'That's my favourite class... I probably show more caring feelings with them in general' (Gina). For other participants though, caring was a holistic, personality-level factor that was a semi-permanent feature of their classrooms. Zoe, for example, appeared to place a strong value on care, which functioned alongside the high degree of empathetic understanding that she held for her students. Her genuine displays of warmth were highly visible in her second observed lesson. As the bell rang for class to begin, Zoe reported feeling that the students 'looked kind of exhausted', and this prompted her to spend the first few minutes of her lesson checking in with the learners: 'How you guys doing? Are you OK? What's going on? Your faces tell me something different... How's reading class?.... How's writing class?.... Did you turn in any assignments yet?' Here we see that Zoe's performance of caring was driven by a recognition that the students were not emotionally ready to learn. She performed caring both through her choice to display warmth, as well as through her use of considered questions aimed at uncovering underlying issues; consequently, like participants in Gkonou and Miller (2017), caring was performed through actions as well as emotional displays.

One of the important findings about the caring emotions exhibited by the participants that I noted was that they were not necessarily driven by a desire to resolve students' issues. To this end, Zoe explained that she 'wanted them to know I'm thinking of them.... I wanted them to know that (0.5) you know, their feelings are valid'. Luke too expressed a similar sentiment as he reported on why he took it upon himself to spend extra time caring for students that he felt were having difficulties:

> The main thing I'm worried about is that I show that I care. Not that I solve their problems or that I'm, uh, you know, building this deep friendship, but rather that I care. So that if there's a late assignment, or they're absent or have some problem. I want them to think 'I know Luke cares.'

Thus, similar to participants in Gkonou and Miller (2017), the emotional labour of caring for learners was frequently performed by the teachers without formal resolution of the difficulties at the heart of their students' situations. In other words, the teachers did not necessarily perform caring because it would bring an immediate instrumental benefit for the learners, but because they felt it was the appropriate thing to do in the emerging situation. This was an indication that these participants were conscious of their responsibilities as teachers in the Japanese education system, as well as of the ethic of care that has been frequently posited as a highly desirable feature of relationships in learning contexts (Noddings, 1995).

In Chapter 5, I wrote about Nathan's strong identity as a caring teacher. His was a moral need to care for his students, even to the degree that he regularly tutored students with extracurricular work, fixed their resumes and prepared them for job interviews (see also Morris, 2022). Nathan also appeared to occasionally share his emotions with students through expressional regulation by using empathetic displays of negative emotions. In these cases, Nathan reported that he 'might kind of express anger with [students] in sympathy' when he felt they had been impacted by 'some kind of injustice'. This is evident in the following excerpt, where Nathan discussed being asked to help students who were suffering 'for lack of a word, bullying' at the hands of another teacher within the International Languages Department:

> I sometimes might feel a bit of sympathetic anger when students have been failed, um, when they have lost motivation and when they feel that they, they feel it difficult to cope with classes. (0.5) Not just that specific class that was taught by that teacher but also other classes where they had a negative- and a real serious negative impact brought on by somebody who's being lazy and, in my view, cruel. That might be when I might express a little bit of sympathetic anger.

As can be seen, because of the negative ways that his colleague's 'lazy' and 'cruel' actions had impacted the students, Nathan chose to share authentic negative emotions. Although Nathan chooses to describe his anger with the word 'sympathy', I noted in my research journal that his anger at the situation remained palpable even during the interview. I took this to be an indication that his feelings were felt in concordance with his students' emotions, meaning that they were somewhat empathetic rather than sympathetic (Mercer, 2016). Although empathy is an important strategy for the building of social relationships (Mercer, 2016), Nathan did not view his actions in this way. When I asked Nathan what goal his empathetic displays might serve, he replied that his displays were 'not really calculated', but instead were his natural reaction to such circumstances: 'the people who are suffering are relatively innocent. (2) I (2) kind of think that most people would get fucked off with that.' In other words, Nathan viewed his displays of empathetic emotions as being instinctive responses to student problems rather than a consciously aware emotion regulation action. This suggests that when performing caring, teachers may interact with authentic emotional output if circumstances arise which are serious in nature, and if the teacher experiences a high degree of empathy for the situation.

9.3.2 Colleagues and response modulation: Tacit competition

I have mentioned numerous times throughout this chapter that the majority of the teachers actively sought to display positive emotions to their students, but one of the interesting contextual factors that influenced the degree of positivity on display was a tacit competition between the participants and their colleagues within the International Languages Department (see also Morris, 2022). Four participants commented on the fact that comparisons with other teachers had led them to modify their emotional output. Tom, for example, felt a clear difference between the energy levels within his classes in comparison to his colleagues'. This feeling was exacerbated by the fact that many of the classrooms had glass walls, which allowed students to see what was happening in the lessons around them: 'you've got kids literally sprinting down corridors, um, running around the building.... It's like so obvious that my lessons are not like those ones.' Such comparisons led him to worry that his classes were 'boring', catalysing him to find new ways to increase displays of positivity in his classroom through activity choices and increased humour. Similarly, Jessica compared herself to another teacher in the International Languages Department, a colleague who she shared a class with, and who she described as 'very (0.5) friendly. Like, I think they see her as a friend'. This colleague's friendliness was a driving force that led Jessica to differentiate herself by modulating her emotional output. To that end, Jessica had decided to employ more genuine expression of her emotions to present a less energetic, more authentic persona: 'it makes me more, not muted, it's not the right word, but more of myself.' Jessica reported that through her honest persona, she was able to connect strongly with some students who appreciated and complimented her on her approach. Moreover, from the perspective of her well-being, Jessica's response modulation choices appeared highly adaptive 'it's less (0.5) tiring, to not have to put on (2) a different face or whatever. (2) But yeah, so I never feel like- I never feel like I don't want to go to work'.

Competitiveness among collegial teachers remains an under-researched topic, with little literature to explore, but the results here suggest that tacit competition can influence the emotional output and well-being of teachers. Language teacher competitiveness is a topic which deserves more attention, and this is particularly true in contexts like Japan, where a shrinking population, commercial forces and short-term unstable employment conditions mean that universities and teachers are increasingly under pressure to please students (e.g. Bradley, 2009; Eades, 2009). Such circumstances are not unique to Japan, and I believe that subjectively perceived competition with colleagues may well emerge as an important psychological feature which increasingly influences teacher emotions and regulation as institutions worldwide come under greater financial pressure.

9.3.3 Classroom content and response modulation: Being clinical

The final contextual factor that I found in the data was the nature of the classroom content being taught. Trends in CLIL and English as a medium of instruction education over the past 10 years mean that the importance of content in language instruction has become undeniable, and many researchers have reported that teachers are not only responsible for teaching the nuts and bolts of language, but also for preparing students to discuss and think critically about emotive world issues (see e.g. Cowie, 2011; Loh & Liew, 2016; Morris & King, 2020, 2023). As part of this role, teachers are liable to bring serious and emotionally sensitive topics into their classrooms, and with such topics comes a significant degree of emotional labour (Cowie, 2011; Loh & Liew, 2016). One of the forms that this emotional labour takes is the desire, or need, for teachers to employ emotional output that matches the seriousness of the topic under discussion, and an important use of response modulation emerged as the participants displayed and suppressed emotions to teach particular topics most effectively. This kind of emotion regulation was reported in the testimonies of five participants, a highly visible example of which came from Vivienne, who described how she regulated her emotional displays when teaching presentation skills:

> I have to help them get in touch with the emotions they want to give to their audience and considering an audience and one's effect on one's audience. And, uh, in giving a travel presentation, the idea is salesmanship and persuasiveness, and smiles almost always help with that. But if you're giving a presentation about terrible things, and you want to show the gravity of the situation to your audience, a smile will not help.

Vivienne is describing a very explicit form of response modulation here that has a direct impact on the tangible output she expects from students in their presentations. She shows a clear awareness that different topics require different emotional displays, referencing the lighter topics covered in her first-year classes (travel) and the more serious topics of her second-year classes (conflict). In order to illustrate the desired emotional displays, she reported to spending time modelling the emotional output she expected from students.

In Vivienne's case, it is clear that her choice of emotional output is related not only the topic of the course (e.g. travel vs conflict), but also to the mode of communication that the students are expected to engage in. In other words, because Vivienne is teaching presentation skills, and because presentations require students to display emotions, her teaching of this skill required her also to model emotional output for her students to emulate. A similar kind of behaviour was exhibited by Gina in her second observed class, though in her case the mode of communication was a written essay:

> I want the students to write cause and effect essays in a very objective way. So, I want them to read a newspaper article and then be able to discuss it and be able to pick out the causes and write about it. I want them to be as objective as possible and I don't want them to use personal examples.... I want to push them to be as clinical as me.... I can't- I don't show any emotion.

Gina's decision to show 'very clinical' emotions to her students is driven by a pedagogic imperative: the use of such emotions is an important part of the register of the academic writing she is teaching. This meant that even when dealing with potentially emotional topics, such as bullying, Gina felt she needed to suppress her emotions and present a neutral face. In both the cases above, the teachers recognised that their response modulation informs the emotional output of the class, and so the teachers decided to tangibly model the emotional displays they wanted.

In Vivienne and Gina's cases, the instrumental goals they were seeking were relatively easy to define and measure, but this was not always the case. Some teachers reported using their emotional displays in a more general way to encourage their students to think more deeply about content. Catherine, for example, in her opening interview, explained how she used strong and passionate emotional displays as an instrumental tool when her students watched a documentary about the sexualisation of young girls in Japanese red-light districts:

> We finished watching the video, and I'm, like 'what do you think about it?' 'It's okay. It's all voluntary, it hurts no one.' And I'm like, okay, let's actually analyse what's going on here. So, the girls, these girls who are 15 and 16 years' old are dancing on a stage.... They have all these guys lined up to meet and shake hands afterwards. I'm like 'watch the faces of the guys. Watch the faces of the girls. Watch their body language. Watch- like what do you notice?' They're like 'he's holding her hand like this and she's trying to pull away and she can't.' I'm like 'exactly. How Is this okay?' Or

(5) like just sheer disgust as I'm helping- well, trying not to indoctrinate but at the same time trying to make them think more critically about what they're watching. Like. Yes. Okay, and on one level, it's a consensual relationship. But on another level, it's not. And on another level, it's just using someone in a terrible way. And we need to be aware of all of these levels. We can't just think at this one. So, in that class, I used my emotion much more because I was much more passionate about it.

In this long passage, Catherine makes clear that she feels it is important for the students in her class to learn more about the social issue she has introduced since, in her eyes, the students have only a surface level understanding of the topic. As such, she employed the genuine expression of 'disgust' to make her feelings on this topic clear to her students. Loh and Liew (2016) have previously reflected on the fact that the decisions language teachers take over the topics they bring into the classroom are inherently emotional and value-laden, and Catherine's testimony clearly reflects the emotional labour involved in such decisions. Her choice to display strong emotions was reminiscent of the motives of 'Emma', a teacher that Jim King and I discussed in an earlier paper (Morris & King, 2020) who employed the same emotion regulation strategy to display highly visible and honest emotions of disgust and anger when dealing with a topic she was passionate about. In that case, Emma wished for her students to recognise that emotional responses to serious topics were welcome, and indeed appropriate in some cases. While Catherine did not report to explicitly modelling emotional displays in the same way, the instrumental purpose of her use of emotions to invoke the seriousness of the topic under discussion and make students think more deeply follows a similar ethos.

9.4 Complex Considerations

In this final section of the chapter, I explore three areas of complexity. The first is in relation to the benefits of the participants' positive emotional displays, the second is in relation to the different ways that emotional displays could be used to influence behavioural issues, and the third is in relation to an important tension that emerged in the participants' emotional display decision-making.

9.4.1 The benefits of positive emotional displays

Earlier in this chapter I reported that non-Japanese teachers are both tacitly and explicitly expected to be positive, but that in the case of the participants at Fukuzaki University, external social pressures were not a significant controlling contextual factor. Instead, the teachers reported that they felt positive emotional displays were simply good teaching practice. As I probed this idea more deeply, two benefits of the participants' choices to display positive emotions emerged. Firstly, they reported adaptive student outcomes. Peter for example, explained the effect that his positive approach to the classroom had on students' oral performances:

> 'My students are so quiet' is something that I hear a lot from teachers at [Fukuzaki University] and Japan in general, but to be honest, I have never had that problem. It's unlikely that I have been lucky with students 6 years in a row, so I think it's all related to how I try to create a safe and friendly environment in the class. Lots of smiles, and as much laughing and good vibes as I can.

Here we see that Peter directly associates his conscious decision to display positive emotions as being a contributing factor in increasing students' spoken output in the classroom. Peter's observations are not surprising, particularly given the vast amount of research concerning the impact of negative emotions like anxiety on student performance (see e.g. Andrade & Williams, 2009; King, 2013a; Maher, 2020; Matsuda & Gobel, 2004; Oya et al., 2004), but what was interesting was that some participants, such as Zoe, felt that emotional classroom considerations should take precedent over other learning and content decisions:

> I remember reading just some random pin on Pinterest of like, uh, what people remember the most from school, and a lot of people don't remember any of the content or like what they learned, but they remember how they felt. (0.5) And I think making these kinds of associations of like, 'this feeling with this place' and 'this place is a learning place' then that-that will probably have a better long-term effect than making sure they remember all of these affixes and stupid grammar points that everyone ignores.

The general sense in the testimonies was that the participating teachers saw enormous instrumental value in their positive emotional displays, and moreover, that the teachers recognized the significant degree of influence they had over the atmospheres of the classroom (see also Morris, 2022). As Stewart noted, 'it's quite uncanny how classes reflect their teachers'. This finding was extremely welcome since research has highlighted that the language teacher is perhaps the primary causal factor in the level of students' enjoyment of foreign language learning (Dewaele & Dewaele, 2020; Dewaele & MacIntyre, 2019; Jiang & Dewaele, 2019). The perspectives of participants like Peter and Zoe show that the teachers had an explicit and conscious awareness of their roles as a 'conductor of an orchestra with junior musicians' (Dewaele et al., 2018: 126), monitoring and regulating classroom atmospheres through their dynamically changing emotional output to maximise positive student emotion.

A second benefit of the participants' choices to display positive emotions was the adaptive impact such displays had on their own well-being (see also Morris, 2022). This was, in part, because being positive is a naturally enjoyable state: 'if you're laughing then you're laughing right?'

(Peter), but it was also attributable to the contagious nature of emotions (Hatfield *et al.*, 1994) which meant that the participants' emotional output was often received by students, magnified and then returned to the teachers 'like a loop' (Nathan). As Catherine noted simply, 'they start laughing and then I start laughing and then it keeps the (0.5) emotion level high in the class'. This emotional transfer was recognised by nine of the participants, and it was again highly indicative of the dynamic and bidirectional interplay that occurs in teacher–student relationships (King, 2016a): Teachers and students do not exist independently of each other in the classroom, and their interactions are located within the histories and futures of relationships (Boiger & Mesquita, 2012). Through their interactions, teachers and students constantly inform each other's emotions both positively and negatively. Displays of positive emotions therefore emerged as more than simply a tool for creating optimum classroom conditions, but frequently as intentional hedonically motivated emotion regulation actions. Simply put, the participants recognised that their positive emotional displays would impact their own subjective well-being as they were reflected back from students, and this in part motivated their display choices.

Before finishing this section, I wish to highlight an extremely important point about these findings: Namely, that they are in direct opposition to other studies on positive emotional displays which have described highly negative psychological outcomes for teachers. A participant in King (2016b) for example, reported on the mental stress that he felt because of the need to be constantly positive, while similarly, an autobiographical study by Lawrence and Nagashima (2020), showed that the first author felt negative emotions and diminished accomplishment when his students labelled him as 'funny' (2020: 51) in class feedback (see also Morris, 2022). One potential reason for the more adaptive orientation experienced by the participants in this study may well be the fact that their displays of positive emotions appeared to be self-chosen rather than explicitly imposed upon them. In previous language education research in Japan, some of the most saliently negative responses to the emotional labour of positivity have been experienced in cases where teachers were explicitly instructed to be positive by their employers and direct managers (e.g. Bailey, 2007; Yarwood, 2020). Of course, the teachers at Fukuzaki University may well be experiencing tacit pressures to be positive, particularly as many had extensive teaching experience in Japan, and it may well also be that the International Languages Department actively sought positively oriented teachers in their hiring processes. That being said, it would seem likely that any emotional stress that teachers may feel from a need to be positive in any given context may well be mitigated through industry-wide acceptance of the pedagogic benefits of positive emotional displays.

9.4.2 Student behaviour and response modulation: Managing the intensity of emotional displays

Earlier, I noted that minor issues with student behaviour were often dealt with through the use of modulated displays of negative emotions. In those cases, the participants found that if they displayed their genuine feelings of frustration and disappointment in a controlled manner, they were able to have a positive impact on the behaviours of students. Generally speaking, I found that the teachers who used this form of emotion regulation to manage small hassles did not report extended feelings of stress. Unfortunately, however, there were occasions when behavioural issues built up over time, which in turn negatively affected the teachers' ability to control their emotional displays. In some cases, the participants became so stressed that they released powerful displays of unregulated negative emotions in front of their classes. I exhibit with Eleanor, who had been struggling for a whole year with a difficult group of three male students in her class who were highly apathetic, and she described an outburst when two of the students in question failed to show up to deliver a presentation towards the end of the semester:

> I would say that day I probably let my (0.5) frustration- more frustration rather than disappointment, show…. I was like, 'you guys need to text the students and find out what's going on.' And one of the students went, 'Oh, such and such student. He's, uh, (2) he's overslept'…. And I'm like, 'tell him he has a choice to either come in and present with you, or he'll get 50% of the grade, tops, (0.5) if he presents later' [spoken in a stern manner]. He dragged his (0.5) sorry self in [laughs].

In this case, Eleanor's anger was compounded by her feelings of exhaustion in relation to the situation. She had simply reached the point where she could no longer tolerate or suppress her emotions: 'like I just think I was so tired that I didn't care anymore…I just- just- didn't- couldn't- couldn't be bothered hiding it at that point.'

The participants not only expressed genuine frustration, but disappointment and sadness too. Vivienne, for example, described a situation where she was struggling to manage her students' use of Japanese in class. After trying numerous strategies, a colleague told her that she should consider displaying her honest emotions to the class, using them as a tool to get the students to realise the impact of their actions. She reported to trying this approach:

> I finished the lesson by telling them 'hey, I'm very frustrated, and I'm very disappointed in this group as a whole.' And to my shock, I started to cry [laughs]. It was a little bit more of a squishy approach… but I thought, 'hey, this is uh- expressing my emotion and it's maybe hitting them in the way that I want to hit them. We'll just see'. I felt kind of bad using tears as a dagger to- to accomplish a classroom goal. But I felt better after crying. Because it was- it was my honest feeling that how upset I was about this particular grievance.

As can be seen, Vivienne reported mixed feelings over her very open display of authentic emotion in this situation, feeling 'kind of bad' about her actions, while also rationalising her display of honesty ('it's maybe hitting them in the way that I want to hit them'). While she reported success in reducing her frustration, which went from 'level 100' to '20 and then back to 80', she also felt 'embarrassed' the next time she saw the students. It appeared that displays of strong negative emotions by the participants at Fukuzaki University brought only mixed successes, both in relation to their impact on student behaviour and their potential for further negative emotions, which themselves had to be regulated.

Many may find it interesting that modulated and unmodulated displays of negative emotions were not the only response modulation strategies reported for dealing with student behavioural issues. In some situations, participants reported to dynamically suppressing negative emotions to achieve similar aims. Stewart, for example, reported an incident where he employed emotional suppression as an instrumental tactic to deal with a student who refused to take part in a silent reading activity. Stewart explained the situation as follows:

> [Student A]'s always demanding the other students' attention. So, I was like 'okay [Student A] if you're gonna mess about just sit outside the class.' And it- I mean it was very jokingly.... And then he went and sat himself outside of the- outside of the class on the chair. And he had his feet up on the glass outside of the chair. So, he's still sort of demanding that- the attention.

When I asked how Stewart dealt with the situation, he reported that rather than getting angry he had hidden his feelings of frustration, explaining 'the best way to deal with it was just to let it pass. To let it pass and then he got bored and he just sort of got down to reading'. For Stewart, it became clear that extensive classroom experience afforded him an understanding of the best course of action in this situation, as he went on to explain:

> It's experience with that particular student (0.5) which has grown over the year... my understanding of the situation was that he- he was looking for- he was demanding the attention. He looks for the attention quite a bit.... He's a positive influence on the classroom, but, you could see some of the other students rolling their eyes sort of like 'oh god [Student A] again? We're trying to read.' And so, it was better to engage in that sort of narrative and just sort of let it pass rather than be adversarial in it.

As can be seen from this testimony, Stewart has a highly informed and nuanced approach to dealing with this incident that was driven by an understanding of his student's behavioural tendencies across the school year. His approach to suppress his emotional display was mediated through in-situ cognitive reappraisal as he had come to reflect on and reassess the student's behaviour in light of what he had learned through their interactions. This example highlights the fact that emotional display decisions are both dynamic and contextual, being influenced not only by momentary behaviours, but also by the history and potential futures of the teacher–student relationship. It reinforces the need for teachers to apply nuanced rather than one-size fits all approaches to dealing with misbehavioural issues, a fact that could well be raised in training and reflective growth sessions, where teachers could be taught to consider multiple emotional response tactics for managing behavioural issues.

9.4.3 The emotion display tension

The final point that I would like to discuss is perhaps also one of the most interesting findings in the data, and it relates to questions over the power of emotional displays that the teachers deemed to be appropriate, and how they dynamically adjusted their displays when interacting with students.

One of the potential dangers of any teacher using their emotions in instrumental ways, such as when managing student behaviour, is that the teacher could end up overpowering students' thinking processes. It was fruitful to find, therefore, that the participants appeared aware of a tension between balancing the ferocity of their passionate emotional displays while also providing the most constructive learning environment. This *emotion display tension* meant that some teachers always kept their authentic emotions out of the classroom (see also Morris & King, 2023). Tom, for example, explained how he never gave students an indication of his opinion on emotive matters:

Tom: It's about their opinion. So, you present the information and you maybe show them different sides to it or something, but my opinion doesn't matter at all. It's not important. And it's not (0.5) um (2) yeah who cares what I think? It's just not relevant at all.

R: Is there any emotion there? Like, sometimes do you feel like you want to step in and say something?

Tom: Yes, sometimes, and I hold that back, because if it's something I'm really interested in or something I really want to give an opinion on it- but I- I try not to because I want to be consistent. It's a conscious decision not to because it just doesn't matter what I think.

Here we see that Tom has a highly principled stance on the use of emotional displays when dealing with discussion-worthy topics, 'holding back' or suppressing any emotions he feels owing to an epistemic notion that teachers should not impress their own opinions upon students. For Tom, it was his past experience as a teacher trainer which had led him to believe that he should suppress his emotions in these cases:

Watching so many observations, I've seen so many people just like bang on about themselves and give their opinion about things. I can't stand it.

> Just like 'who cares?' Like, they are not doing it on purpose, they just can't help it because they got like an audience and, you know, somebody will give them a good listening to.

Catherine too, was highly cognisant of the emotion display tension, giving a nuanced explanation of how she managed her emotional output. For example, she reported to tempering her displays when she felt the issues under discussion were not black and white:

> Usually- I try to treat- I try to treat most things objectively.... I'm against [the topic that Catherine's students chose in class], but I don't feel like I have the right to just push- force that on anyone else. That's my own opinion.... And I could have just gotten angry with them and be like, 'that's not an appropriate topic'. But that's- that's me, forcing my opinion on them. Using my anger as a manipulative tool.... So, if it was something that I happen to very much disagree with the students, usually I would take a step back and be more neutral and objective with how I approached it.

In this excerpt, Catherine describes a great deal of awareness that any emotion she felt for particular topics might end up, in fact, silencing students and reducing any room for critical discussion. The behaviour she describes appears antithetical to her use of passionate emotional displays that she reported when teaching students about the sexualisation of young girls described above, and this suggests that Catherine walks a balancing act in her classes. Indeed, one of the interesting findings about Catherine's emotional displays was that her response modulation fluctuated dynamically, not just from topic to topic, but on a moment-to-moment basis within a single interaction. This was revealed as the interview continued:

> R: If it's a topic you think probably everybody does agree with you- probably it's a clear-cut issue. Orphans. (3) Then does that allow you to display-
> C: That allows me to display more emotion and more honest opinion. Except for when like a student disagrees, and then I will usually, again, dial back the emotion, because I don't want to overwhelm their argument with my righteous anger. Um, I want to engage them in the discussion, and (3) critically- not, not like not as in critical discourse analysis, but thinking critically about the topic. Like, why do you hold that particular opinion? Why are you angry at me for having this opinion? Let's explore that.

Here in this excerpt, we can see that Catherine reports to 'dial back' emotional displays when students disagree with her. In other words, while presenting her authentic passionate emotions, Catherine also remains acutely aware of her students' responses and, in reaction to those responses, modulates the displays of her emotions on a momentary basis. In her final interview, it emerged that Catherine's decision-making in these kinds of circumstances had been strongly influenced by a critical incident involving complaints she had received from students. The incident in question occurred within a class of adult learners who attended the university on weekends for leisure purposes, and Catherine reported that some of the students were 'for lack of a better word, attacking' her because she had chosen to teach a class on Japanese human rights violations. Catherine reported that she felt the management at Fukuzaki University did not support her on the issue:

> I wasn't explicitly told 'you have to teach this' or 'you cannot teach this', but they're like, 'you must work with the students.' And I didn't really get support from the faculty from the school, that I could continue teaching what I was teaching. It was more 'you have to change to please the students' was the definite feeling that I was getting.

The impact of this event complicated Catherine's thought processes when displaying content-related emotions to students, and indeed provoked her to feel a greater degree of anxiety. Such anxiety was visible during her second observed class where, after showing students the trailer of her favourite movie *Ip Man* – a kung-fu action movie set during Japan's occupation of China during the 1940s, I observed Catherine to spend a long time explaining the movie to the students, repeatedly highlighting that she felt the 'action is fantastic' and that '*Donnie Yen* is amazing'. When I asked her about this, she explained she was having an emotional response which prompted her to 'contextualise' her movie choice to her students: 'I realized, oh, they could possibly interpret [the themes of the movie] to mean that I am like anti-Japanese. And that's why I think it's a good movie'. Catherine's testimony throughout this section is indicative of the emotion display tension that teachers may feel as they regulate their emotional output continually in response to live student feedback. It also shows how critical incidents in which teachers feel unsupported by management can cause a great deal of stress, not only within the moment, but moving forward, influencing future emotion display decisions. Her behaviour highlights the dynamic complexity of classroom emotions as teachers adapt their emotional output continually in response to classroom events as they endeavour to maintain the most effective working relationships and language learning conditions within the constraints of institutional and sociopolitical pressures.

9.5 Lessons Learned: Holistic and Responsive Emotional Displays

In this chapter I have explored the ways that response modulation was used by the participants, particularly in relation to expression management and the use of self-disclosure. The actions the participants took were driven by a wide range of contextual factors, and the participants negotiated a number of tensions in their decision-making.

The data on response modulation in the study was incredibly complex and rich, and in bringing the chapter to a close, one final point I wish to highlight is that the participants' response modulation was both holistic and responsive. It was holistic in the sense that many of the participants' decisions were informed by internal notions of identity and good teaching practice, which were relatively stable over time, and it was reactive in the sense that the participants employed emotion regulation in a dynamic and responsive way as the interpreted the events that were happening in their own classrooms. The tensions that the participants' experienced and the decisions that they made were to a great deal informed by conflict between these two areas. As language teachers, how should we negotiate our holistic beliefs on good teaching practice in the face of classroom realities? Such a question is surely important for all to consider.

Notes

(1) It should be noted here that the word harassment has been adopted from English into the Japanese language, where it is known as *harasumento*. Many compound nouns now exist in Japanese to describe the varying forms of harassment that affect workers, including *pawaa harasumento* (power harassment) when superiors abuse junior workers, and *matanitii harasumento* (maternity harassment) when pregnant women are discriminated against in the workplace. Karaoke harassment is a real though relatively new idea, and advice exists within Japan on recruitment websites and blogs for how workers might deal with this issue.
(2) This excerpt has also been published in Morris and King (2023).

10 Conclusion: Language Teacher Emotion Regulation

> I feel like a class is like an orchestra playing a symphony. When everything is working, it's like the best music you've ever heard, but if people are out of tune or playing the wrong notes, it sounds (and feels) terrible.
>
> I think it's based on how I used to feel as a student in language classes. Some teachers were so intimidating, and I just didn't want to be there, but others were so friendly, and I loved the class.
>
> The best piece of advice I got when I was doing my high school teacher training was this: 'students don't care what you know until they know that you care.'
>
> Continuous improvement is definitely one place where I find my joy in teaching.
>
> Extracts from correspondence with Peter

A few days after completing our final interview, I received an email from Peter. He said that he had greatly enjoyed the research process (I was very glad), and that he felt motivated to share some additional thoughts with me about emotion regulation and teaching. We sent emails back and forth for a few weeks, and it is those insights which I have included at the opening of this chapter. Peter apologised for the length of his emails and what he called his 'stream of consciousness writing', but he shouldn't have – I was incredibly grateful! Peter had managed to summarise almost everything that I had been studying, thinking about and writing about for the previous six months, and he'd done it in only a few paragraphs.

At the outset of this book, I stated that I had important goals that I wanted to achieve. My first goal was to give practicing teachers such as Peter a voice on their emotion regulation, my second goal was to provide a model of language teacher emotion regulation to support teachers and researchers in their own investigations, and my third goal was to present lessons for the wider field. In this final chapter, I return to these goals.

10.1 Goal 1: The Voices of Practicing Professionals

To begin, I wish to break down Peter's words as I summarise what I think are some of the most important things that can be taken away from this book.

10.1.1 'I feel like a class is like an orchestra playing a symphony'

The conductor is the head of the orchestra, and their actions consider each of the individual players. Similarly at Fukuzaki University, the teachers continually performed emotion regulation with their students in mind. They built relationships, managed misbehaviour, modelled appropriate emotions and supported students through the enaction of caring and supportive personas. These motives were often achieved through the use of response modulation with the participants regulating their facial displays to communicate desires to students.

In many previous studies, emotion regulation has only been explored from the perspective of the teacher's well-being, but at Fukuzaki University, the teachers' regulation of their own emotional states frequently achieved secondary and tertiary instrumental motives with students. The most memorable example of this for me was in Luke's testimony, presented in Chapter 7. Therein, Luke reported that his colleague had been having relational issues with a class that they both shared, and this colleague had consequently caused Luke to feel significant stress. In that situation, Luke employed distraction to reduce negative emotions and present himself as a professional teacher, while simultaneously protecting his learners from unproductive and unwelcome emotional states. Of course, the use of emotion regulation in aid of multiple emotion regulation motives could possibly lead to emotion goal conflict (Morris & King, 2020), and unfortunately, these kinds of tensions sometimes emerged as the participants at Fukuzaki University wrestled with their emotional responsibilities against their hedonic needs. Nevertheless, I strongly believe that studies of emotion regulation need to take seriously the fact that the strategies teachers employ are often driven by multiple motives that relate to both the teacher and the students simultaneously.

10.1.2 'When everything is working, it's like the best music you've ever heard'

One of the most important things I came to understand about emotion regulation was its impact on positive well-being. The participants viewed positive emotions to be utterly essential for the performance of their teaching duties, and they were able to generate these through diverse strategies including job crafting, mental time travel and ontogenetic reappraisal.

A salient contextual factor underscoring the participants' ability to generate positive emotional experiences was the institutional freedom that Fukuzaki University afforded its teaching staff. The fact that the participants were generally free to decide on course directions, materials and activities, meant that they could plan and manage their lessons in accordance with their own notions of best practice. This allowed them to perform emotional personas in line with their personal desires and to use mental time travel effectively.

I want to acknowledge that institutional factors simultaneously had a powerful negative effect on the teachers' well-being, particularly in relation to the working conditions that the participants were employed under. This was seen most saliently in Richard's descriptions of his emotional distancing that was, to a great degree, a result of dissatisfaction with the looming end of his tenure at Fukuzaki University. This finding is a potent reminder that employment insecurity has a salient negative impact on well-being and performance (King, 2016b; Morris & King, 2018). Overall, the evidence in the study suggests that a secure, supportive and flexible approach to teacher management by programme directors and institutions may be what allows teachers to experience the 'best music they've ever heard'.

10.1.3 'If people are out of tune or playing the wrong notes, it sounds (and feels) terrible'

But of course, teaching is a profession that is full of stress, and 'wrong notes' were the result of both the teachers' and students' actions. Fortunately, the participants routinely employed strategies that both pre-empted stress (e.g. proactive coping, emotional distancing, distraction and ontogenetic reappraisal,) and also that responded to the emergence of negative emotions in real time (e.g. problem-directed action and reactive forms of response modulation). While cognitive change in general, and cognitive reappraisal in particular, are most often associated with adaptive well-being (Gross & John, 2003; McRae & Gross, 2020; Troy *et al.*, 2013), I was impressed with the fact that the participants in this study seemingly used all forms of emotion regulation strategies to manage their emotional health.

Luke and Vivienne's attempts to engage with their students on non-class matters showed how teachers may successfully develop a more empathetic understanding of their students' circumstances. Given the highly adaptive nature of these actions, which enabled the participants to experience lower levels of stress in the face of classroom adversity, I believe that ontogenetic reappraisal is perhaps the most potent form of emotion regulation that leads not only to improved well-being in general terms, but also to increased resilience for teachers in future stressful situations. The evidence in this study certainly lends support to attempts to intervene and train teachers in emotion regulation (such as Gregersen *et al.*, 2020). I hope we see much more of this kind of work!

10.1.4 'Some teachers were so intimidating, and I just didn't want to be there, but others were so friendly, and I loved the class'

Teachers are people too, with their own successes, triumphs, fears and failures, and in all of the interviews I was continually impressed by the complexity of the intrapersonal contextual factors underpinning the participants' emotion regulation. The teachers' own histories, both as educators and learners, had a particularly powerful impact on their emotion regulation motives and goals. Nowhere was this seen more than when the participants regulated their emotions for identity-related reasons. It seems that the teachers recognised that choosing to be 'intimidating', or 'friendly', or 'engaging', or 'authoritative' would exert a powerful influence on both the students and themselves. Nathan, for example, felt a congruence between his identity as a caring teacher and his performance of caring emotions that meant he didn't feel undue tension under potentially stressful situations.

Perhaps unsurprisingly, the desire to be fun, positive, caring and motivating was prolific in the data, affirming other studies which suggest that non-Japanese teachers enact these expected classroom identities. I believe it was hugely important, though, that the experiences of the teachers at Fukuzaki University challenged previous literature on the motivational burden in Japan (King, 2016b; Lawrence & Nagashima, 2020). The results showed that it was possible for teachers to be fun, positive and caring in ways that actually increased their subjective well-being when such emotional personas aligned with the teachers' own notions of good teaching (see also Morris, 2022).

10.1.5 'Students don't care what you know until they know that you care'

Strong arguments have been made to view language teaching as essentially a relational endeavour (Gkonou, 2022; Gkonou & Mercer, 2017, 2018; Gkonou & Miller, 2023), and following this study I can only echo and offer my support to these calls. Students emerged as an important source of both positive and negative emotion, and throughout the testimony it was seen that the ways the teachers carried themselves in interactions led to repercussions which reverberated across time. The teachers had a clear awareness of this fact, as evidenced by their discussions of why they chose to implement creative and engaging activities and perform positive emotional displays. Both of these decisions were often driven by the realisation that students' experiences of positive emotions would be reflected back onto the teacher.

Importantly, teacher–student relationships influenced not only the emotions that the teachers experienced, but also the emotion regulation actions that they engaged in. The quality of the relationships between individual students and teachers, for example, were particularly important factors guiding the use of two strategies: physical avoidance, which was employed when the relationships were strained, and in-situ reappraisal, which was employed when the relationships were positive. Empathy was a key facilitator in these kinds of emotion regulation decisions, with those teachers who had developed empathy for their students' personal and learning circumstances more able to manage their emotional responses during interactions.

10.1.6 'Continuous improvement is definitely one place where I find my joy in teaching'

The final point that I want to emphasise is the extraordinary degree to which emotion regulation featured in the participants' lives and work. Emotion regulation was ubiquitous in the observed classes, influencing almost every moment of teaching, and each of the participants employed a diverse range of strategies in accordance with all categories described by the process model of emotion regulation. The motives of the participants' uses of emotion regulation were also highly variable, and the teachers at Fukuzaki University showed a keen awareness of how emotional decision-making affected virtually all aspects of their teaching. In addition to helping them find their joy in teaching, emotion regulation informed the ways that the participants planned courses, the ways that they created and selected materials, the ways that they prepared in the mornings, the ways that they dealt with stress, the ways that they presented content, the ways that they engaged students in their materials, the ways that they interacted with students they liked, the ways that the interacted with students they didn't like, the ways that they organised their classrooms, the ways that they dealt with classroom difficulties, the ways that they developed and projected their identities and the ways that they addressed institutional and sociopolitical expectations. The study left me under no doubt that emotion regulation is a critical classroom competence that was skilfully employed by the participants for diverse purposes in the pursuit of most effective teaching. While Zembylas (2002: 89) observed that emotions influence 'almost everything' a teacher does, I would like to advance that sentiment by asserting that it is emotion regulation which is at the heart of almost every decision a teacher makes.

10.2 Goal 2: The Language Teacher Emotion Regulation Model (LTERM)

In Chapter 2 of this book, I presented a preliminary model of language teacher emotion regulation. The model was tentative because at that point I was unable to present any taxonomy of emotion regulation strategies and motives. Now, at the completion of the study central to this book, I am in a position to complete this model.

10.2.1 Language teacher emotion regulation strategy choices

This study reaffirmed numerous other studies (e.g. Bielak & Mystkowska-Wiertelak, 2020; Heydarnejad et al., 2021) by revealing that teachers employ a diverse range of emotion regulation strategies during the course of their work in accordance with all categories of strategy described by the process model of emotion regulation: namely, situation selection strategies, situation modification strategies, attention deployment strategies, cognitive change strategies and response modulation strategies (Gross, 1998, 2014, 2015). These strategies were used to regulate both positive and negative emotions, and as has been suggested in general psychology (Heiy & Cheavens, 2014), multiple strategies were frequently employed simultaneously to achieve required outcomes.

10.2.2 Language teacher emotion regulation motive choices

In general psychology, Tamir and colleagues (Mauss & Tamir, 2014; Tamir, 2016; Tamir et al., 2020) have proposed that emotion regulation motives can be split into two general categories: hedonic motives, referring to the use of emotion regulation for the purpose of generating and maintaining positive well-being, and instrumental motives, for purposes relating to pragmatic outcomes not related to well-being. This study affirmed this general finding, but also revealed four subcategories of hedonic motives and six categories of instrumental motives, which are valuable for future teachers and researchers exploring this topic. These subcategories are visualised in Figure 10.1.

The diagram highlights that hedonic emotion regulation was performed with four distinctive submotives? The participants regulated their emotions by increasing positive emotions (*prohedonic: increase positive*),

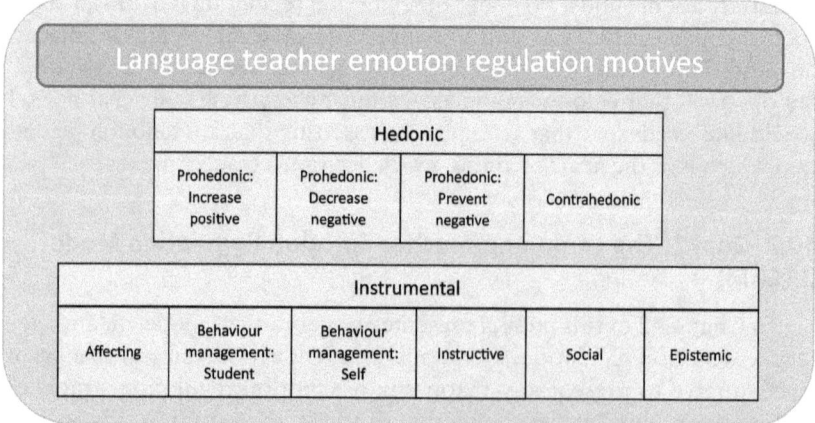

Figure 10.1 Language teacher emotion regulation motives

by decreasing negative emotions (*prohedonic: decrease negative*), by actively preventing negative emotions from arising (*prohedonic: prevent negative*) and by increasing their experiences of negative emotions (*contrahedonic*).

The diagram also indicates that there were six instrumental submotives. Firstly, the teachers regulated for *affecting* purposes. In other words, they regulated emotions to influence the emotional states of their students. The teachers aimed to increase their students' positive emotional experiences, build encouraging emotional atmospheres and ensure that their students were engaged with the content of the lessons. Secondly and thirdly, the teachers employed their emotion regulation for behaviour management purposes. Some strategies, such as the modulated and unmodulated expression of negative emotions, helped the participating teachers to direct the off-task behaviours of students (*behaviour management: student*), while other strategies, such as mental time travel, targeted the teacher's own behaviours (*behaviour management: self*). Given their different targets, it is appropriate to view behavioural management towards teachers and students as two distinct emotion regulation motives. Fourthly the teachers regulated for *instructive* purposes. In these cases, the emotion regulation used by the participants was directly related to the teaching of lessons, allowing the teachers to build emotional connections between the students and the materials being taught. The fifth motive was for *social* purposes. Emotion regulation supported the teachers to build strong relationships with their students. The sixth and final instrumental motive that emerged in the data was the use of emotion regulation for *epistemic* purposes. Through such emotion regulation, the participants enacted desired or expected personas in the presence of their students.

10.2.3 Mapping motives and strategies

The various emotion regulation motives listed above emerged through the central study in this book, but they are affirmed by the fact that they each motive was achieved with almost an entirely unique variety of emotion regulation strategies. To highlight this fact, I have mapped each emotion regulation motive to the strategies that were employed in aid of them by the participants at Fukuzaki University (see Figure 10.2). As can be seen in the diagram, each motive was achieved by a unique set of strategies. To exemplify with one example, it can be seen in the figure that the strategy choices used by the participants to influence the behaviour of their students (*behaviour management: student*) were entirely different from those used to manage their own behaviour (*behaviour management: self*). While student behaviours were managed through three forms of response modulation, the teachers' own behaviours were managed through mental time travel and in-situ cognitive reappraisal.

10.2.4 The completed language teacher emotion regulation model (LTERM)

Finally, I am in a position to present the completed language teacher emotion regulation model (LTERM), which can be seen in Figure 10.3. Astute observers will note that the left side of the diagram remains unchanged from the preliminary model proposed in Chapter 2 of this book. In other words, the model of language teacher emotional experiences that was theorised from psychological literature proved to be accurate and relevant to the study at Fukuzaki University. In brief, this side of the model illustrates that teacher emotions have both intrapersonal and interpersonal dimensions that emerge through processes of appraisal as teachers interact with various stakeholders in their professional sphere. Simultaneously, it also shows that these emotions are informed by the teacher's historical experiences and bound up within institutional and sociopolitical circumstances.

The right-hand side of the model has changed significantly and now highlights the various emotion regulation strategies and motives that language teachers employ in their work. All 10 of the emotion regulation motives that emerged in the data have been included, as well as all forms of emotion regulation strategy. The arrows between indicate the interaction between the various motives and strategy choices.

Figures 10.2 and 10.3 are not meant to be final products, but snapshots. The diagrams reveal how the teachers at Fukuzaki University regulated their emotions using a variety of strategies for a variety of motives, but it is likely, given the vast range of emotion regulation motives and strategies that exist, that the diagrams will continue to be developed as emotion regulation receives further attention in different contexts. What I hope and believe is that the diagrams provide important visual representations of language teacher emotion regulation and a roadmap for others wishing to explore this crucial skill. I welcome readers to employ the language teacher emotion regulation model in their own research, to adapt it and refine it, to interrogate it and critique it. In doing so, we can continue to push our understanding forward, supporting teachers in new ways. After all, improving the lives and work of those in the classroom is undoubtedly the most important goal of any study.

10.3 Goal 3: Lessons for the Field

My final goal for this book was to reveal lessons for the many stakeholders in the language teaching industry. In the final moments of the introductory chapter, I presented a number of questions related to this aim, and to conclude this book I wish to answer them.

Conclusion: Language Teacher Emotion Regulation 157

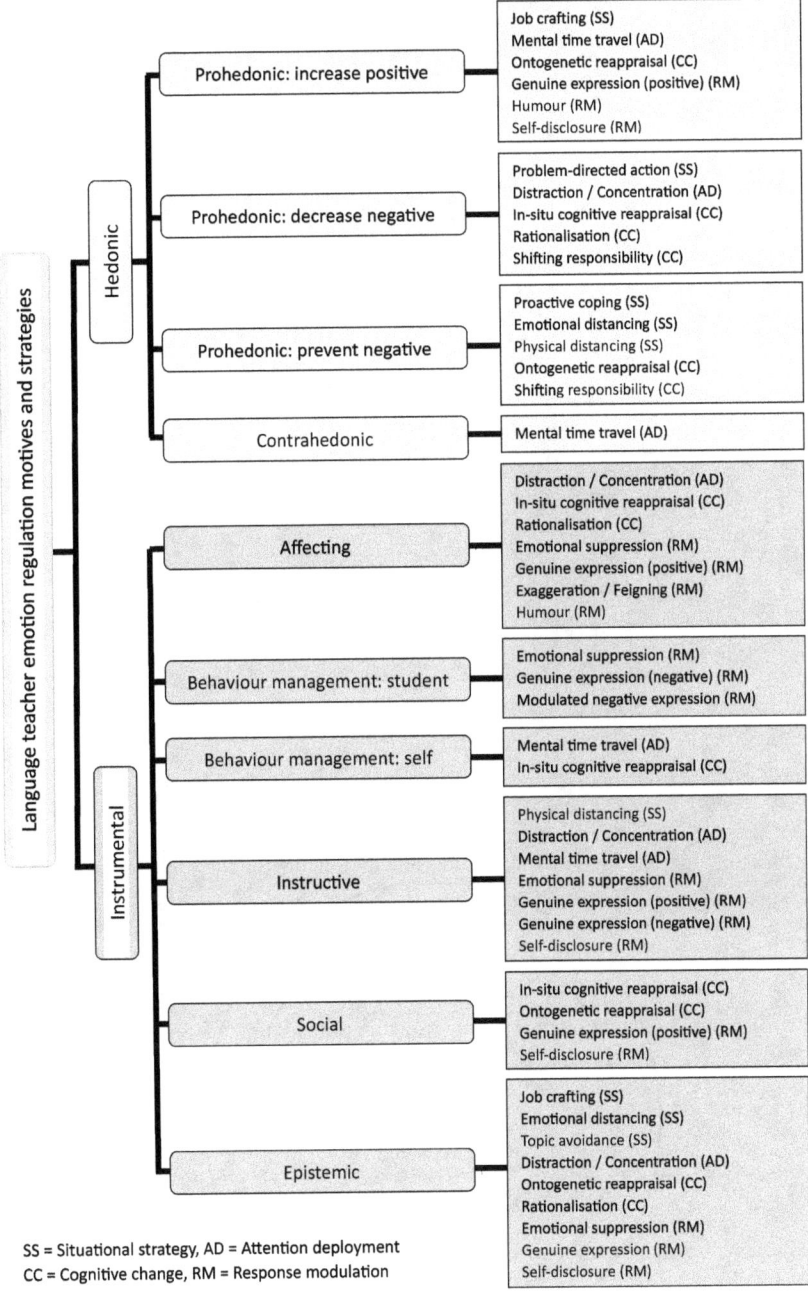

Figure 10.2 Emotion regulation motives and corresponding strategies

158 Language Teacher Emotion Regulation

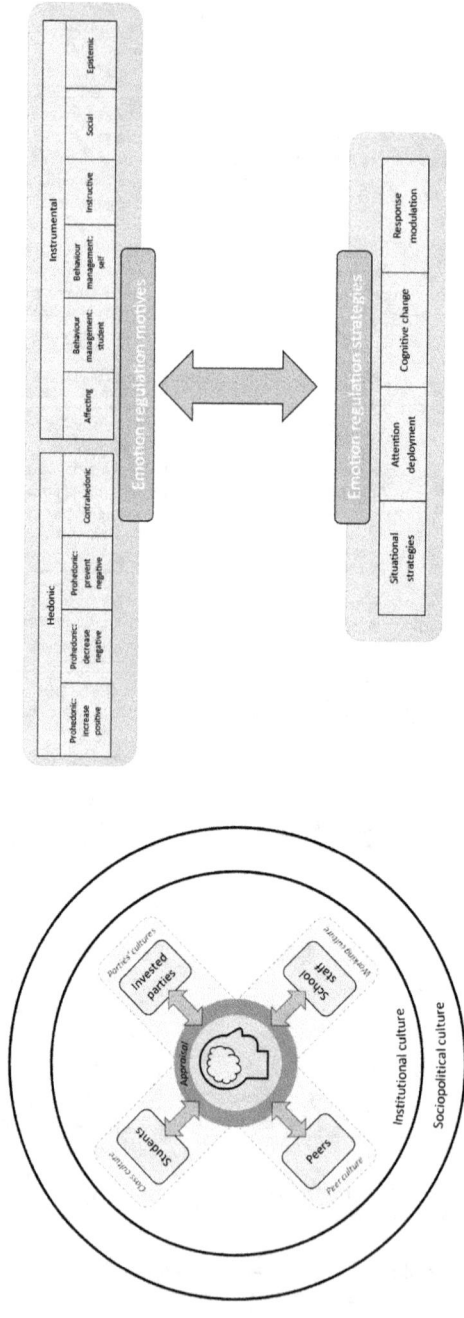

Figure 10.3 The language teacher emotion regulation model (LTERM)

10.3.1 How can language teachers understand their own emotion regulation practices more deeply, and make more adaptive choices for themselves and their students?

This study revealed some very potent emotion regulation strategies that simultaneously supported classroom learning and emotional wellbeing. Therefore, teachers who are struggling with the emotional dimension of their classroom practice may receive a significant amount of benefit from finding ways to craft more meaning and joy from their work, from maintaining stress-reducing routines to proactively manage the potential for negative emotions, from generating positive emotional states by planning interesting classes, and from developing a habit of using mental time travel to become excited about the teaching of classes. Moreover, since positive emotional displays were frequently reflected back from the students in this study, there is the potential that teachers could have a powerful influence over their own emotions simply by choosing to display more positive expressions.

Dealing with negative emotions and classroom issues is equally a salient part of teaching work. The results here suggest that while it is not problematic to distract attention away from sources of stress for a short time, it is most effective for teachers to resolve any problems they are facing with students quickly in a direct and controlled manner.

One of the most effective, and indeed basic, strategies for the proactive regulation of emotions in this study was the use of learning logs. These took the form of structured or unstructured journals in which the students could record reflections of their lives and learning (see e.g. Murphey, 1993; Woo & Murphey, 1999). They helped to build an empathetic understanding of students' life experiences, which afforded a greater ability to reappraise classroom stressors. Such logs may have a particularly strong effect on teachers when they are moving to work in unfamiliar cultures.

Teachers should not simply be left to their own devices when considering emotional issues in their classrooms, and trainers should consider being proactive in helping teachers to reflect on emotion regulation. Reflection is likely to help teachers to better understand the motives and factors lying underneath their decision-making, as well as provide them with alternative and more adaptive strategy choices. Since critical incidents emerged as valuable catalysts for growth, asking teachers to recall recent emotionally demanding events is a potentially fruitful starting point. Reflective journaling tools that address emotion regulation choices may also be powerful, and I have created and detailed one such framework, the *frustration regulation journal*, elsewhere (Morris, 2019).

I also agree with other researchers (e.g. King *et al.*, 2020; Martínez Agudo, 2018b) who have suggested that overt emotion regulation training programmes be established. Certainly, educators at all levels of experience would benefit from a greater understanding of the various ways that they can manage their emotions, both in consideration of their own well-being, and of how their choices might influence the students in their classrooms. Since student behavioural concerns emerged as a salient source of stress in this study, a focal point for training programmes would be to consider how teachers may employ their emotional displays to negotiate classroom issues while also simultaneously managing stress. More direct instruction on the emotional responsibilities and expectations that exist in different cultures would also be a useful addition, particularly for teachers who are to be working in unfamiliar contexts. I welcome recent studies like those of Gregersen et al. (2020), Maher (2020) and Nakamura et al. (2021), who have begun to explore emotion regulation training with teachers and students, and hope that such work continues in the future.

10.3.2 Must institutions do more to support the emotional demands of teaching?

The most important recommendations that emerged from this study for Japanese higher education institutions concerned the ways that they can support and also inhibit teachers' subjective well-being through their management practices. For the participants at Fukuzaki University, an admirable degree of autonomy was afforded teachers with regards to classroom and content decisions, as well as with their identity enaction and emotion display choices. This allowed the participants to teach in ways which best suited their own notions of best practice and, equally, gave them the power they needed to regulate their emotions in highly adaptive ways. The level of autonomy desired may vary by teacher, but supportive and flexible approaches are likely to allow teachers to employ more adaptive emotion regulation.

Since employment conditions emerged as a salient factor negatively influencing well-being, this study reaffirms other findings that have suggested that the use of insecure, limited-term employment contracts in Japan may have a negative impact on teachers (King, 2016b; Morris & King, 2018; Murray, 2013). Of course, the use of adjunct lecturers is a worldwide issue, and it is hoped that this study reveals, at least in part, how these kinds of conditions can negatively influence language teachers and the work they do with students. The obvious recommendation for institutions here is to provide more support and security for teachers.

10.3.3 How should researchers best explore emotional decision-making?

Throughout this book I have asserted and shown that researchers should remain open to the fact that emotion regulation is not a singularly motivated activity. The impact of emotion regulation on well-being cannot be fully understood without also considering what other higher-order motives are being sought. Complexity-informed methods afford explorations which can attend to motive, strategy and context simultaneously, and should be seriously contemplated by other researchers along with the use of multiple data collection methods.

For those researchers seeking to explore emotion regulation within their own contexts I cannot stress enough the power of observational and introspective data collection. The use of stimulated recall in this study proved invaluable, providing a whole host of benefits. Firstly, the observations provided rich contextualisation of the general emotion regulation practices participants described in their initial interviews. This meant that when a teacher described themselves as 'caring', or 'fun' or 'serious', I was able to understand in great detail how such emotions were conveyed in front of the class and in interactions with individual students. Secondly, the observations allowed me to pinpoint key incidents and focus on these during subsequent interviews. This meant that I was able to understand the participants' explanations in greater clarity as they discussed their thoughts and decision-making on incidents that we had both been present for. Thirdly, the stimulated recalls afforded me detailed notes of crucial emotional moments during the participants' lessons. This meant that I was more able to provide thick and interesting descriptions of the emotional incidents and experiences to you, the reader. A final benefit, which was also reported by Gkonou and Mercer (2017), was that the stimulated recall sessions helped to reveal emotion regulation decisions and behaviours which might have otherwise gone unnoticed even by the participants themselves. Consequently, there were moments of realisation in the interviews which were both inherently interesting, and also ethically important – certainly a benefit of the research for the participants may have been these opportunities for new understanding and growth.

10.3.4 Where should we go next?

What a wonderful time to begin researching emotion regulation! The field is still in its infancy and the possibilities are numerous. Personally, I have been surprised that so few studies have integrated teachers' and students' perspectives. Teachers might report that they regulate their emotions for a particular purpose, but this does not mean that their desired goals are corroborated, or even understood by learners. In fact, given the complex ways that the contextual factors in this study interacted with emotional displays and behaviours, it seems critical to now investigate emotion regulation from the perspective of language teachers and their students simultaneously. One way that this could be done is by employing stimulated recall protocols with both teachers and students on the same classroom event to ascertain what triangulation or divergence may be seen.

While this study is wholly qualitative in nature, it seems prudent to quantify the results through, for example, surveying or psychological testing. A relevant second future research direction would be to try to understand to what degree the results that were obtained herein apply more broadly to the experiences of other language teachers in other contexts. Such data may ultimately afford greater understanding of how emotion regulation actions can support teachers to deal with issues that affect us all.

This study dealt with a single and defined context. While I chose the focus of non-Japanese EFL teachers working at a Japanese university with care, there remains a need to investigate other teacher groups. Work need not be limited to tertiary institutions, nor to Japan, and certainly I would welcome investigations with other teaching levels and in other cultural contexts.

Finally, while there have been some recent attempts at emotion regulation interventions with teachers and students (Gregersen *et al.*, 2020; Maher, 2020; Nakamura *et al.*, 2021), the results to date have not always been successful. Certainly, one of the main goals of emotion regulation research should be to improve the emotional lives of teachers. My own opinion is that the intervention studies thus far have adopted an overtly cognitive approach, focusing primarily on cognitive change strategies. I believe that a more substantial and holistic training programme that attends to the whole range of emotion regulation strategies may well be the answer.

10.4 Concluding Remarks

Hargreaves (1998) commented over 25 years ago on the fact that educators need to be skilled in their use of emotions to most ably reach their students:

> It is not just a matter of knowing one's subject, being efficient, having the correct competences, or learning all the right techniques. Good teachers are not just well-oiled machines. They are emotional, passionate beings who connect with their students and fill their work and their classes with pleasure, creativity, challenge and joy. (1998: 835)

This book, I hope, takes some steps towards showing how language teachers, specifically non-Japanese EFL teachers working in the Japanese university context, achieve good teaching through processes of emotion regulation, while also showing that teachers and their emotions do not exist independently of the historical, internal, interpersonal and wider social climates that they live and work within.

Appendices

Appendix A: Semi Structured Interview Protocol

A version of this instrument has also been published in Morris & King, 2023

A. Opening speech

Thank you for agreeing to take part in this research. Today, I am going to ask you about a number of topics related to emotions. For example I will ask about the emotions you feel and display when you teach, and how and why you control your emotions when you teach. This should take no more than 45-60 minutes. I'd once again like to assure you that your answers will be kept confidential, and that if you do not feel comfortable with a question, then you do not have to answer it. That said, your honest answers will be very valuable to my study. I would also like to remind you that your participation in this research is voluntary. If you have any questions about the research, or if you wish to withdraw, please email me at any time. Do you have any questions before we begin the interview? I would also like to introduce emotion regulation. Emotion regulation means altering your emotions, and this could mean many things such as extending or shortening emotions, hiding emotions, exaggerating emotions, trying to stop emotions, trying to start an emotion.

B. Opening questions: setting the tone and building success

- ☐ Please tell me a little about your teaching career so far and what has led you to this point.

C. Content questions * questions are adapted from Sutton (2004), ** from Gross and Richards (2006)

Opening

- ☐ I would like you to think of a time in the past week or two when you tried to manage your emotions in the classroom. Go ahead and take a few moments to think of a time when you tried to alter your emotions. When you're ready, I'd like you to describe this to me in as much detail as you can**.

- [ ] You mentioned the emotion(s) _____. Other common emotions are on this list. Could you look at the list and tell me which 2 or 3 seem most relevant to you when teaching?*

Emotional labour/epistemic motives
- [ ] What kinds of emotions do you think teachers should display in the classroom?
- [ ] What kinds of emotions do you think teachers should hide in the classroom?

Performance/social motives
- [ ] Do you use your emotions as a tool when teaching? Why? How do you use them?
- [ ] How do you use your emotions to influence the relationships you form with students?
- [ ] Have you got a student who is brilliant? Why? What do you do when you interact with them?
- [ ] Have you got a student who frustrates you? Why? What do you do when you interact with them?

Well-being motives
- [ ] How do you deal with negative emotions (e.g. frustration and anger) in the classroom?
- [ ] What things do you do as part of your work to generate more joy from teaching?
- [ ] What classroom incident has caused you the most stress this year?

General questions
- [ ] How do you use humour in your teaching?
- [ ] What impact does your preparation have on your emotions?
- [ ] How does this institution influence your emotions in the classroom and how you manage them?
- [ ] How does being in Japan influence your emotions in the classroom and how you regulate them?

Keep focusing on questions of how, why, and on ER strategies!

D. Closing questions
- [ ] What should I have asked you that I didn't think to ask?

List of emotions

Anger, joy, frustration, fear, sadness, excitement, disgust, surprise, love/affection, disappointment, embarrassment/shame, guilt, anxiety.

Appendix B: Observation Instrument

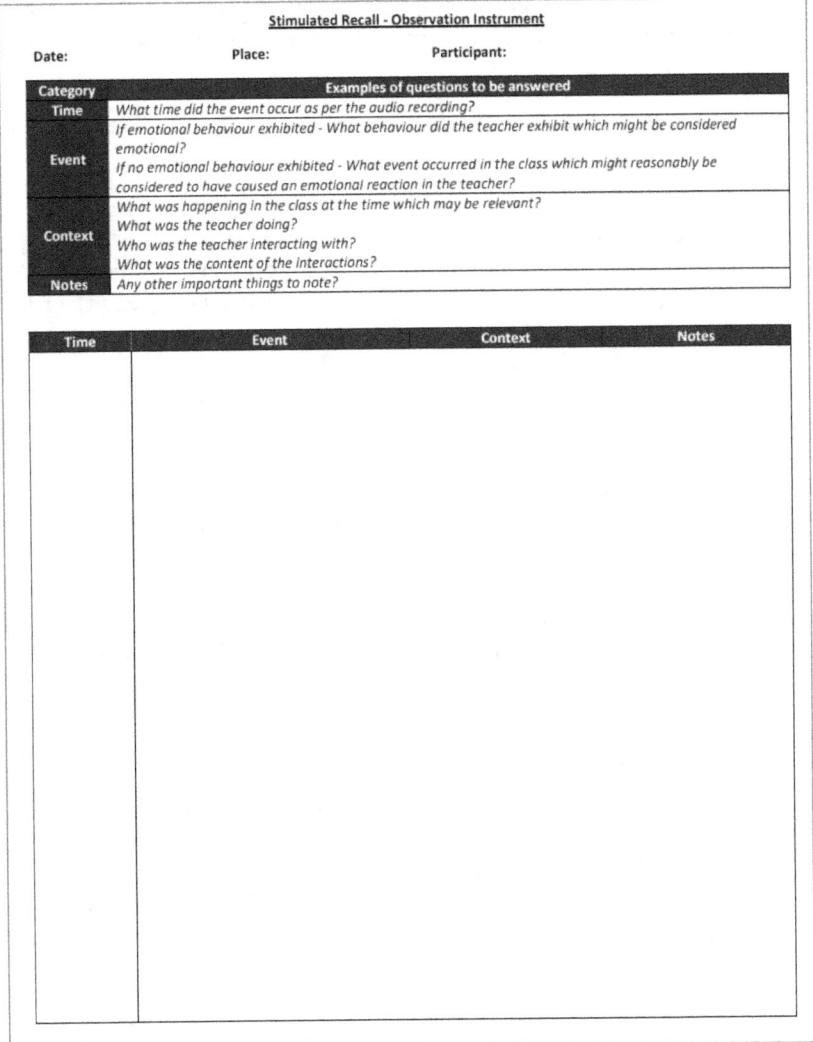

Appendix C: Stimulated Recall Interview Protocol

Adapted from Gass & Mackey, 2017.

Goals of the stimulated recall

1. To understand the internal thoughts and processes of teachers during incidents of outwardly displayed emotions during the observed class.

2. To understand the internal thoughts and processes of teachers during incidents which may reasonably be considered to have caused an emotional reaction in the teacher, which may or may not have been outwardly displayed.

A: During observed class

1. Arrive at class in good time (10 minutes before class), greet the teacher and then take a seat at the front of the classroom at the side.
2. Set the main recording device in a location where I can read the time on it, and ensure that it is facing the teacher. Set up the back-up recording device and begin recording on both.
3. During the observation, take notes on the lesson using the observation instrument form. Record:
   a. The time from the audio recorder.
   b. The events. That it, either the emotional behaviour exhibited by the teacher, or in the absence of observable behaviour, the classroom event which may reasonably be considered to have caused an emotional reaction in the teacher.
   c. The context. That is, the antecedents of the emotional event, the interactions the teacher is engaged in at the time of the event etc.
   d. Any additional notes.

B: Stimulated recall protocol

1. After moving to the interview room, ask the participant if they are comfortable and ready to begin (Drink? Bathroom?).
2. Begin recording the interview.
   Say: *The purpose of the interview today is to examine some of the events that happened in the class. Although I was able to observe and record these events, I wasn't able to know what you were feeling and thinking, so I'd like to ask you questions about your internal thoughts and feelings. Discussing emotions is very personal. I'd once again like to assure you that your answers will be kept confidential, and that if you do not feel comfortable with a question, then you do not have to answer it. That said, your honest answers will be very valuable to my study.*

   I'm going to ask you about different events from the class. I'd like you to try to remember what you were thinking and feeling then, when the incident took place, not what you think and feel about it now. This is very important.

   I'm going to be using two sources to help you recall the events. Firstly, I'm going to be using the notes that I took in class, which I can describe to you. Secondly, I have the recording of the class.

Are these instructions clear?

3. Hand the participant a blank sheet of paper. Explain the following: *Please think about the class you taught. On this paper, could you please write a list of emotions that you experienced while teaching the class.* Answer any questions the participant may have, and give them time to write their list.
4. Ask the teacher which emotion word they would like to begin by discussing. Following this, proceed through the list of emotion words. If required, describe events to the teacher using my notes, and play the recording as necessary.
Questions to ask about each emotion word and incident:

What emotion were you feeling right then?

What caused you to feel that emotion?

What were you thinking right then?

What were you doing to control/regulate your emotions then?

Why did you want to control your emotions? (focus on context)

Why did you want to control your emotions by using that method? (focus on context)

If the participant cannot answer, ask: *thinking about that situation now, why do you think you felt that way? Do you think you were regulating your emotion in any way there? Why and how?*

Try not to interrupt too much, other than providing back channelling responses such as:

Oh, mmm, great, good, I see, Uh-huh, Ok.

5. When all the events have been discussed, ask:
Were there any other times during the class where you remember feeling strong emotions?

If the participant gives an answer, then refer back and ask them what they were thinking at the time.

C: Follow up to initial interviews

If I have any follow-up questions that I would like to ask concerning the initial interviews, I would ask them now.

D. Ending the interview

Thank the participant for their time and help with this research

Appendix D: Transcription Conventions

Adapted from Wray & Bloomer, 2006

Symbol	Meaning	Example
(0.5)	Short pause of less than 1 second	I don't really kind of (0.5) get that upset about it
(#)	Pause of # seconds	... but (2) yeah it's like...
xxx...	Indicates text has been removed for the sake of readability. The text is less than a whole sentence.	whoever the leader of the group is... they know that they're going to be called
xxx....	Indicates text has been removed for the sake of readability. The text is more than a whole sentence.	I get a lot of joy out of their joy.... Pride in helping them
xxx-	Indicates an unfinished utterance	I arrived shortly bef- It was earlier than usual.
[indecipherable]	Unclear utterance	...stressed and things got [indecipherable] and you just think actually
[xxx]	Indicates a non-linguistic feature	Sure, please do [laughs]
[pseudonym]	Redacted sections for reasons of confidentiality and ease of understanding	When I met [Student Y]
[translation]	Indicates an English translation of a Japanese word	'carrying their own *bento* [lunchbox] and injuries',

Appendix E: Member Checking Instructions

The following written instructions were provided to participants when checking their testimonies.

Thank you very much for agreeing to member check the testimony from the interviews for my study.

Over the following pages, I have included excerpts of my final paper, and in each of these excerpts, your testimony places a significant role. In the excerpts below your pseudonym is 'xxx'. In each of the excerpts, you will find extracts of your testimony from the interviews. You will also find some of my interpretations of the testimonies. The interviews we recorded have been transcribed verbatim, and include pausing, errors and back tracking. It may feel strange to read your words in this way, but they reflect the interview itself and are an important part of the final report. Since the excerpts are a work in progress, I would be grateful if you would not share them with other people.

Purpose of the member checking

The purpose of the member checking is to help me to ensure that I am interpreting your words in a way that fairly represents your testimony. Importantly, I wish to ensure that I have not misunderstood the ideas that you discussed in the interviews, and so I am seeking comments from you as to whether you agree with the testimony and my interpretations.

It must be acknowledged that a significant amount of time has elapsed since the interviews took place, and undoubtedly you are not the same teacher that you were. For this reason, please do not contribute new insights on who you are as a teacher now. Instead, please focus on the testimonies as snapshots of the time when they took place.

What to do

When checking the testimony, I would be grateful if you could do the following:

a. If you agree with what is written, please do nothing, or add a short comment indicating that you agree.
b. If you disagree with what is written, or feel that I have misunderstood your words, please add a comment explaining what you think is incorrect.
c. If you cannot remember saying the words, or are not sure what the idea represents, please add this as a comment.
d. If you have a question about the testimony, or are worried about something, please feel free to leave a comment.

When checking the testimony, please do not do the following:

a. Please do not fix grammatical errors
b. Please do not elaborate on points unless you think that I have misunderstood your testimony.

Once again, I would like to thank you for your support with my study and for all the time you have donated to this project.

References

Acheson, K., Taylor, J. and Luna, K. (2016) The burnout spiral: The emotion labor of five rural U.S. foreign language teachers. *The Modern Language Journal* 100 (2), 522–537.
Aida, Y. (1994) Examination of Horwitz, Horwitz and Cope's construct of foreign language anxiety: The case of students of Japanese. *The Modern Language Journal* 78 (2), 155–168.
Amirian, S.M.R. and Behshad, A. (2016) Emotional intelligence and self-efficacy of Iranian teachers: A research study on university degree and teaching experience. *Journal of Language Teaching and Research* 7 (3), 548–558.
Andrade, M. and Williams, K. (2009) Foreign language learning anxiety in Japanese EFL university classes: Physical, emotional, expressive and verbal reactions. *Sophia Junior College Faculty Journal* 29, 1–24.
Appleby, R. (2013a) Desire in translation: White masculinity and TESOL. *TESOL Quarterly* 47 (1), 122–147.
Appleby, R. (2013b) Singleness, marriage, and the construction of heterosexual masculinities: Australian men teaching English in Japan. *PORTAL: Journal of Multidisciplinary International Studies* 10 (1), 1–21.
Arnold, M.B. (1959) From perception to emotion and action. *Acta Psychologica* 15, 406–417.
Arnold, J. and Brown, H.D. (1999) A map of the terrain. In J. Arnold (ed.) *Affect in Language Learning* (pp. 1–24). Cambridge University Press.
Ashforth, B.E. and Humphrey, R.H. (1993) Emotional labor in service roles: The influence of identity. *The Academy of Management Review* 18 (1), 88–115.
Aspinall, R.W. (2005) University entrance in Japan. In J.S. Eades, R. Goodman and Y. Hada (eds) *The 'Big Bang' in Japanese Higher Education: The 2004 Reforms and the Dynamics of Change* (pp. 199–218). Trans Pacific Press.
Aspinall, R.W. (2006) Using the paradigm of 'small cultures' to explain policy failure in the case of foreign language education in Japan. *Japan Forum* 18 (2), 255–274.
Aspinwall, L.G. and Taylor, S.E. (1997) A stitch in time: Self-regulation and proactive coping. *Psychological Bulletin* 121 (3), 417–436.
Auerbach, E.R. (1993) Reexamining English only in the ESL classroom. *TESOL Quarterly* 27 (1), 9–32.
Azari Noughabi, M., Fekri, N. and Kazemkhah Hasankiadeh, F. (2022) The contribution of psychological wellbeing and emotion-regulation to foreign language teaching enjoyment. *Frontiers in Psychology* 13, 889133.
Bailey, K. (2007) Akogare, ideology, and Charisma Man mythology: Reflections on ethnographic research in English language schools in Japan. *Gender, Place and Culture* 14 (5), 585–608.
Barrett, L.F. (2014) The conceptual act theory: A précis. *Emotion Review* 6 (4), 292–297.
Barrett, L.F. (2017) *How Emotions are Made: The Secret Life of the Brain*. Pan Books.
Batstone, R. (2010) Issues and options in sociocognition. In R. Batstone (ed.) *Sociocognitive Perspectives on Language Use and Language Learning* (pp. 3–23). Oxford University Press.

Bekleyen, N. (2009) Helping teachers become better English students: Causes, effects, and coping strategies for foreign language listening anxiety. *System* 37 (4), 664–675.

Benesch, S. (2017) *Emotions and English Language Teaching: Exploring Teachers' Emotion Labour*. Routledge.

Benesch, S. (2018) Emotions as agency: Feeling rules, emotion labor, and English language teachers' decision-making. *System* 79, 60–69.

Benesch, S. (2020) Theorising emotions from a critical perspective: English language teachers' emotion labour when responding to students writing. In C. Gkonou, J.-M. Dewaele and J. King (eds) *The Emotional Rollercoaster of Language Teaching* (pp. 53–69). Multilingual Matters.

Bielak, J. and Mystkowska-Wiertelak, A. (2022) Language teachers' interpersonal learner-directed emotion-regulation strategies. *Language Teaching Research* 26 (6), 1082–1105.

Biesta, G.J.J. and Burbules, N.C. (2003) *Pragmatism and Educational Research*. Rowman and Littlefield Publishers Inc.

Boiger, M. and Mesquita, B. (2012) The construction of emotion in interactions, relationships, and cultures. *Emotion Review* 4 (3), 221–229.

Borg, S. (2006) *Teacher Cognition and Language Education: Research and Practice*. Bloomsbury Publishing Plc.

Brackett, M.A., Palomera, R., Mojsa-Kaja, J., Reyes, M.R. and Salovey, P. (2010) Emotion-regulation ability, burnout, and job satisfaction among British secondary-school teachers. *Psychology in the Schools* 47 (4), 406–417.

Bradley, W. (2009) Administrative work as reform in Japanese higher education. In G.S. Poole and C. Ya-Chen (eds) *Higher Education in East Asia: Neoliberalism and the Japanese Professoriate* (pp. 33–48). Sense Publishers.

Braunstein, L.M., Gross, J.J. and Ochsner, K.N. (2017) Explicit and implicit emotion regulation: A multi-level framework. *Social Cognitive and Affective Neuroscience* 12 (10), 1545–1557.

Breckenridge, Y. and Erling, E.J. (2011) The native speaker English teacher and the politics of globalisation in Japan. In P. Seargeant (ed.) *English in Japan in the Era of Globalisation* (pp. 80–100). Palgrave Macmillan.

Breen, L. (2007) The researcher 'in the middle': Negotiating the insider/outsider dichotomy. *The Australian Community Psychologist* 19 (1), 163–174.

Breen, M.P. (1985) The social context for language learning – A neglected situation? *Studies in Second Language Acquisition* 7 (2), 135–158.

Britzman, D. (1986) Cultural myths in the making of a teacher: Biography and social structure in teacher education. *Harvard Educational Review* 56 (4), 442–457.

Bryant, A. and Charmaz, K. (2011) Grounded theory. In M. Williams and W.P. Vogt (eds) *The SAGE Handbook of Innovation in Social Research Methods* (pp. 205–227). SAGE Publications.

Bryant, F. (2003) Savoring Beliefs Inventory (SBI): A scale for measuring beliefs about savouring. *Journal of Mental Health* 12 (2), 175–196.

Bryman, A. (2006) Integrating quantitative and qualitative research: How is it done? *Qualitative Research* 6 (1), 97–113.

Butler, C. (2019) The ronin teacher: Making a living as a full-time part-timer at Japanese universities. In P. Wadden and C.C. Hale (eds) *Teaching English at Japanese Universities: A New Handbook* (pp. 25–31). Routledge.

Butzkamm, W. (2003) We only learn language once. The role of the mother tongue in FL classrooms: Death of a dogma. *The Language Learning Journal* 28 (1), 29–39.

Candela, A.G. (2019) Exploring the function of member checking. *The Qualitative Report* 24 (3), 619–628.

Carlson, J.A. (2010) Avoiding traps in member checking. *The Qualitative Report* 15 (5) 1102–1113.

Cayanus, J.L. (2004) Effective instructional practice: Using teacher self-disclosure as an instructional tool. *Communication Teacher* 18 (1), 6–9.

Cayanus, J.L. and Martin, M.M. (2008) Teacher self-disclosure: Amount, relevance, and negativity. *Communication Quarterly* 56 (3), 325–341.

Cayanus, J.L., Martin, M.M. and Goodboy, A.K. (2009) The relation between teacher self-disclosure and student motives to communicate. *Communication Research Reports* 26 (2), 105–113.

Chang, M.-L. (2013) Toward a theoretical model to understand teacher emotions and teacher burnout in the context of student misbehavior: Appraisal, regulation and coping. *Motivation and Emotion* 37 (4), 799–817.

Charmaz, K. (2014) *Constructing Grounded Theory* (2nd edn). Sage Publications Ltd.

Cho, J. and Trent, A. (2016) Validity in qualitative research revisited. *Qualitative Research* 6 (3), 319–340.

Council of Local Authorities for International Relations [CLAIR] (2013) The JET Programme: ALT handbook. http://jetprogramme.org/wp-content/MAIN-PAGE/current/publications/altcirseahandbook/alt-2013.pdf

Cook, V. (1999) Going beyond the native speaker in language teaching. *TESOL Quarterly* 33 (2), 185–209.

Corcoran, R.P. and Tormey, R. (2012) How emotionally intelligent are pre-service teachers? *Teaching and Teacher Education* 28 (5), 750–759.

Cowie, N. (2011) Emotions that experienced English as a Foreign Language (EFL) teachers feel about their students, their colleagues and their work. *Teaching and Teacher Education* 27 (1), 235–242.

Creswell, J.W. and Miller, D.L. (2000) Determining validity in qualitative inquiry. *Theory Into Practice* 39 (3), 124–130.

Creswell, J.W. and Creswell, J.D. (2018) *Research Design: Qualitative, Quantitative and Mixed Methods Approaches* (5th edn). Sage Publications Inc.

Cutrone, P. (2009) Overcoming Japanese EFL learners' fear of speaking. *University of Reading Language Studies Working Papers* 1, 55–63.

Dale, P.N. (1986) *The Myth of Japanese Uniqueness*. Croom Helm Ltd.

Day, C. and Leitch, R. (2001) Teachers' and teacher educators' lives: The role of emotion. *Teaching and Teacher Education* 17 (4), 403–415

de Bot, K., Lowie, W. and Verspoor, M. (2007) A dynamic systems theory approach to second language acquisition. *Bilingualism: Language and Cognition* 10 (1), 7–21.

De Costa, P.I., Rawal, H. and Li, W. (eds) (2018) Emotions in second language teaching: Theory, research and teacher education [Special issue]. *Chinese Journal of Applied Linguistics* 41 (4).

De Costa, P.I., Li, W. and Hima, R. (2020) Should I stay or leave? Exploring L2 teachers' profession from an emotionally inflected framework. In C. Gkonou, J.-M. Dewaele and J. King (eds) *The Emotional Rollercoaster of Language Teaching* (pp. 211–227). Multilingual Matters.

Dewaele, J.-M. and MacIntyre, P. (2019) The predictive power of multicultural personality traits, learner and teacher variables on foreign language enjoyment and anxiety. In M. Sato and S. Loewen (eds) *Evidence-based Second Language Pedagogy: A Collection of Instructed Second Language Acquisition Studies* (pp. 263–286). Routledge.

Dewaele, J.-M. and Dewaele, L. (2020) Are foreign language learners' enjoyment and anxiety specific to the teacher? An investigation into the dynamics of learners' classroom emotions. *Studies in Second Language Learning and Teaching* 10 (1), 45–65.

Dewaele, J.-M., Gkonou, C. and Mercer, S. (2018) Do ESL/EFL teachers' emotional intelligence, teaching experience, proficiency and gender affect their classroom practice? In J.D. Martínez Agudo (ed.) *Emotions in Second Language Teaching: Theory, Research and Teacher Education* (pp. 125–144). Springer International Publishing.

Dörnyei, Z. (2001) *Motivational Strategies in the Language Classroom*. Cambridge University Press.
Dörnyei, Z. (2007) *Research Methods in Applied Linguistics*. Oxford University Press.
Dörnyei, Z. and Ryan, S. (2015) *The Psychology of the Language Learner Revisited*. Taylor and Francis Group.
Eades, J.S. (2009) Local thinking, global dreams. In G.S. Poole and C. Ya-Chen (eds) *Higher Education in East Asia: Neoliberalism and the Professoriate* (pp. 151–173). Sense Publishers.
Eades, J.S., Goodman, R. and Hada, Y. (eds) (2005) *The 'Big Bang' in Japanese Higher Education: The 2004 Reforms and the Dynamics of Change*. Trans Pacific Press.
Ekman, P. and Cordaro, D. (2011) What is meant by calling emotions basic. *Emotion Review* 3 (4), 364–370.
Elahi Shirvan, M. and Taherian, T. (2021) Relational influences of a teacher's self-disclosure on the emergence of foreign language enjoyment patterns. In M. Simons and T.F.H. Smits (eds) *Language Education and Emotions: Research into Emotions and Language Learners, Language Teachers and Educational Processes* (pp. 135–148). Routledge.
Elliot, A.J. and Thrash, T.M. (2002) Approach-avoidance motivation in personality: Approach and avoidance temperaments and goals. *Journal of Personality and Social Psychology* 82 (5), 804–818.
English, T. and Eldesouky, L. (2020) We're not alone: Understanding the social consequences of intrinsic emotion regulation. *Emotion* 20 (1), 43–47.
Falout, J. and Murphey, T. (2018) Teachers crafting job crafting. In S. Mercer and A. Kostoulas (eds) *Language Teacher Psychology* (pp. 211–230). Multilingual Matters.
Fan, J. and Wang, Y. (2022) English as a foreign language teachers' professional success in the Chinese context: The effects of well-being and emotion regulation. *Frontiers in Psychology* 13, 952503.
Fredrickson, B.L. (2000) Cultivating positive emotions to optimize health and well-being. *Prevention and Treatment* 3.
Fredrickson, B.L. (2001) The role of positive emotions in positive psychology: The broaden-and-build theory of positive emotions. *The American Psychologist* 56 (3), 218–226.
Gass, S.M. and Mackey, A. (2017) *Stimulated Recall Methodology in Applied Linguistics and L2 Research* (2nd edn). Routledge.
Geluso, J. (2013) Negotiating a professional identity: Non-Japanese teachers of English in pre-tertiary education in Japan. In S.A. Houghton and D.J. Rivers (eds) *Native-Speakerism in Japan: Intergroup Dynamics in Foreign Language Education* (pp. 92–104). Multilingual Matters.
Ghanizadeh, A. and Moafian, F. (2009) The role of EFL teachers' emotional intelligence in their success. *ELT Journal* 64 (4), 424–435.
Ghanizadeh, A. and Royaei, N. (2015) Emotional facet of language teaching: Emotion regulation and emotional labor strategies as predictors of teacher burnout. *International Journal of Pedagogies and Learning* 10 (2), 139–150.
Gilmore, A. (2016) Language learning in context: Complex dynamic systems and the role of mixed methods research. In J. King (ed.) *The Dynamic Interplay Between Context and the Language Learner* (pp. 194–224). Palgrave Macmillan.
Gkonou, C. (2022) Teacher-learner relationships. In T. Gregersen and S. Mercer (eds) *The Routledge Handbook of the Psychology of Language Learning and Teaching* (pp. 275–284). Routledge.
Gkonou, C. and Mercer, S. (2017) Understanding emotional and social intelligence among English language teachers. *ELT Research Papers 17.03*. British Council.
Gkonou, C. and Mercer, S. (2018) The relational beliefs and practices of highly socio-emotionally competent language teachers. In S. Mercer and A. Kostoulas (eds) *Language Teacher Psychology* (pp. 158–177). Multilingual Matters.

Gkonou, C. and Miller, E.R. (2017) Caring and emotional labour: Language teachers' engagement with anxious learners in private language school classrooms. *Language Teaching Research* 23 (3), 372–387.

Gkonou, C. and Miller, E.R. (2020) 'Critical incidents' in language teacher's narratives of emotional experiences. In C. Gkonou, J.-M. Dewaele and J. King (eds) *The Emotional Rollercoaster of Language Teaching* (pp. 131–149). Multilingual Matters.

Gkonou, C. and Miller, E.R. (2021) An exploration of language teacher reflection, emotion labor, and emotional capital. *TESOL Quarterly* 55 (1), 134–155.

Gkonou, C. and Miller, E.R. (2023) Relationality in language teacher emotion regulation: Regulating emotions through, with and for others. *System* 115, 103046.

Gkonou, C., Dewaele, J.-M. and King, J. (eds) (2020a) *The Emotional Rollercoaster of Language Teaching*. Multilingual Matters.

Gkonou, C., Dewaele, J.-M. and King, J. (2020b) Introduction to the emotional rollercoaster of language teaching. In C. Gkonou, J.-M. Dewaele and J. King (eds) *The Emotional Rollercoaster of Language Teaching* (pp. 1–12). Multilingual Matters.

Glomb, T.M. and Tews, M.J. (2004) Emotional labor: A conceptualization and scale development. *Journal of Vocational Behavior* 64 (1), 1–23.

Goleman, D. (1995) *Emotional Intelligence: Why it can Matter More than IQ*. Bantam Books.

Goleman, D. (2006) *Social Intelligence: The New Science of Human Relationships*. Bantam Dell.

Golombek, P. (2016) Grappling with language teacher identity. In G. Barkhuizen (ed.) *Reflections on Language Teacher Identity* (pp. 151–157). Routledge.

Golombek, P. and Klager, P. (2015) Play and imagination in developing language teacher identity-in-activity. *Ilha do Desterro* 68 (1), 17–32.

Goodman, R. (2005) W(h)ither the Japanese university? An introduction to the 2004 higher education reforms in Japan. In J.S. Eades, R. Goodman and Y. Hada (eds) *The 'Big Bang' in Japanese Higher Education: The 2004 Reforms and the Dynamics of Change* (pp. 1–31). Trans Pacific Press.

Grandey, A.A. (2000) Emotional regulation in the workplace: A new way to conceptualize emotional labor. *Journal of Occupational Health Psychology* 5 (1), 95–110.

Greene, M.J. (2014) On the inside looking in: Methodological insights and challenges in conducting qualitative insider research. *The Qualitative Report* 19 (29), 1–13.

Greenglass, E.R. and Fiksenbaum, L. (2009) Proactive coping, positive affect, and wellbeing: Testing for mediation using path analysis. *European Psychologist* 14 (1), 29–39.

Gregersen, T., Macintyre, P.D. and Meza, M.D. (2014) The motion of emotion: Idiodynamic case studies of learners' foreign language anxiety. *The Modern Language Journal* 98 (2), 574–588.

Gregersen, T., MacIntyre, P.D. and Macmillan, N. (2020) Dealing with the emotions of teaching abroad: Searching for silver linings in a difficult context. In C. Gkonou, J.-M. Dewaele and J. King (eds) *The Emotional Rollercoaster of Language Teaching* (pp. 228–246). Multilingual Matters.

Gross, J.J. (1998) The emerging field of emotion regulation: An integrative review. *Review of General Psychology* 2 (3), 271–299.

Gross, J.J. (1999) Emotion regulation: Past, present, future. *Cognition and Emotion* 13 (5), 551–573.

Gross, J.J. (2014) Emotion regulation: Conceptual and empirical foundations. In J.J. Gross (ed.) *Handbook of Emotion Regulation* (2nd edn, pp. 3–20). The Guilford Press.

Gross, J.J. (2015) Emotion regulation: Current status and future prospects. *Psychological Inquiry* 26 (1), 1–26.

Gross, J.J. and John, O.P. (2003) Individual differences in two emotion regulation processes: Implications for affect, relationships, and well-being. *Journal of Personality and Social Psychology* 85 (2), 348–362.

Gross, J.J. and Richards, J.M. (2006) Emotion regulation in everyday life. In D.K. Snyder, J. Simpson and J.N. Hughes (eds) *Emotion Regulation in Couples and Families: Pathways to Dysfunction and Health* (pp. 13–35). American Psychological Association.
Gyurak, A. and Etkin, A. (2014) A neurobiological model of implicit and explicit emotion regulation. In J.J. Gross (ed.) *Handbook of Emotion Regulation* (2nd edn, pp. 76–92). The Guilford Press.
Gyurak, A., Gross, J.J. and Etkin, A. (2011) Explicit and implicit emotion regulation: A dual process framework. *Cognition and Emotion* 25 (3), 401–412.
Hadley, G. (2017) *Grounded Theory in Applied Linguistics Research*. Routledge.
Haeussler, S. (2013) Emotional regulation and resilience in educational organisations: A case of German school teachers. Doctoral dissertation, Northumbria University. Northumbria Research Link.
Hagenauer, G. and Volet, S.E. (2014) 'I don't hide my feelings, even though I try to': Insight into teacher educator emotion display. *The Australian Educational Researcher* 41 (3), 261–281.
Hale, C.C. and Wadden, P. (2019) The landscape of Japanese higher education: An introduction. In C.C. Hale and P. Wadden (eds) *Teaching English at Japanese Universities: A New Handbook* (pp. 3–10). Routledge.
Hall, J.K. (1995) (Re)creating our worlds with words: A sociohistorical perspective of face-to-face interaction. *Applied Linguistics* 16 (2), 206.
Hallett, R.E. (2013) Dangers of member checking. In W. Midgley, P.A. Danahar and M. Baguley (eds) *The Role of Participants in Education Research: Ethics, Epistemologies and Methods* (pp. 29–39). Routledge.
Hargreaves, A. (1998) The emotional practice of teaching. *Teaching and Teacher Education* 14 (8), 835–854.
Hargreaves, A. (2000) Mixed emotions: Teachers' perceptions of their interactions with students. *Teaching and Teacher Education* 16 (8), 811–826.
Hargreaves, A. (2005) Educational change takes ages: Life, career and generational factors in teachers' emotional responses to educational change. *Teaching and Teacher Education* 21 (8), 967–983.
Hashimoto, K. (2000) 'Internationalisation' is 'Japanisation': Japan's foreign language education and national identity. *Journal of Intercultural Studies* 21 (1), 39–51.
Hatfield, E., Cacioppo, J.T. and Rapson, R L. (1994) *Emotional Contagion*. Cambridge University Press.
Hayes, B.E. (2013) Hiring criteria for Japanese university English-teaching faculty. In S.A. Houghton and D.J. Rivers (eds) *Native-speakerism in Japan: Intergroup Dynamics in Foreign Language Education* (pp. 132–146). Multilingual Matters.
Heigham, J. and Sakui, K. (2009) Ethnography. In J. Heigham and R. Croker (eds) *Qualitative Research in Applied Linguistics: A Practical Introduction* (pp. 91–111). Palgrave Macmillan.
Heiy, J.E. and Cheavens, J.S. (2014) Back to basics: A naturalistic assessment of the experience and regulation of emotion. *Emotion* 14 (5), 878–891.
Henry, A. and Thorsen, C. (2018) Teachers' self-disclosures and influences on students' motivation: A relational perspective. *International Journal of Bilingual Education and Bilingualism* 24 (1), 1–15.
Heydarnejad, T., Zareian, G., Ghaniabadi, S. and Adel, S.M.R. (2021) Measuring language teacher emotion regulation: Development and validation of the Language Teacher Emotion Regulation Inventory at Workplace (LTERI). *Frontiers in Psychology* 12.
Hino, N. (1988) Yakudoku: Japan's dominant tradition in foreign language learning. *JALT Journal* 10 (1, 2), 45–53.
Hobfoll, S.E. (1989) Conservation of resources: A new attempt at conceptualizing stress. *American Psychologist* 44 (3), 513–524.

Hobfoll, S.E. (2001) The influence of culture, community, and the nested-self in the stress process: Advancing conservation of resources theory. *Applied Psychology: An International Review* 50 (3), 337–370.

Hochschild, A.R. (1983) *The Managed Heart: Commercialization of Human Feeling*. University of California Press.

Hofstadler, N., Talbot, K., Mercer, S. and Lämmerer, A. (2020) The thrills and ills of content and language integrated learning. In C. Gkonou, J.-M. Dewaele and J. King (eds) *The Emotional Rollercoaster of Language Teaching* (pp. 13–30). Multilingual Matters.

Holliday, A. (2007) *Doing and Writing Qualitative Research* (2nd edn). Sage Publications Ltd.

Hollis, M. (2002) Introduction: Problems of structure and action. In M. Hollis (ed.) *The Philosophy of Social Science: An Introduction* (pp. 1–22). Cambridge University Press.

Hooper, D. (2022) Action logs as mediational means for teacher development. *Language Teaching Research* 26 (5), 1034–1046.

Hooper, D. and Snyder, B. (2017) Becoming a 'real' teacher: A case study of professional development in eikaiwa. *The European Journal of Applied Linguistics and TEFL* 6 (2), 183–201.

Hooper, D. and Hashimoto, N. (2020) Moving beyond 'McEnglish'. In D. Hooper and N. Hashimoto (eds) *Teacher Narratives from the English Classroom: Moving beyond McEnglish* (pp. 14–30). Candlin and Mynard ePublishing Limited.

Horiguchi, S., Imoto, Y. and Poole, G.S. (2015) Introduction. In S. Horiguchi, Y. Imoto and G.S. Poole (eds) *Foreign Language Education in Japan: Exploring Qualitative Approaches* (pp. 1–18). Sense Publishers.

Horwitz, E.K. (1986) Preliminary evidence for the reliability and validity of a foreign language anxiety scale. *TESOL Quarterly* 20 (3), 559–562.

Horwitz, E.K. (1996) Even teachers get the blues: Recognizing and alleviating language teachers' feelings of foreign language anxiety. *Foreign Language Annals* 29 (3), 365–372.

Horwitz, E.K., Horwitz, M.B. and Cope, J. (1986) Foreign language classroom anxiety. *The Modern Language Journal* 70 (2), 125–132.

Hosotani, R. and Imai-Matsumura, K. (2011) Emotional experience, expression, and regulation of high-quality Japanese elementary school teachers. *Teaching and Teacher Education* 27 (6), 1039–1048.

Humphrey, R.H., Ashforth, B.E. and Diefendorff, J.M. (2015) The bright side of emotional labor. *Journal of Organizational Behavior* 36 (6), 749–769.

Humphries, S. (2020) 'Please teach me how to teach': The emotional impact of educational change. In C. Gkonou, J.-M. Dewaele and J. King (eds) *The Emotional Rollercoaster of Language Teaching* (pp. 150–172). Multilingual Matters.

Ito, H. (2017) Rethinking active learning in the context of Japanese higher education. *Cogent Education* 4 (1).

Jiang, Y. and Dewaele, J.-M. (2019) How unique is the foreign language classroom enjoyment and anxiety of Chinese EFL learners? *System* 82, 13–25.

Jones, R.H. and Richards, J.C. (2016) *Creativity in Language Teaching: Perspectives from Research and Practice*. Routledge.

Kafetsios, K., Nezlek, J.B. and Vassilakou, T. (2012) Relationships between leaders' and subordinates' emotion regulation and satisfaction and affect at work. *The Journal of Social Psychology* 152 (4), 436–457.

Kanner, A.D., Coyne, J.C., Schaefer, C. and Lazarus, R.S. (1981) Comparison of two modes of stress measurement: Daily hassles and uplifts versus major life events. *Journal of Behavioral Medicine* 4 (1), 1–39.

Kasai, M., Lee, J.A. and Kim, S. (2011) Secondary EFL students' perceptions of native and nonnative english-speaking teachers in Japan and Korea. *Asian EFL Journal* 13 (3), 272–300.

Kemper, T.D. (1981) Social constructionist and positivist approaches to the sociology of emotions. *American Journal of Sociology* 87 (2), 336–362.

King, J. (2013a) *Silence in the Second Language Classroom*. Palgrave Macmillan.

King, J. (2013b) Silence in the second language classrooms of Japanese universities. *Applied Linguistics* 34 (3), 325–343.

King, J. (2016a) Introduction to the dynamic interplay between context and the language learner. In J. King (ed.) *The Dynamic Interplay between Context and the Language Learner* (pp. 1–10). Palgrave Macmillan.

King, J. (2016b) 'It's time, put on the smile, it's time!': The emotional labour of second language teaching within a Japanese university. In C. Gkonou, D. Tatzl and S. Mercer (eds) *New Directions in Language Learning Psychology* (pp. 97–112). Springer International Publishing.

King, J. and Ng, K.-Y.S. (2018) Teacher emotions and the emotional labour of second language teaching. In S. Mercer and A. Kostoulas (eds) *Language Teacher Psychology* (pp. 141–157). Multilingual Matters.

King, J. and Morris, S. (2022) Social interaction. In T. Gregersen and S. Mercer (eds) *The Routledge Handbook of the Psychology of Language Learning and Teaching* (pp. 313–324). Routledge.

King, J., Dewaele, J.-M. and Gkonou, C. (2020) Concluding thoughts on the emotional rollercoaster of language teaching. In C. Gkonou, J.-M. Dewaele and J. King (eds) *The Emotional Rollercoaster of Language Teaching* (pp. 288–295). Multilingual Matters.

King, N., Horrocks, C. and Brooks, J. (2019) *Interviews in Qualitative Research* (2nd edn). SAGE Publications Ltd.

Kinmouth, E.H. (2005) From selection to seduction: The impact of demographic change on private higher education in Japan. In J.S. Eades, R. Goodman and Y. Hada (eds) *The 'Big Bang' in Japanese Higher Education: The 2004 Reforms and the Dynamics of Change* (pp. 106–135). Trans Pacific Press.

Koby, C.J. (2015) Communicative competence in high school? Really? In P. Clements, A. Krause and H. Brown (eds) *JALT 2014 Conference Proceedings* (pp. 126–132). The Japan Association for Language Teaching.

Koole, S.L. (2009) The psychology of emotion regulation: An integrative review. *Cognition and Emotion* 23 (1), 4–41.

Koole, S.L. and Fockenberg, D.A. (2011) Implicit emotion regulation under demanding conditions: The moderating role of action versus state orientation. *Cognition and Emotion* 25 (3), 440–452.

Koole, S.L. and Rothermund, K. (2011) 'I feel better but I don't know why': The psychology of implicit emotion regulation. *Cognition and Emotion* 25 (3), 389–399.

Kostoulas, A. and Lämmerer, A. (2018) Making the transition into teacher education: Resilience as a process of growth. In S. Mercer and A. Kostoulas (eds) *Language Teacher Psychology* (pp. 247–263). Multilingual Matters.

Kostoulas, A. and Lämmerer, A. (2020) Resilience in language teaching: Adaptive and maladaptive outcomes in pre-service teachers. In C. Gkonou, J.-M. Dewaele and J. King (eds) *The Emotional Rollercoaster of Language Teaching* (pp. 89–110). Multilingual Matters.

Kubota, R. (1999) Japanese culture constructed by discourses: Implications for applied linguistics research and ELT. *TESOL Quarterly* 33 (1), 9–35.

Kubota, R. (2011) Learning a foreign language as leisure and consumption: Enjoyment, desire, and the business of eikaiwa. *International Journal of Bilingual Education and Bilingualism* 14 (4), 473–488.

Kubota, R. (2015) Foreword. In S. Horiguchi, Y. Imoto and G.S. Poole (eds) *Foreign Language Education in Japan: Exploring Qualitative Approaches* (pp. vii–ix). Sense Publishers.

Kyriacou, C. (2001) Teacher stress: Directions for future research. *Educational Review* 53 (1), 27–35.
Larsen, R.J. and Prizmic, Z. (2007) Regulation of emotional well-being: Overcoming the hedonic treadmill. In M. Eid and R.J. Larsen (eds) *The Science of Subjective Well-being* (pp. 258–289). The Guilford Press.
Larsen-Freeman, D. and Cameron, L. (2008) *Complex Systems and Applied Linguistics*. Oxford University Press.
Larson-Hall, J. and Stewart, J. (2018) Making a career of university teaching in Japan: Getting (and keeping) a full-time job. In P. Wadden and C.C. Hale (eds) *Teaching English at Japanese Universities: A New Handbook* (pp. 11–24). Routledge.
Lawrence, L. and Nagashima, Y. (2020) The intersectionality of gender, sexuality, race, and native-speakerness: Investigating ELT teacher identity through duoethnography. *Journal of Language, Identity and Education* 19 (1), 42–55.
Lazarus, R.S. (1991) Cognition and motivation in emotion. *American Psychologist* 46 (4), 352–367.
Lee, M., Pekrun, R., Taxer, J.L., Schutz, P.A., Vogl, E. and Xie, X. (2016) Teachers' emotions and emotion management: Integrating emotion regulation theory with emotional labor research. *Social Psychology of Education* 19 (4), 843–863.
Lemarchand-Chauvin, M.-C. and Tardieu, C. (2018) Teachers' emotions and professional identity development: Implications for second language teacher education. In J.D. Martínez Agudo (ed.) *Emotions in Second Language Teaching: Theory, Research and Teacher Education* (pp. 425–443). Springer International Publishing AG.
Lievens, F. and Chan, D. (2017) Practical intelligence, emotional intelligence, and social intelligence. In J.L. Farr and N.T. Tippins (eds) *Handbook of Employee Selection* (2nd edn, pp. 342–364). Routledge.
Littleton, A. (2021) Emotion regulation strategies of kindergarten ESL teachers in Japan: An interview-based survey. *The Language Learning Journal* 49 (2), 203–218.
Lively, K.J. and Weed, E.A. (2016) The sociology of emotions. In L. Feldmann Barrett, M. Lewis and J.M. Haviland-Jones (eds) *Handbook of Emotions* (4th edn, pp. 66–81). The Guilford Press.
Loh, C.E. and Liew, W.M. (2016) Voices from the ground: The emotional labour of English teachers' work. *Teaching and Teacher Education* 55, 267–278.
Lowe, R.J. (2015) A matter of degrees: Native-speakerism and centre qualification bias in Japan. *The Journal of English as an International Language* 10 (2), 1–17.
MacIntyre, P.D. and Gardner, R.C. (1989) Anxiety and second-language learning: Towards a theoretical clarification. *Language Learning* 44 (2), 283–305.
MacIntyre, P.D. and Gardner, R.C. (1994) The subtle effects of language anxiety on cognitive processing in the second language. *Language Learning* 44 (2), 283–305.
MacIntyre, P.D., Mercer, S. and Gregersen, T. (2021) Reflections on researching dynamics in language learning psychology. In R.J. Sampson and R.S. Pinner (eds) *Complexity Perspectives on Researching Language Learner and Teacher Psychology* (pp. 15–34). Multilingual Matters.
Maher, K. (2020) Examining L2 learners' silent behaviour and anxiety in the classroom using an approach based on cognitive-behavioural theory. In J. King and S. Harumi (eds) *East Asian Perspectives on Silence in English Language Education* (pp. 80–104). Multilingual Matters.
Mann, S. (2016) *The Research Interview: Reflective Practice and Reflexivity in Research Processes*. Palgrave MacMillan.
Martínez Agudo, J.D. (ed.) (2018a) *Emotions in Second Language Teaching: Theory, Research and Teacher Education*. Springer International Publishing.
Martínez Agudo, J.D. (2018b) Introduction and overview. In J.D. Martínez Agudo (ed.) *Emotions in Second Language Teaching: Theory, Research and Teacher Education* (pp. 1–16). Springer International Publishing.

Matikainen, T. (2019) Beyond the native speaker fallacy: Internationalizing English-language teaching at Japanese universities. In P. Wadden and C.C. Hale (eds) *Teaching English at Japanese Universities: A New Handbook* (pp. 174–179). Routledge.

Matsuda, A. (2011) 'Not everyone can be a star': Students' and teachers' beliefs about English teaching in Japan. In P. Seargeant (ed.) *English in Japan in the Era of Globalization* (pp. 38–59). Palgrave Macmillan.

Matsuda, S. and Gobel, P. (2004) Anxiety and predictors of performance in the foreign language classroom. *System* 32 (1), 21–36.

Matsumoto, D., Yoo, S.H., Nakagawa, S. and Multinational Study of Cultural Display Rules. (2008) Culture, emotion regulation, and adjustment. *Journal of Personality and Social Psychology* 94 (6), 925–937.

Mauss, I.B. and Tamir, M. (2014) Emotion goals: How their content, structure, and operation shape emotion regulation. In J.J. Gross (ed.) *Handbook of Emotion Regulation* (2nd edn, pp. 361–375). Guilford Press.

Mayer, J.D. and Salovey, P. (1997) What is emotional intelligence? In P. Salovey and D.J. Sluyter (eds) *Emotional Development and Emotional Intelligence: Implications for Educators* (pp. 3–31). Basic Books.

McDermid, F., Peters, K., Jackson, D. and Daly, J. (2014) Conducting qualitative research in the context of pre-existing peer and collegial relationships. *Nursing Research* 21 (5), 28–33.

McRae, K. and Gross, J.J. (2020) Emotion regulation. *Emotion* 20 (1), 1–9.

McVeigh, B.J. (2002) *Japanese Higher Education As Myth*. M.E. Sharpe.

Mercer, J. (2007) The challenges of insider research in educational institutions: Wielding a double-edged sword and resolving delicate dilemmas. *Oxford Review of Education* 33 (1), 1–17.

Mercer, S. (2016) Seeing the world through your eyes: Empathy in language learning and teaching. In P.D. MacIntyre, T. Gregersen and S. Mercer (eds) *Positive Psychology in SLA* (pp. 91–111). Multilingual Matters.

Mercer, S. and Kostoulas, A. (eds) (2018) *Language Teacher Psychology*. Multilingual Matters.

Mercer, S. and Gregersen, T. (2020) *Teacher Wellbeing*. Oxford University Press.

Mesquita, B. (2022) *Between us: How Cultures Create Emotions*. W. W. Norton and Company.

Mesquita, B., De Leersnyder, J. and Albert, D. (2014) The cultural regulation of emotions. In J.J. Gross (ed.) *Handbook of Emotion Regulation* (2nd edn, pp. 284–304). The Guilford Press.

Mesquita, B., De Leersnyder, J. and Boiger, M. (2016) The cultural psychology of emotions. In L. Feldmann Barrett, M. Lewis and J.M. Haviland-Jones (eds) *Handbook of Emotions* (4th edn, pp. 393–411). The Guilford Press.

Mevarech, Z.R. and Maskit, D. (2015) The teaching experience and the emotions it evokes. *Social Psychology of Education* 18 (2), 241–253.

Miller, E.R. and Gkonou, C. (2018) Language teacher agency, emotion labor and emotional rewards in tertiary-level English language programs. *System* 79, 49–59.

Ministry of Economy, Trade and Industry (2019) *Monthly Report on the Current Survey of Selected Service Industries, December 2018*. Ministry of Economy, Trade and Industry http://www.meti.go.jp/statistics/tyo/tokusabido/result/pdf/hv201812kj.pdf

Ministry of Education, Culture, Sports, Science and Technology (2011a) *Course of Study for Lower Secondary Education: Section 9 Foreign Languages*. Ministry of Education, Culture, Sports, Science and Technology – Japan. http://www.mext.go.jp/a_menu/shotou/new-cs/youryou/eiyaku2/gai.pdf

Ministry of Education, Culture, Sports, Science and Technology (2011b) *The Revisions of the Courses of Study for Elementary and Secondary Schools*. Ministry of Education, Culture, Sports, Science and Technology – Japan. http://www.mext.go.jp/en/policy/education/elsec/title02/detail02/__icsFiles/afieldfile/2011/03/28/1303755_001.pdf

Ministry of Education, Culture, Sports, Science and Technology (2012) *Higher Education in Japan*. Ministry of Education, Culture, Sports, Science and Technology – Japan. http://www.mext.go.jp/en/policy/education/highered/title03/detail03/__icsFiles/afieldfile/2012/06/19/1302653_1.pdf

Ministry of Education, Culture, Sports, Science and Technology (2014) *English Education Reform Plan Corresponding to Globalisation*. Ministry of Education, Culture, Sports, Science and Technology – Japan. https://www.mext.go.jp/en/news/topics/detail/__icsFiles/afieldfile/2014/01/23/1343591_1.pdf

Ministry of Education, Culture, Sports, Science and Technology (2016) *Statistical Abstract*. Ministry of Education, Culture, Sports, Science and Technology – Japan. http://www.mext.go.jp/en/publication/statistics/title02/detail02/1379369.htm

Ministry of Education, Culture, Sports, Science and Technology (2023) *Gakkoukihonchousa* [Basic statistics]. Ministry of Education, Culture, Sports, Science and Technology – Japan. https://www.mext.go.jp/b_menu/toukei/chousa01/kihon/1267995.htm

Ministry of Education, Culture, Sports, Science and Technology (MEXT) and British Council (2013) *ALT Handbook*. MEXT and British Council. https://www.britishcouncil.jp/sites/default/files/alt-handbook-en_0.pdf

Minter, R.L. (2009) Faculty burnout. *Contemporary Issues in Education Research* 2 (2), 1–8.

Miyake-Warkentin, K., Hooper, D. and Murphey, T. (2019) Student action logging creates teacher efficacy. In P. Clements, A. Krause and R. Gentry (eds) *Teacher Efficacy, Learner Agency* (pp. 341–349). The Japan Association for Language Teaching.

Miyoshi, M. and Harootunian, H.D. (1991) Japan in the world. *Boundary 2* 18 (3), 1–7.

Moors, A. (2014) Flavors of appraisal theories of emotion. *Emotion Review* 6 (4), 303–307.

Moors, A., Ellsworth, P.C., Scherer, K.R. and Frijda, N.H. (2013) Appraisal theories of emotion: State of the art and future development. *Emotion Review* 5 (2), 119–124.

Morris, S. (2019) The frustration regulation journal: A reflective framework for educators. *Relay Journal* 2 (2), 294–305.

Morris, S. (2022) Performing motivating and caring identities: The emotions of non-Japanese university teachers of English. In M. Mielick, R. Kubota and L. Lawrence (eds) *Discourses of Identity: Language Learning, Teaching and Reclamation Perspectives in Japan* (pp. 341–358). Palgrave Macmillan.

Morris, S. and King, J. (2018) Teacher frustration and emotion regulation in university language teaching. *Chinese Journal of Applied Linguistics* 41 (4), 433–452.

Morris, S. and King, J. (2020) Emotion regulation among university EFL teachers in Japan: The dynamic interplay between context and emotional behaviour. In C. Gkonou, J.-M. Dewaele and J. King (eds) *The Emotional Rollercoaster of Language Teaching* (pp. 193–210). Multilingual Matters.

Morris, S. and King, J. (2023) University language teachers' contextually dependent uses of instrumental emotion regulation. *System* 116, 103080.

Morris, S., Yamamoto, K. and King, J. (2023) Practitioner researcher intuition in stimulated recall studies. *Journal for the Psychology of Language Learning* 5 (2), 34–44.

Murphey, T. (1993) Why don't teachers learn what learners learn? Taking the guesswork out with action logging. *English Teaching Forum* 31 (1), 6–10.

Murray, A. (2013) Teacher burnout in Japanese higher education. *The Language Teacher* 37 (4), 51–55. https://jalt-publications.org/tlt/archive

Nagatomo, D.H. (2012) *Exploring Japanese University English Teachers' Professional Identity*. Multilingual Matters.

Nagatomo, D.H. (2016) *Identity, Gender and Teaching English in Japan*. Multilingual Matters.

Nakamura, S., Darasawang, P. and Reinders, H. (2021) A practitioner study on the implementation of strategy instruction for boredom regulation. *Language Teaching Research* 28 (2), 786–808.

Namaziandost, E., Heydarnejad, T. and Rezai, A. (2022) Iranian EFL teachers' reflective teaching, emotion regulation, and immunity: Examining possible relationships. *Current Psychology* 42 (3), 2294–2309.

Nayer, P.B. (1994) Whose English is it? *Teaching English as a Second or Foreign Language* 1 (1), 1–7.

Neff, K.D. (2011) Self-compassion, self-esteem, and well-being. *Social and Personality Psychology Compass* 5 (1), 1–12.

Neustupný, J.V. and Tanaka, S. (2004) English in Japan: An overview. In V. Makarova and T. Rodgers (eds) *English Language Teaching: The Case of Japan* (pp. 11–28). LINCOM GmbH.

Nias, J. (1996) Thinking about feeling: The emotions in teaching. *Cambridge Journal of Education* 26 (3), 293–306.

Noddings, N. (1995) Themes of care. *The Phi Delta Kappan* 76 (9), 675–679.

Nuske, K. (2020) Charisma man or critical pedagogue? Eikaiwa and unexpected paths of professional development. In D. Hooper and N. Hashimoto (eds) *Teacher Narratives from the Eikaiwa Classroom: Moving Beyond 'McEnglish'* (pp. 149–158). Candlin and Maynard ePublishing Limited.

Nyklíček, I., Vingerhoets, A. and Zeelenberb, M. (2011) Emotion regulation and well-being: A view from different angles. In I. Nyklicek, A. Vingerhoets and M. Zeelenberb (eds) *Emotion Regulation and Well-Being* (pp. 1–9). Springer.

Ochsner, K.N. and Gross, J.J. (2014) The neural bases of emotion and emotion regulation: A valuation perspective. In J.J. Gross (ed.) *Handbook of Emotion Regulation* (2nd edn, pp. 23–42). The Guilford Press.

Oda, M. and Takada, T. (2005) English language teaching in Japan. In G. Braine (ed.) *Teaching English to the World: History, Curriculum and Practice* (pp. 93–102). Routledge.

Oxford, R.L. (1999) Anxiety and the language learner: New insights. In J. Arnold (ed.) *Affect in Language Learning* (pp. 58–67). Cambridge University Press.

Oya, T., Manalo, E. and Greenwood, J. (2004) The influence of personality and anxiety on the oral performance of Japanese speakers of English. *Applied Cognitive Psychology* 18, 841–855.

Parrott, W.G. (2007) Components and the definition of emotion. *Social Science Information* 46 (3), 419–423.

Poole, G.S. (2010) *The Japanese Professor: An Ethnography of a University Faculty*. Sense Publishers.

Poole, G.S. and Ya-Chen, C. (2009) Introduction. In G.S. Poole and C. Ya-Chen (eds) *Higher Education in East Asia: Neoliberalism and the Professoriate* (pp. 1–12). Sense Publishers.

Pring, R. (2004) *Philosophy of Educational Research* (2nd edn). Continuum.

Pring, R. (2015) *Philosophy of Education Research* (3rd edn). Bloomsbury Publishing.

Prior, M.T. and Haneda, M. (eds) (2023) Language teacher emotion research: Contemporary developments and challenges [Special issue]. *System*.

Qiu, X. and Lo, Y.Y. (2016) Content familiarity, task repetition and Chinese EFL learners' engagement in second language use. *Language Teaching Research* 21 (6), 681–698.

Quoidbach, J., Berry, E.V., Hansenne, M. and Mikolajczak, M. (2010) Positive emotion regulation and well-being: Comparing the impact of eight savoring and dampening strategies. *Personality and Individual Differences* 49 (5), 368–373.

Quoidbach, J., Mikolajczak, M. and Gross, J.J. (2015) Positive interventions: An emotion regulation perspective. *Psychological Bulletin* 141 (3), 655–693.

Rajagopalan, K. (2005) Non-native speaker teachers of English and their anxieties: Ingredients for an experiment in action research. In E. Llurda (ed.) *Non-Native Language Teachers: Perceptions, Challenges and Contributions to the Profession* (pp. 283–303). Springer US.

Research Institute for Higher Education (2022) *Statistics of Japanese Higher Education: 18-Year-Old Population*. RIHE. https://rihe.hiroshima-u.ac.jp/en/statistics/synthesis/

Richards, J.C. (2013) Creativity in language teaching. *Iranian Journal of Language Teaching Research* 1 (3), 19–43.
Rivers, D.J. (2013) Institutionalised native-speakerism: Voices of dissent and acts of resistance. In S.A. Houghton and D.J. Rivers (eds) *Native-Speakerism in Japan: Integroup Dynamics in Foreign Language Education* (pp. 75–91). Multilingual Matters.
Rosenberg, E.L. (1998) Levels of analysis and the organization of affect. *Review of General Psychology* 2 (3), 247–270.
Roth, S. and Cohen, L.J. (1986) Approach, avoidance, and coping with stress. *American Psychologist* 41 (7), 813–819.
Russell, J.A. (2014) Four perspectives on the psychology of emotion: An introduction. *Emotion Review* 6 (4), 291.
Safdar, S., Friedlmeier, W., Matsumoto, D., Yoo, S.H., Kwantes, C.T., Kakai, H. and Shigemasu, E. (2009) Variations of emotional display rules within and across cultures: A comparison between Canada, USA, and Japan. *Canadian Journal of Behavioural Science / Revue canadienne Des Sciences Du Comportement* 41 (1), 1–10.
Sakamoto, R. (2014) Resolving the culture clash in the team-taught classroom. *Teaching English Now* 28, 10–11.
Sakui, K. (2004) Wearing two pairs of shoes: Language teaching in Japan. *ELT Journal* 58 (2), 155–163.
Saldaña, J. (2016) *The Coding Manual for Qualitative Researchers* (3rd edn). Sage Publications Ltd.
Sampson, R.J. and Pinner, R.S. (eds) (2021) *Complexity Perspectives on Researching Language Learner and Teacher Psychology*. Multilingual Matters.
Sanchez, H.S. and Grimshaw, T. (2020) Stimulated recall. In J. Mckinley and H. Rose (eds) *The Routledge Handbook of Research Methods in Applied Linguistics* (pp. 312–324). Routledge.
Scherer, K.R. (2001) Appraisal considered as a process of multilevel sequential checking. In K.R. Scherer, A. Schorr and T. Johnstone (eds) *Appraisal Processes in Emotion: Theory, Methods, Research* (pp. 92–120). Oxford University Press.
Scherer, K.R. (2005) What are emotions? And how can they be measured? *Social Science Information* 44 (4), 695–729.
Scherer, K.R. (2009) The dynamic architecture of emotion: Evidence for the component process model. *Cognition and Emotion* 23 (7), 1307–1351.
Schutz, P.A. and DeCuir, J.T. (2002) Inquiry on emotions in education. *Educational Psychologist* 37 (2), 125–134.
Seargeant, P. (2009) *The Idea of English in Japan: Ideology and the Evolution of a Global Language*. Multilingual Matters.
Shimizu, K. (1995) Japanese college students attitudes towards English teachers: A survey. *The Language Teacher* 19 (10), 5–8.
Shuman, V. and Scherer, K. (2014) Concepts and structure of emotions. In R. Pekrun and L. Linnenbrink-Garcia (eds) *International Handbook of Emotions in Education* (pp. 13–35). Routledge.
Simons, M. and Smits, T.F.H. (eds) (2021) *Language Education and Emotions: Research into Emotions and Language Learners, Language Teachers and Educational Processes*. Routledge.
Smith, L. and King, J. (2018) Silence in the foreign language classroom: The emotional challenges for L2 teachers. In J.D. Martínez Agudo (ed.) *Emotions in Second Language Teaching* (pp. 323–340). Springer.
Song, H., Kim, J. and Luo, W. (2016) Teacher–student relationship in online classes: A role of teacher self-disclosure. *Computers in Human Behavior* 54, 436–443.
Song, J. (2021) Emotional labour and professional development in ELT. *ELT Journal* 75 (4), 482–491.
Sowden, C. (2007) Culture and the 'good teacher' in the English Language classroom. *ELT Journal* 61 (4), 304–310.

Suri, G. and Gross, J.J. (2016) Emotion regulation: A valuation perspective. In L.F. Barrett, M. Lewis and J.M. Haviland-Jones (eds) *Handbook of Emotions* (4th edn, pp. 453–466). The Guilford Press.

Sutton, R.E. (2004) Emotional regulation goals and strategies of teachers. *Social Psychology of Education* 7 (4), 379–398.

Tahira, M. (2012) Behind MEXT's new course of study guidelines. *The Language Teacher* 36 (3), 3–8.

Tajino, A. and Tajino, Y. (2000) Native and non-native: What can they offer? Lessons from team-teaching in Japan. *ELT Journal* 54 (1), 3–11.

Talbot, K. and Mercer, S. (2018) Exploring university ESL/EFL teachers' emotional well-being and emotional regulation in the United States, Japan and Austria. *Chinese Journal of Applied Linguistics* 41 (4), 410–432.

Tamir, M. (2016) Why do people regulate their emotions? A taxonomy of motives in emotion regulation. *Personality and Social Psychology Review* 20 (3), 199–222.

Tamir, M., Vishkin, A. and Gutentag, T. (2020) Emotion regulation is motivated. *Emotion* 20 (1), 115–119.

Taxer, J.L. and Frenzel, A.C. (2015) Facets of teachers' emotional lives: A quantitative investigation of teachers' genuine, faked, and hidden emotions. *Teaching and Teacher Education* 49, 78–88.

Thoits, P.A. (1989) The sociology of emotions. *Annual Review of Sociology* 15, 317–342.

Thoits, P.A. (2007) Extending Scherer's conception of emotion. *Social Science Information* 46 (3), 429–433.

Thorne, S. (2016) *Interpretive Description: Qualitative Research for Applied Practice* (2nd edn). Routledge.

Tracy, K. and Robles, J.S. (2013) *Everyday Talk: Building and Reflecting Identities*. The Guilford Press.

Tripp, D. (2012) *Critical Incidents in Teaching (Classic Edition): Developing Professional Judgement*. Taylor and Francis Group.

Troy, A.S., Shallcross, A.J. and Mauss, I.B. (2013) A person-by-situation approach to emotion regulation: Cognitive reappraisal can either help or hurt, depending on the context. *Psychological Science* 24 (12), 2505–2514.

Tsai, J.L., Levenson, R.W. and McCoy, K. (2006) Cultural and temperamental variation in emotional response. *Emotion* 6 (3), 484–497.

Tsuneyoshi, R. (2013) Communicative English in Japan and 'native speakers of English'. In S.A. Houghton and D.J. Rivers (eds) *Native-speakerism in Japan: Intergroup Dynamics in Foreign Language Education* (pp. 119–131). Multilingual Matters.

Turley, E.D. and Gallagher, C.W. (2008) On the 'uses' of rubrics: Reframing the great rubric debate. *The English Journal* 97 (4), 87–92.

Walkinshaw, I. and Oanh, D.H. (2014) Native and non-native English language teachers: Student perceptions in Vietnam and Japan. *SAGE Open* 4 (2).

White, C. (2018) The emotional turn in applied linguistics and TESOL: Significance, challenges and prospects. In J.D. Martínez Agudo (ed.) *Emotions in Second Language Teaching* (pp. 19–34). Springer.

Woo, L. and Murphey, T. (1999) Activating metacognition with action logs. *The Language Teacher* 23 (5), 15–18.

Wray, A. and Bloomer, A. (2006) *Projects in Linguistics* (2nd edn). Hodder Education Group.

Wrzesniewski, A. and Dutton, J.E. (2001) Crafting a job: Revisioning employees as active crafters of their work. *The Academy of Management Review* 26 (2), 179–201.

Yamagami, M. and Tollefson, J.W. (2011) Elite discourses of globalization in Japan: The role of English. In P. Seargeant (ed.) *English in Japan in the Era of Globalisation* (pp. 15–37). Palgrave Macmillan.

Yano, Y. (2001) World Englishes in 2000 and beyond. *World Englishes* 20 (2), 119–132.

Yarwood, A. (2020) Emotional labour in the eikaiwa classroom. In D. Hooper and N. Hashimoto (eds) *Teacher Narratives from the Eikaiwa Classroom: Moving beyond 'McEnglish'* (pp. 82–93). Candlin and Mynard ePublishing Limited.

Yazawa, O. (2017) Student's perception of native English speaking teachers and Japanese teachers of English: The effect on students' self-efficacy and emotional state. *Eruditi* 1, 61–72.

Yin, H. (2016) Knife-like mouth and tofu-like heart: Emotion regulation by Chinese teachers in classroom teaching. *Social Psychology of Education* 19, 1–22.

Yin, H. and Lee, J.C.-K. (2012) Be passionate, but be rational as well: Emotional rules for Chinese teachers' work. *Teaching and Teacher Education* 28 (1), 56–65.

Yin, H., Lee, J.C.K., Zhang, Z.-H. and Jin, Y.-L. (2013) Exploring the relationship among teachers' emotional intelligence, emotional labor strategies and teaching satisfaction. *Teaching and Teacher Education* 35, 137–145.

Yin, H., Huang, S. and Wang, W. (2016) Work environment characteristics and teacher well-being: The mediation of emotion regulation strategies. *International Journal of Environmental Research and Public Health* 13 (9), 907.

Zaki, J. and Ochsner, K. (2016) Empathy. In L.F. Barrett, M. Lewis and J.M. Haviland-Jones (eds) *Handbook of Emotions* (pp. 871–884). The Guilford Press.

Zaki, J., Ochsner, K.N. and Ochsner, K. (2012) The neuroscience of empathy: Progress, pitfalls and promise. *Nature Neuroscience* 15 (5), 675–680.

Zembylas, M. (2002) Constructing genealogies of teachers' emotions in science teaching. *Journal of Research in Science Teaching* 39 (1), 79–103.

Zembylas, M. (2003) Emotions and teacher identity: A poststructural perspective. *Teachers and Teaching* 9 (3), 213–238.

Zembylas, M. (2004) The emotional characteristics of teaching: An ethnographic study of one teacher. *Teaching and Teacher Education* 20 (2), 185–201.

Index

Affecting motives 154–155, 157–158
Anger xvii, 9, 11, 14, 16, 17, 20, 22, 30, 33, 38–39, 71, 96, 103–104, 108, 111, 117–118, 131, 136, 140, 143, 146
Anxiety 26–27, 29, 31, 42, 61, 81, 89, 98, 102, 107, 141, 147
Appraisal 9–11, 13–14, 16, 20–23
Attentional strategies (Attention deployment) 6, 20–21, 39–42, 72, 88, 96–107, 154, 158
Automaticity 10, 18, 61, 75, 104–105
Avoidance
  Avoidance and approach 21, 40, 76, 82–84, 90, 94–95, 101
  Problem avoidance 82, 87, 95
  Topic avoidance 87–88, 157

Behaviour management: self motives 154–155, 157–158
Behaviour (of students) 11, 92–94, 100–101, 130–131, 143–145, 150, 155, 160
Behaviour management: student motives 82–85, 122–123, 143–145, 154–155, 157–158
Broaden-and-build theory 36

Caring 33, 86, 121, 124, 126, 134–137, 150, 152, 161
Coding 64, 70–72
Cognitive change 6, 20–22, 32, 35, 37, 40–43, 71–72, 88, 108–128, 151, 154, 158, 162
Cognitive reappraisal (see under Reappraisal)
Colleagues (impact on emotion regulation) 15, 34, 40–41, 54, 79, 137–138
Competition (between colleagues) 137–138

Complex dynamic systems theory (CDST) 61, 63–64
Concentration 97–98, 100, 102–104, 159
Conceptual evaluations 10
Content (lesson content and emotion regulation) 26, 61, 85–86, 133, 138–141, 145–147, 153, 155, 160
Contextual evaluations 10
Contrahedonic motives 19, 154–155, 157–158
Core evaluations 10
Core features of emotion regulation 15–18

Daigaku (statistics of) 49
Deep acting 31–32
Disappointment xvii, 43, 89, 92, 93, 108, 122, 130, 143, 164
Distancing (physical and emotional) 30, 82–84, 90–92, 94, 151, 157
  Dynamic emotional distancing 90–92
Distraction 97–98, 100, 102–105, 150–151, 157, 159

Eigo vs eikaiwa 54–55, 124, 134
Eikaiwa gakkou 51, 52
Emotion
  Components of 10–11, 13, 14–15, 21–22, 129
  Definition of 9–13
  vs feelings, moods, etc. 9
Emotional intelligence 27–30, 61
Emotional labour 7, 30–35, 37, 52, 67, 72, 86, 129, 134, 138, 140, 142
Emotion display tension 145–147
Emotion regulation
  Definition of 2, 8, 14–24
  Implicit vs explicit 17–19, 104–105
  Intrinsic vs extrinsic 17–18
  Requirements of second language teaching 25–26

Emotion regulation (*Continued*)
  Research considerations 56, 61–66, 160–161
  Trait 34–35
Emotion regulation goals 16, 18–19, 30, 34, 152
Emotion regulation motives 2, 16, 18–20, 22–24, 32, 38, 56, 70–72, 150, 152–159, 161
Emotion regulation outcomes 16–20, 123, 154
Emotion regulation strategies 2, 4, 8, 15–24, 32, 35–43, 56, 62, 70–72, 104, 150–151, 153–159, 162
Empathy
  and emotion regulation 122–128, 136–137, 153
  in research 74
English education in Japan
  History of 46–47
  Reasons for 47–48
Enjoyment (see under Joy)
Epistemic motives 20, 38, 42, 67, 84–86, 88, 94, 102, 104, 113, 125, 133, 145, 154–155, 157–158, 164
Ethics 73
Eudaimonic motives 20
Exaggeration (see under Modulated expression)
Explicit emotion regulation (see under Emotion regulation)
Expressional regulation 92–94, 130–131
Extrinsic emotion regulation (see under Emotion regulation)

Feigning (see under Modulated expression)
Frustration xvii, 10, 14, 21, 33, 42, 68, 76, 80, 83, 84, 92, 97–98, 100, 103–104, 110–111, 116, 119, 131, 143–144, 159, 164
Frustration regulation journal 159
Fun 54, 75, 78, 132, 134–135, 152, 161

Genuine expression 28, 31–32, 133, 135, 137, 140, 143–145, 157
Grounded theory 60, 62–63, 65
Guilt 68, 84, 90, 94, 106, 112–114, 129, 132, 164

Hedonic motives 19–20, 24, 40–42, 77–78, 83–84, 94, 97, 102–104, 110, 112, 114, 122–124, 133, 142, 150, 154–155, 157–158
History of emotions in language teaching 27
Humour 38, 99, 130, 137, 157, 164

Identity 22, 29, 33–34, 48, 85–86, 105, 119–122, 134–137, 148, 152, 160
Implicit emotion regulation (see under Emotion regulation)
Insider/outsider 60
In-situ reappraisal (see under Reappraisal)
Institutions
  Impact on emotion regulation xviii, 2–3, 7, 15, 24, 30–32, 64, 77, 79, 83–84, 88–89, 94, 99–100, 118, 134, 138, 147, 151, 153, 156, 160, 162
  in Japan 46, 48–50
Instructive motives 154–155, 157–158
Instrumental motives 19–20, 24, 36, 38, 41–43, 72, 84, 94, 98–99, 102–104, 130–133, 136, 139–141, 144–145, 150, 154–155, 157–158
Interpersonal 2, 6, 8–9, 11, 13–15, 22–23, 28, 41, 152, 156
Interventions with teachers 37, 40, 162
Intrapersonal 2, 6, 8–9, 11, 13–14, 22–23, 28, 152, 156
Intrinsic emotion regulation (see under Emotion regulation)

Japanese higher education
  Issues with 50
  Role of 49–50
Job crafting 77–79, 85–86, 94, 150, 157
Joy 22, 35, 39–40, 52–54, 71, 76, 78–79, 85, 98, 101, 105, 113, 119, 124, 134, 141, 149, 153, 159, 162, 164
Juken eigo 48, 53, 54

Kokusaika 48

Language teacher emotion regulation model (LTERM) 153–158
Language teacher emotion regulation model, preliminary (LTERM-P) 22–23

Member checking 72–73, 168–169
Mental time travel 97–99, 101–102, 105–107, 126, 150–151, 155, 157, 159
Misbehaviour (see under Behaviour (of students))
Modulated expression 29, 92–94, 130–131, 143–144, 155, 157
Motives (see under Emotion regulation motives)

Negative emotions (see under Anger, Anxiety, Disappointment, Frustration, Guilt, Stress)
Nihonjinron 48
Non-Japanese teachers in Japan 51–55

Observation procedures 61–62, 68, 165
Ontogenetic reappraisal (see under Reappraisal)
Outcomes (see under Emotion regulation outcomes)

Participants (demographics) 58–59
Performance motives 20, 27, 29, 67, 98, 104, 150, 157–158, 164
Personal histories xviii, 3, 5, 12, 117–119, 131, 152, 156
Personality 82, 87, 90, 94, 100–102, 134–135
Positive emotions (see under Caring, Fun, Joy)
Proactive coping 79–82, 94, 151, 157
Problem-directed action 40, 82–84, 87, 92–94, 121, 157
Process model of emotion regulation 6, 20–22, 154
Prohedonic motives 19, 77–78, 154–155, 157–158
Psychological resources 31, 36–37, 101, 105, 117, 128

Rationalisation 111–113, 128, 144, 157
Reappraisal 16, 35–36, 42–43
  In-situ reappraisal 109–111, 116–117, 122–123, 128, 144, 155, 157
  Ontogenetic reappraisal 109–111, 117–119, 123–128, 150–151, 157
Recommendations
  for institutions 160
  for researchers 160–161
  for teachers 159–160
  for trainers 159–160
Relationship crafting (see under Job crafting)
Relationships 12–13, 15, 20, 23–24, 28–29, 33, 38–42, 60, 64, 86–88, 91, 108, 115–117, 119–122, 125, 136–137, 142, 147, 150–155, 164
Reminiscence 22, 98
Resilience 36–37, 119, 126, 151
Response modulation 6, 20–21, 29, 32, 41–43, 71–72, 92–94, 104, 129–148, 150–151, 154–155, 158
Responsibility
  Emotional responsibilities in Japanese higher education 33–34, 40, 51–55
  and emotion regulation 5, 26, 36, 41, 67, 79, 83–84, 86–88, 100, 106, 112–115, 119–122, 134–136, 150, 160

Savouring 22, 40, 98, 101
Self-disclosure 30, 131–134, 147, 157
Self-presentation 28
Semi-structured interview procedures 43–44, 61–62, 65–67, 163–164
Shifting the onus of responsibility 114–115, 157
Situational strategies 6, 20–21, 35, 40–42, 71–72, 76–95, 111, 154, 158
  Situation modification 20–21, 39, 76, 154
  Situation selection 20–21, 76, 154
Situation-attention-appraisal-response cycle 9, 20
Social intelligence 28–29, 61
Social motives 20, 29–30, 38, 67, 125, 132, 154–155, 157–158, 164
Socioemotional competencies 28–30, 61
Stimulated recall
  Procedures of 3, 43–44, 61–65, 69–70, 75, 161, 165–167
  in relation to findings 85, 90, 101, 132
Strategies (see under Emotion regulation strategies)
Stress
  Definition of 9, 36
  Experiences of 14, 20, 28, 31–34, 53, 67, 86, 92, 105–107, 124, 126–127, 142–143, 147, 150

Stress (*Continued*)
 Regulation of 4, 15, 16, 33, 36–38, 40, 80–82, 87, 90, 94, 100–101, 105, 114, 117–120, 122–123, 128, 151–153, 159–160
Suppression xvii–xviii, 13, 33, 35–36, 38–39, 68, 92–94, 130, 138–147, 157
Surface acting 31–32

Task crafting (see under Job crafting)
Trait emotion regulation (see under Emotion regulation)

Transcription 70, 73, 168

Well-being xviii, 7, 9, 16–17, 19, 31, 34–40, 43, 67, 72, 150–152, 154, 160
 and attention deployment 99–100, 107
 and cognitive change 109, 111, 117, 119, 121, 123, 125
 and response modulation 133, 137–138, 141–142
 and situation selection 78, 84, 92

Yakudoku 47, 53

For Product Safety Concerns and Information please contact our EU Authorised Representative:

Easy Access System Europe

Mustamäe tee 50

10621 Tallinn

Estonia

gpsr.requests@easproject.com